Teaching Adolescents Who Struggle with Reading

Practical Strategies

David W. Moore
Arizona State University West

Kathleen A. Hinchman
Syracuse University

Foreword by

Richard T. Vacca
Professor Emeritus, Kent State University

Boston   New York   San Francisco
Mexico City   Montreal   Toronto   London   Madrid   Munich   Paris
Hong Kong   Singapore   Tokyo   Cape Town   Sydney

Senior Series Editor: *Aurora Martínez Ramos*
Editorial Assistant: *Kevin Shannon*
Senior Marketing Manager: *Krista Groshong*
Editorial-Production Service: *Omegatype Typography, Inc.*
Manufacturing Buyer: *Andrew Turso*
Composition Buyer: *Linda Cox*
Cover Administrator: *Joel Gendron*
Electronic Composition: *Omegatype Typography, Inc.*

Library of Congress Cataloging-in-Publication Data

Moore, David W.
    Teaching adolescents who struggle with reading : practical strategies / David W. Moore, Kathleen A. Hinchman ; foreword by Richard T. Vacca.
        p. cm.
    Rev. ed. of: Starting out. c2003.
    Includes bibliographical references and index.
    ISBN 0-205-46606-0 (pbk.)
    1. Reading (Secondary) 2. Language arts (Secondary) I. Hinchman, Kathleen A.
II. Moore, David W. Starting out. III. Title.

LB1632.M62 2006
428.4'071'2—dc22

2005041119

Printed in the United States of America

10 9 8 7 6 5 4 3 2 1   10 09 08 07 06 05

Credits: p. 1, Tony Freeman/PhotoEdit; pp. 11, 139, David Young-Wolff/PhotoEdit; p.16, Nancy Sheehan/PhotoEdit; pp. 21, 42, 86, Will Hart/PhotoEdit; pp. 39, 151, Will Hart; p. 51, Jonathon Nourok/PhotoEdit; p. 59, 129, Michael Newman/PhotoEdit; p. 106, Brian Smith; pp. 131, 191, Myrleen Ferguson Cate/PhotoEdit; p. 171, Prentice Hall, Inc.

CONTENTS

Foreword   vii
Preface   ix

1 Perspectives   1

An Instructional Setting for All Learners   2
Passion 3 / Purpose 3 / Partnership 4 / Plans 5

Metaphors for Adolescent Literacy and Instruction   6
Builders 6 / Apprentice 12

Background on Adolescents Who Struggle as Readers   13
Why Are So Many Adolescents Illiterate? 13 / Shouldn't Adolescent
Literacy Instruction Concentrate on Remediating Disabilities? 16

Conclusion   18

References   19

2 Before School Starts   21

Classroom Culture   22
Naming Classroom Culture 23 / General Positives 26

Classroom Structure   27
Room Arrangement 27 / Procedures 29 / Discipline Plan 36

Conclusion   41

References   42

3 Framing and Launching Units of Instruction   43

Framing Units   44
Topics 45 / Standards-Based Outcomes 45 / Central
Questions 48 / Culminations 50 / Framing Units Coherently 51

Launching Units   52
Real-World Observing/Participating 52 / Reading Aloud 53 /
Previewing Passages 53 / Brainstorming 54 / Writing 56

Conclusion   57

References   57

4 Weaving Literacy through Units of Instruction   59

Selecting Literacy Strands   60

Isolating and Integrating Literacy Strands   61

Examples of Literacy Strands   64
Builder 64 / Learner 68 / Experiencer 71 / Doer 74 /
Analyzer 82

Conclusion   83

References   84

5 Moving toward Differentiation   86

Initiating Group Instruction   88
New Beginnings 89 / Features of the Course Opening 99 /
Final Word 101

Accommodating Individuals   101
Instructional Choices 101 / Partners 103

Conclusion   104

References   104

6 Interventions in Special Classes   106

Dimensions of Responsive Interventions   108
Positive Relationships 108 / A Shared Agenda 109 / Adolescents'
Existing Literacies 110 / Models of Proficient Performance 111 /
Engaged, Extended Reading and Writing 112 / Planning Interventions
with Balance and Breadth 113

Interventions Using the Four Resources Model   115
Code Breaker 115 / Meaning Makers 118 / Text User 122 /
Text Analyzer 123

Conclusion   124

References   126

7 Connections beyond the Classroom   129

Home–School Partnerships   130
Family Book Talks 132 / Interviews 133 / Compacts 134 /
Family Resource Centers 135

Cross-Age Partnerships   135
Buddy Reading   136   /   Tutoring   137

Community–School Partnerships   137
Volunteer   138   /   After-School Programs   139

Cultural Ties   140

Professional Development   141
Study Groups   141   /   Professional Associations   142

School Structures   144
Literacy across the Curriculum   144   /   Library–Media Centers   144   /
School Success Courses   145   /   Personalized Schools   146   /
Full-Service Schools   147

Conclusion   147

References   148

8   Classroom Assessments   151

Uses of Assessment   152
High-Stakes Assessments   153   /   Classroom-Support Assessments   155

Classroom-Support Assessments   156
Rubrics   156   /   Portfolios   159   /   Teacher–Student
Conferences   160   /   Diagnostic Inventories   161

Grading   162
Components   163   /   Weights   164   /   Performance Norms   166   /
Fairness   166

Conclusion   169

References   169

9   Program Leadership   171

Beginning a Schoolwide Literacy Program   172
Literacy Teams   174   /   Setting Goals   175   /   Involving Staff   177   /
Creating a Culture   179

Structures for Schoolwide Literacy Improvement   180
Literacy across the Curriculum   180   /   Academic Literacy
Development Classes   181   /   Intervention Services   183   /
Resource Support   186   /   Out-of-School Extensions   187

Conclusion   188

References   188

10 **Program Profiles**   **191**

Schoolwide Offerings   **193**
Service Agencies   193   /   Local Designs   197   /
School Restructuring   199

Intervention Offerings   **201**
Status of Interventions   201   /   Cases for Pull-Out Support   202   /
Avoiding Stigma   202   /   After-School Programs   203   /
Commercial Resources   203

Conclusion   **206**

References   **207**

Index   **209**

FOREWORD

This book belongs in the hands of all middle or high school teachers who have ever wondered what they can do to help students who struggle with reading. David Moore and Kathleen Hinchman, the authors of *Teaching Adolescents Who Struggle With Reading,* have written a timely book in an era of standards-based educational reform. It is for every teacher of adolescents who at one time or another has thought about throwing in the towel, giving up on reading as a vehicle for classroom-related learning experiences. Adolescents who struggle with reading in academic contexts often resist outright or go through the motions of reading without ever engaging in the process. In this book, Moore and Hinchman show you how to break the cycle of resistance and disengagement in which struggling adolescent readers often find themselves.

Adolescents who struggle with reading, regardless of ability level, often get lost in a maze of words. They can recall bits and pieces of information but the text doesn't make sense to them in ways that permit them to think deeply about ideas. Indeed, periodic national assessments show that the majority of American students in grades 4, 8, and 12 have obtained at least basic levels of literacy. These assessments, known as the National Assessment of Educational Progress (NAEP) surveys for reading and writing suggest that many students in middle and high school struggle with complex literacy tasks. They may appear skillful in their ability to answer factual questions, but struggle with reading tasks that require interpretation and critical thinking. One of the strengths of Moore and Hinchman's book is that they provide a user-friendly guide for showing teachers how to embed critical literacy strategies into regular subject matter instructional units.

Teaching adolescents is no easy task. Their lives are complex. Not only are they undergoing great physical changes, but they also are faced with ongoing cognitive, emotional, and social challenges. In middle and high school classrooms, numerous interrelated factors influence adolescents' ability to use reading as a tool for learning. For example, as teachers embed reading into instructional units, they often make instructional decisions and use strategies based on their students' prior knowledge of, attitude toward, and interest in the subject. In doing so, they take seriously the role of purpose in literacy and learning. The learner's purpose for engaging in reading, writing, and discussion are of critical concern in the teaching of adolescents. Not only are learner-related variables taken into account, but teachers also recognize that they need to plan strategies around the language and conceptual difficulty of the text material, the assumptions that the text writers make about their audience of readers, and the text structures that writers use to organize ideas and information.

One of the underlying assumptions of Moore and Hinchman's book is that many adolescents who struggle with literacy tasks must begin to feel confident in their ability to be successful with reading and writing. If students believe, for example, that they have a good chance to succeed at a reading task, they are likely to exhibit a willingness to engage in reading and to complete the task. In other words, they will bring to learning situations a high level of self-efficacy—an "I can" belief that leads to a sense of competence. One of the strengths of Moore and Hinchman's book lies in the use of innovative instructional routines that enhance self-efficacy and motivation by influencing adolescent learners' judgments of what they can do with whatever skills and learning strategies they bring to classroom-related experiences requiring literacy.

The ability to read—and read well—for a variety of purposes has taken on unprecedented importance for human beings in the twenty-first century. In the late 1990s, The Commission on Adolescent Literacy of the International Reading Association, of which David Moore and Kathleen Hinchman were founding members, asserts in its position statement that tomorrow's adults "will need advanced levels of literacy to perform their jobs, run their households, act as citizens, and conduct their personal lives. They will need literacy to cope with the flood of information they will find everywhere they turn" (International Reading Association, 1999, p. 3). If teachers use the strategies in Moore and Hinchman's book, they will undoubtedly make a difference in the literate lives of adolescents.

Richard T. Vacca, Professor Emeritus
Kent State University

PREFACE

Middle and high school teachers regularly come upon adolescents whose reading does not fit mainstream expectations. *Teaching Adolescents Who Struggle with Reading* describes classroom teaching and learning that acknowledges these individuals.

When writing *Teaching Adolescents Who Struggle with Reading,* we envisioned an audience mainly of educators new to this topic. You might be a preservice teacher enrolled in an initial preparation program or a practicing teacher engaged in staff development efforts. You might be part of a mentor–protégé team formed during a teacher induction period. You might teach in a reading or special education program, or you might teach subject matter. Finally, you might serve as a curriculum supervisor, staff developer, or school administrator wanting an update on this topic. Welcome.

When planning and writing this book, we drew on the professional knowledge base of adolescent literacy as well as on our combined experience. David Moore taught social studies in an Arizona high school for 2 years when he first realized that some adolescents' reading interfered with their subject matter learning and that other adolescents' reading, which was considered proficient, actually could be developed much further. After earning a master's degree in reading education, he taught reading for 6 years in middle and high schools. Since earning a doctorate in reading education in 1980, his teaching, research, and service have centered on adolescent literacy. Among other positions in David's professional career, he has served recently as co-chair of the International Reading Association's Commission on Adolescent Literacy.

Kathy Hinchman began taking reading education courses and tutoring as an undergraduate English education major. She continued this work through 5 years of teaching middle school English/language arts and developmental, corrective, and remedial reading, earning a master's degree in reading education along the way. Kathy taught college study strategies for several years and has worked in reading clinics for more than 20 years, supervising the tutoring of children in grades kindergarten through high school. Her research has been concerned with adolescent literacy since finishing her doctoral dissertation, which examined teachers' and students' understandings of literacy and literacy instruction. Kathy frequently works with school districts that are concerned with developing programs to address the literacy needs of their adolescent students.

Scope of the Book

The title of this book suggests the range of ideas and information that we offer. *Teaching Adolescents Who Struggle with Reading* concentrates on instruction for middle and high school students who experience school literacy difficulties. This book presents classroom and schoolwide programs that fit youth who struggle as readers in school.

This is an introductory text, one that presents basic instructional practices. It is meant to serve as a primer, describing entry-level fundamentals. We emphasize beginning-of-the-year course plans—what to accomplish the first few days and weeks of school to get classroom reading, writing, and learning off to a good start. We introduce preliminary actions for establishing literacy programs inside and outside classroom walls.

Finally, we present down-to-earth direction that is meant to be in touch with the real world of teaching. We offer feasible advice for providing quality instruction. Chapter contents are applicable and adaptable for educators who need information now.

Special Features

Reviewers of *Teaching Adolescents Who Struggle with Reading* have noted several of its special features. The following features were most often mentioned.

Chapter Opening and Closing Questions

Each chapter opens with a question that invites engagement and focuses attention, preparing the reader for upcoming contents. The questions are distilled from ones we have encountered during our many years of teaching and consulting. For instance, Chapter 1 opens with the query, How am I supposed to teach adolescents who can't read? Revisiting the questions after reading the chapters is a good way to review and develop what you have learned.

Presentation

We have made every effort to present concise and comprehensible prose. We have explained unfamiliar terminology when first introducing it and have organized the chapters as logically as possible. We have devised metaphors and vignettes to help the reader access complex ideas. Each chapter contains numerous references to support our assertions and promote additional reading.

Multiple Connections

This book highlights the multiple connections among reading and adolescents' school lives. For instance, we explain how adolescents' personal identities are enmeshed with their reading performance, subject matter learning, and family and community status. We accentuate adolescent reading instruction that links routines, lessons, units, and programs of instruction. We relate topics that range from designing appropriate bell work to full-service schools that provide substance abuse counseling and career pathways. We connect school structures (e.g., seating arrangements, available reading materials, daily procedures) with school cultures (e.g., passion, purpose, partnership). In brief, we portray adolescents and their literacies amid a web of shaping forces.

Specifics

Each chapter of this book contains specifics that illustrate the general ideas we offer. For instance, we present concrete examples for naming the classroom culture you might desire, central questions for framing your instructional units, and practices for helping your students experience literary worlds. Our ending chapters contain websites of professional associations that address adolescent literacy, of agencies that help those interested implement schoolwide reading programs, and of publishers that market commercial products.

A Final Word

Adolescents who struggle with reading in school often have been doing so for many years. Engaging these young men and women in meaningful school-related literacy can be complicated, but they deserve nothing less. We hope this book contributes to your efforts in providing adolescents the instruction they deserve!

Acknowledgments

We thank the following reviewers for this edition: Deborah Doty, Northern Kentucky University; Kathy Lennox, Mattacheese Middle School; Roxanne Reedyk, Riverview Alternative High School; and Lynn Romeo, Monmouth University.

CHAPTER

1 Perspectives

CENTRAL QUESTION: THINK AHEAD

How am I supposed to teach adolescents who can't read?

This question, or one very much like it, comes up regularly when we interact with secondary school educators during staff development sessions. It reminds us of circumstances not so many years ago when we first realized that many adolescents in middle school and high school struggle as readers and writers. Both of us have taken this question to heart, responding to it most of our professional lives.

Addressing the literacy of adolescents now is especially timely. Renewed attention to upper-grade reading and writing began in the 1990s and continues today. Expectations that everyone be highly literate for the demands of the new economy, the advances in technology and communication, and the state-mandated reading standards and assessments are unprecedented. The news media now regularly compares test scores reported for schools, school districts, states, and the nation. During this time, educators and the public have expressed great concern over reading achievement disparities among groups that differ by race, language, and class. And whereas much attention has been devoted to reading test scores, others maintain that personal values such as intellectual curiosity, recreation, and aesthetic experience are being neglected.

This book presents our best response to these expectations and concerns. We begin by describing an instructional setting that benefits all learners, including adolescents who struggle as readers. A good first step toward promoting literacy development is to commit to a setting that supports everyone.

An Instructional Setting for All Learners

Instructional settings shape teaching and learning. They are the classroom conditions surrounding individuals. Like air, settings are difficult to point to; they are expressions of beliefs and attitudes, which circulate invisibly among teachers, students, and others. However, settings substantially influence students' school experiences in general (Ryan & Patrick, 2001) and literacy in particular (Moje & O'Brien, 2001). For instance, students' classroom experiences with study guides are not all alike. One study guide about a passage might serve mainly to keep students busy and control their behavior; another might stimulate thought, encourage independent thinking, and promote discussion. A discussion in one classroom might consist of a debate with members belittling one another; a discussion in another classroom might be a conversation that respectfully explores multiple viewpoints about a passage. Even though two classrooms might set aside the same amount of time for study guides and discussions, one might promote students' reading and writing proficiencies more than another because the settings differ.

In this section we characterize a general classroom setting that promotes literacy productively. It benefits those who find reading and writing easy as well as those who find it difficult. This setting is characterized by what we call the *Four Ps:* passion, purpose, partnership, and plans.

Passion

Passion is a term infrequently applied to literacy development, but it expresses what we consider to be a crucial aspect. The best teachers, the ones who truly make a difference in students' lives, have a passionate belief in what they are doing, and students come to embrace this belief, too. Teachers who are passionate about literacy fervently advocate it as essential for a full life. They are totally committed to the value of reading and writing well now and in the future. Some teachers express their passion for reading by regularly recounting favorite books and reading experiences, sharing current readings with students, and having guests attest to the value of literacy. The enthusiasm they project for reading and writing rubs off on students, who come to demonstrate a commitment to reading, too (Allen, 1995; Krogness, 1995).

Passionate teachers also are fervent advocates of students, aiming for whatever is in individuals' best interests. Passionate teachers have a deep and unshakable belief that all students can learn; they especially believe that all students are capable of developing their reading and writing. They express this belief in part by maintaining high expectations. They aim for excellence, being convinced that with reasonable effort all learners can reach it. This is a positive and affirming mindset, one that creates an "anything's possible" atmosphere and enables students to take control of their literacy development. Students become willing and able to exert reasonable effort to do better.

Purpose

Along with a passion for reading and writing, coupled with a passion for adolescents' reading and writing development, effective classroom settings have purpose, or vision. Teachers and students know where they are going. The following two sayings vividly express this principle:

> You've got to think about big things while doing small things so that all the small things go in the right direction.

> When you're up to your neck in alligators, it's hard to remember that your initial objective was to drain the swamp.

As these expressions suggest, having in mind a purpose focuses attention on what is important. It provides coherence to classroom activities. With an endpoint in mind, teachers and students can allocate their attention and energies appropriately, leading to results rather than to wasted time.

Purpose unites classrooms. It helps learners collaborate because they know where they are going. Purpose motivates classroom involvement and commitment. It fosters a sense of progress as learners see their efforts continually going toward something.

A statement of purpose, or a goal, expresses where you see yourself and others in the future. It is a sign pointing in a certain direction rather than a blueprint of specifics. Educators who affirm literacy as a goal for secondary schools, in concert with Graham (1981) and countless others, might convey this to students as shown in Figure 1.1. Displaying the terms on a bulletin board, talking about them, and referring to them during the year helps establish direction.

Terms such as *opportunities*, *voice*, and *insight* (in Figure 1.1) express a purpose better than expressions such as, "To effectively organize text information" or, "To adjust speed of reading according to the difficulty of the material." Organizing information and adjusting speed are the means to an end; they are not the ultimate end. Focusing too much on organizing and adjusting can be shortsighted and counterproductive because they are not educational purposes; they are strategies that enable individuals to accomplish purposes.

Ultimate purposes never can be mastered because they always grow. Concepts such as power and self-sufficiency resemble balloons that continually touch new space as they expand. Being committed to statements of purpose keeps everyone pressing forward. Such lofty, far-reaching, and long-ranging goals capture imagination and sustain action.

Partnership

Effective classroom settings also are characterized by partnership (Roeser, Eccles, & Sameroff, 2000). Partnership is evident when people come together as a community, united in their efforts. Everyone acts as a member of the

FIGURE 1.1   Literacy Vision Statement

club—an insider; no one is marginalized and treated as an outsider. Learners might work alone, but a climate of mutual support and solidarity prevails. Individuals ally with one another in different combinations to help each other out, providing input and support. People's contributions are treated respectfully. The key to any partnership is collaboration; people accomplish things by working together.

Numerous partnership arrangements are visible in effective classrooms. Various teacher–student and student–student configurations form to accomplish tasks. Teachers address students collectively as a whole class, in small groups, in pairs, and one at a time in conferences. Class members collaborate face to face to accomplish projects. With regard to literacy, individuals might collectively brainstorm what they know about a topic before reading or writing about it. They might come together in small groups to talk about what they read. They might form a group, separate to learn aspects of a topic, then rejoin to share what each one learned.

At the schoolwide level, counselors, librarians, and other resource personnel assist with classroom plans. They might contribute reading materials, or they might support individuals' efforts with materials. Older students might work with younger ones and peers might work with one another in tutoring/mentoring projects.

Partnerships involving people outside the school also are evident in effective classroom settings. Family members join with educators to support adolescents' reading and writing efforts. Community members acting on their own and as representatives of local businesses, trade groups, service agencies, and government offices promote the value of literacy and assist with reading and writing practices. Community colleges, technical schools, and universities provide assistance.

Plans

Planning is another aspect of effective settings. Teachers devise structures for students so they can devote their attention productively. Teachers set a stage that maximizes opportunities for success. As the saying goes, "A failure to plan is a plan for failure."

An important part of classroom planning involves establishing an overall learning arrangement (Danielson, 1996). For instance, teachers plan classroom space to best accommodate their teaching practices. If frequent one-to-one reading conferences are planned, then appropriate furniture is placed in back of the class to avoid disruptions. If small-group sessions are to occur frequently, then student desks or tables are placed accordingly. Other classroom plans involve routines that facilitate class work, grading practices, and discipline procedures. When a planful attitude circulates in a classroom, students come to class with appropriate materials and mindsets. They are ready to learn when class begins.

Planning also involves deciding on directions for learning and the practices to achieve them. Teachers equip themselves and their students to accomplish literacy goals. If students are to learn how to produce a persuasive argument, then teachers plan structure and support for that to happen. They decide what will enable their students to accomplish the task. Similarly, students who internalize reading and writing plans know what is needed to succeed; they can design a path to success.

Metaphors for Adolescent Literacy and Instruction

The Four Ps of effective classroom settings name conditions conducive to learning anything. Teaching and learning characterized by passion, purpose, partnership, and plans enable learners of all ages and abilities to do well, whether they're in a sports camp, music class, outdoor education experience, or academic classroom. In this section, we begin narrowing the focus. We turn to reading, in general, and reading instruction, in particular. We offer metaphor as a way to think about them.

Representing life metaphorically is more than a literary flourish. People think, communicate, and live by metaphor, considering one thing in terms of another (Lakoff & Johnson, 1980). Metaphors effectively characterize the beliefs people have about situations. To illustrate, educators who view students as factory workers, colleagues as competitors, and schools as bureaucracies differ from those who see students as researchers, colleagues as partners, and schools as communities. Underlying metaphors about literacy shape—and are shaped by—the way teachers and students engage it. The following presents builder as the primary metaphor for adolescents when reading; it presents apprentice as the primary metaphor for adolescents when learning to improve their reading.

Builders

Readers acting as builders assemble ideas. They actively construct meaning in response to what print offers. Readers produce an internal text in response to the external one being read. This metaphor is in contrast to a computer-oriented one that envisions readers simply downloading predigested information into their brains.

Reading researchers and educators have supported a metaphor of reading as building, or constructing, for many years (Pearson, 1992). To illustrate, E. L. Thorndike's influential report *Reading as Reasoning*, published in 1917, expressed this view:

Reading is a very elaborate procedure, involving the weighing of many elements in a sentence, their organization in the proper relations one to another, the selection of certain of their connotations and the rejection of others, and the cooperation of many forces to determine final response. (p. 323)

To draw out the metaphor of adolescent readers as actively building ideas from print, think of four related aspects:

1. *Materials.* The construction materials used during assembly are readers' prior experiences and knowledge—the mental contents brought to the page.
2. *Blueprints.* The construction blueprints are the authors' words, the print. Readers consult the blueprints to know how to shape their prior experiences and knowledge according to the author's blueprint.
3. *Architects.* The construction architects are the passage authors, those who set down the printed message.
4. *Tools.* The construction tools are the comprehension strategies readers use to build meaning. Proficient readers have available numerous strategies in their mental toolboxes for comprehending passages.

To see how this metaphor plays out with a brief passage, consider the following sentence from John McPhee's classic book, *Basin and Range* (1990, p. 183).

If by some fiat I had to restrict all this writing to one sentence, this is the one I would choose: The summit of Mt. Everest is marine limestone.

To make sense of this passage, readers need to actively construct a message. For instance, following the author's architectural blueprint, we first focus mainly on what comes after the colon. Taking what we already know about limestone, we next form a visual image of it making up Mt. Everest's summit. We then compare this image with other mountain summits we know that consist of volcanic rock. Finally, by synthesizing our knowledge that ocean deposits produce limestone, and by realizing that what was once an ocean floor now is the highest point on Earth, we are able to access McPhee's message about the incredible power of plate tectonics on the Earth's surface.

The reader-as-builder metaphor leads to classrooms that support readers as they construct ideas. These classrooms have students put what they read into their own words, expressing content through oral, written, and graphic mediums. They have students build new ideas through multiple forms of writing, drama, group talk, graphic organizers, and so on.

This metaphor calls attention to readers' materials (i.e., prior experiences and knowledge) used to produce ideas in response to the architect's plan. Readers with limited understandings of *fiat, summit, Mt. Everest, marine,* and *limestone* have little to mold in response to McPhee's words.

This metaphor also calls attention to readers' tools for constructing ideas—their expertise with strategies. Some of the more productive strategies that deserve attention in secondary classrooms include the following:

- Determining importance: reading selectively
- Discerning the organization of text and using that organization as a tool for understanding
- Using context to determine the meanings of apparently important yet unfamiliar words encountered in the text
- Being strategic: monitoring, reviewing, and repairing one's comprehension performance; clarifying what is unclear; planning future actions
- Summarizing: condensing ideas and information
- Forming visual, auditory, and other sensory images
- Predicting: anticipating upcoming information and ideas
- Grasping explicitly stated literal information: noting what's stated right there on the page
- Connecting authors' ideas across different parts of a passage: thinking and searching to get it all together
- Relating authors' ideas with the ones already in mind: associating what authors say with what is known; paraphrasing
- Evaluating: judging the quality of the authors' writings and the trustworthiness of authors' messages; considering alternatives
- Applying: thinking about how to use the text ideas in the future; using the passage as a springboard to new ideas
- Synthesizing information from various sources

In brief, the reader-as-builder metaphor directs attention to the active role individuals play when constructing meaning. It focuses on what readers bring to a page, emphasizing the incredible amount of prior knowledge and thinking skills needed to produce a valid internal text in response to what is on the page.

Now think of four roles that readers and writers enact within the builder metaphor: learner, experiencer, doer, and analyzer. These roles signal the major types of building that occur. As Figure 1.2 shows, builder is the main metaphor and the four subdivisions represent specific aspects of it.

Learner.   Especially with adolescents, reading often is linked with learning. Adolescent readers frequently are viewed metaphorically as learners because print provides access to countless ideas, concepts, and facts. Readers make sense of print to build knowledge of something, to become informed.

Stable learning of what is expressed in the previous John McPhee quote begins with building meaning about it, but this is only the beginning. Stable learning also comes with additional actions to expand and store in long-term memory what one gets from print. Enmeshing comprehension strategies

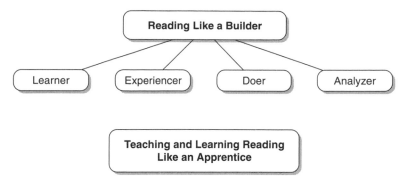

FIGURE 1.2   Metaphors for Reading and Reading Instruction

with study strategies promotes learning. To commit ideas about the summit of Mt. Everest to long-term memory, one might perform the following five tasks:

1. Paraphrase the message in a notebook or learning log
2. Produce a flowchart or set of illustrations depicting plate tectonics and land surface formations
3. Talk about plate tectonics and land surface formation with others
4. Test oneself and clarify misconceptions on several succeeding days
5. Inquire further into the topic

The reader-as-learner metaphor connects well with adolescents' progressions to lifelong learning. Advocates of this metaphor make learning with texts important to school success. They accentuate short- and long-term inquiry projects and guide students' learning efforts with multiple texts. They teach study strategies (sometimes without distinguishing them from comprehension strategies) that enable learners to link and retrieve information. For instance, they might promote note taking, regular review sessions during the week, and test preparation techniques such as practicing with potential test items.

Experiencer.   David Moore recalls visiting the Grand Canyon several times as a boy and well into his youth without ever really knowing what the fuss was all about. He would stand on the rim, looking out over the canyon, then after about 20 minutes—if there were no squirrels to feed—be ready to go. It was like looking at a nice picture.

When David returned to the canyon in the early 1990s with some hiking friends, he again looked at the picture somewhat impassively. Then he and his friends located the trail they were to hike down—and stepped *into* the picture. What a difference! On that trip and the many that followed, David came to more fully experience and truly appreciate the canyon. Among his experiences were a lunar eclipse while camping near the Colorado River; near–heat exhaustion while walking in 100 degree weather, then finding a spring gushing out of the sandstone with water to drink, a place to swim, and trees for shade; a hike up the canyon walls with his sons in a gentle snowfall that eventually gave way to sunlight blazing across the canyon and revealing startlingly white buttes.

Stepping into the picture is a good way to express literary experience. Experiencers vicariously step into text worlds and live through an event, feeling the sensations and emotions of the virtual reality. People refer to intense literary experiences as events that immerse one in the moment, merging the intellect and the emotions. It's not just what is said, it is the way it is said.

Viewing readers as constructing experiences entails the personal connections they make with authors, with story characters, with other readers, and with the overall situation. Consider this passage from Helen Keller's (1954) *The Story of My Life:*

> The mystery of language was revealed to me. I knew then that "w-a-t-e-r" meant the wonderful cool something that was flowing over my hand. That living word awakened my soul, gave it light, joy, set it free.

This passage has always spoken to us. The description of water as the "wonderful cool something" has always seemed inspired. And the poetry of the last line, "awakened my soul, gave it light, joy, set it free," allows us to share with Helen Keller—at least to some degree—the moment when language was revealed to her. Those who view readers as experiencers seem to resonate with these words from Richard Wright (1966):

> I hungered for books, new ways of looking and seeing. It was not a matter of believing and disbelieving what I read, but of feeling something new, of being affected by something that made the look of the world different.

It is important to add here that experiencers also derive simple pleasures and entertainment through print, along with occasionally intense literary experiences. They find comfort and delight in what they read; they enjoy books by Stephen King, Dave Barry, Barbara Cartland, and other light reading, too.

Advocates of the reader-as-experiencer metaphor provide encouragement and opportunities for adolescents to read widely for recreation and enrichment (Abrahamson, 1997). These advocates also have readers share personal reactions to what they encounter, structuring response-centered activities that involve journal responses, artistic expressions, and oral sharings. They encourage readers to explore multiple possibilities of reacting to literature.

Following a cookbook recipe
exemplifies reading as doing.

Doer. Now take a look at a sentence from a user manual accompanying some computer software (Nova Development Corporation, 1996):

> Double-click your desktop publishing, graphics, or word processing program and open your document. Choose the appropriate command and specify the format (EPS, TIFF, JPEG), if necessary, in the resulting dialog box.

On first encountering this message, the words do not speak to us in a manner similar to the quotation of Helen Keller's words just shared. In fact, a corporation—not an individual—is named as the author. Nor do we want to commit this to long-term memory. We are trying to get something done as efficiently as possible. Readers in situations such as this can be seen metaphorically as doers.

Doers accomplish procedures in response to print; they follow directions to perform tasks. They read to accomplish specific tasks:

- Assembling products
- Navigating the Internet, libraries, and other sources of information
- Responding to email messages

- Synthesizing information and producing an original message
- Completing long-term projects
- Running appliances, machinery, and software
- Completing legal documents and contracts

Advocates of the reader-as-doer metaphor engage students with procedural operations as part of ongoing instruction. They provide appropriate instruction to complete whatever task is at hand. They emphasize self-monitoring and control of emotions when performing especially painstaking tasks. This aspect of reading often receives less instructional attention than others, although it deserves ever-increasing attention as the pace of change in the workplace and the home continues.

Analyzer.   Analysis is a process of determining central features. Analyzers break things down for investigation; they scrutinize what they encounter. They hold things up to the light for purposes of examination.

Readers as analyzers assume a critical perspective on print. Like accomplished scientists, they are skeptical about what they read. Readers as analyzers know full well that because human beings produce print, the product always is tied up with human aspirations, attitudes, and limitations. Consequently, these readers regularly question what is presented, wondering about authors' unstated assumptions and flaws.

Readers who analyze the John McPhee quote previously presented might question several aspects of this brief piece. Does the sentence describing the highest point on Earth once being an ocean floor truly fit with what McPhee presents? How well does reading this encapsulate McPhee's statement? Further, why does McPhee add this statement at this point? Is this the most appropriate location? Readers as analyzers also might wonder about McPhee's choice of the word *fiat*. Why did he select such a Latinate word—is he being ostentatious, or does *fiat* best fit the message? How does this word position its readers—does it include or exclude readers from the text?

Apprentice

While thinking of literacy as a building, or constructing, process (with four aspects), think of literacy learning as an apprenticeship. The metaphor of readers as apprentices calls attention to how adolescents improve literacy (Brown, Collins, & Duguid, 1989). Adolescents improve their literacy when people who are more knowledgeable show them how to use it to accomplish projects. Adolescents become expert builders through master–apprentice relationships.

For students who have mastered the basic processes of reading by the time they reach adolescence, much still needs to be accomplished. In one school day, an adolescent might variously read and write like a learner, experiencer, doer, and analyzer in classes individually devoted to language arts, history, algebra, technology, and biology. When they leave school for home or work, they encounter other situations that call for literacy. Individuals learn to participate in these multiple situations by acting as apprentices in each.

Newcomers learn appropriate ways of acting by participating with those who are more competent. Master–apprentice relationships are formed. Apprentices are involved with valued projects, and masters support efforts as needed. Masters and apprentices collaborate, with the masters guiding the apprentices through what is needed to accomplish the project. Apprentices learn the strategies, goals, attitudes, and resources needed to be successful.

Those who advocate the view of reader as apprentice guide students to read, write, and think as those who already are adept in the particular situation. They immerse students in a community of like-minded individuals attempting to accomplish similar goals. For instance, they focus learners on the ways newspaper editors read copy submitted to them, on the ways biologists digest professional articles, and on the ways technicians scan manuals. They highlight the special vocabulary of each practice, the organizational formats of typical readings, and the mindset practitioners adopt. Teachers, acting as masters, regularly acculturate their apprentices into the different ways of using literacy in their specializations.

Background on Adolescents
Who Struggle as Readers

Adolescents who struggle as readers are not in a class by themselves. They benefit as much as adolescents who excel with reading by being in meaningful, print-rich situations described in the first two sections of this chapter. Everyone profits from settings characterized by passion, purpose, partnership, and plan. Everyone's literacy is enhanced when approached as builders, learners, experiencers, doers, analyzers, and apprentices. However, adolescents who struggle as readers also benefit from educational decisions informed by clear understandings of and sensitivities to their particular circumstances (Davidson & Koppenhaver, 1993; Moore, Alvermann, & Hinchman, 2000). Misconceptions readily interfere with appropriate instruction. In this section we answer two questions that shed light on common misconceptions about adolescent literacy.

Why Are So Many Adolescents Illiterate?

Because literacy is multidimensional—meaning it does not lie on one scale, nor is it all or nothing—the conception that many adolescents are illiterate is faulty. Practically all U.S. adolescents can read and write to some degree (Campbell, Hombo, & Mazzeo, 2000). Rather than addressing illiteracy among adolescents, we find it more productive to address basic literacy, aliteracy, and multiple literacies.

Basic Literacy. When all goes well during the preschool and primary school years, young children learn how print is arranged on a page and how letters connect with sounds. These are major accomplishments, but they are only basic steps toward growth into fully developed reading and writing.

Consider the following well-known quote from Shakespeare's *Hamlet:*

> *To be, or not to be: that is the question.*

Each word in this quote can be found in any primary grade classroom, but great maturity in reading and in life is needed to comprehend fully what this particular combination of words is saying. To make full sense of the nuances and implications of Shakespeare's language, readers orchestrate, refine, and extend the basic skills they learned in the early grades.

Now consider the increased sophistication of language and ideas that occur further in Hamlet's soliloquy on suicide:

> *To die, to sleep;*
> *To sleep? Perchance to dream. Ay, there's the rub;*
> *For in that sleep of death what dreams may come*
> *When we have shuffled off this mortal coil,*
> *Must give us pause.*

When reading this brief passage, unsophisticated students probably would be mystified by the terms *perchance* and *mortal coil,* misled into expecting the phrase *what dreams may come* to signal a question, and confused about what the *rub* actually is referring to, among other things.

The traditional reading tests administered by the National Assessment of Educational Progress (NAEP) regularly show that a majority of U.S. adolescents have mastered basic skills (Campbell, Hombo, & Mazzeo, 2000). Most upper-grade students are able to decode words that follow predictable spelling patterns and answer literal-level questions about simple passages. However, far fewer students have gone beyond these basic literacy skills to interpreting complex academic prose and extending the meanings they encounter. Most U.S. adolescents can read school materials at a basic level; however, far fewer can read materials at advanced levels.

Additionally, the average NAEP reading scores for 9- and 13-year old children in 1999 are statistically significantly higher than their scores in 1971. But the average reading scores for 17-year old youths show no statistically significant improvement from 1971 to 1999. The average NAEP reading scores among adolescents have remained virtually unchanged for about 3 decades. In a scholarly review of research on beginning reading instruction, Hiebert and Taylor (2000) expressed this situation as follows:

> The early reading interventions by themselves are not sufficient to guarantee success with the tasks of the middle grades. When subsequent instruction fails to attend to what children continue to need, the successes of the early grades—while real at the time—wane. (p. 477)

Aliteracy.   Youth in the upper grades are taught reading skills, tested on them, and exhorted to improve them from the time they enter school. By the time they reach adolescence, individuals have formed distinctive approaches to print, generating deeply held attitudes about books and methods for dealing with them. They have responded to family, peer group, and community perspectives on the value of reading. When individuals decide that school reading offers little value, they disdain it for other outlets. These students tend toward *aliteracy,* or being unwilling to read, more than *illiteracy,* or being unable to read.

Addressing aliteracy is important not only because adolescents who follow this path miss worthwhile recreational and aesthetic experiences, but because volume of reading is connected directly with intellectual proficiencies (Cunningham & Stanovich, 1998). Wide reading has consequences for adolescents' academic futures in rich-get-richer/poor-get-poorer cycles. Adolescents who either won't read or can't read miss tremendous opportunities for developing their vocabularies, knowledge of the world, and literacy competencies. Avid readers develop verbal proficiencies substantially beyond those who read little.

Multiple Literacies.   Outside of school, adolescents encounter print through advertisements, magazines, catalogs, paperbacks, and notes, to name a few sources. Many teens function with these forms of print in quite sophisticated ways (Moje, 2000). They adeptly and avidly navigate through technical manuals, websites, teen culture magazines, and special interest publications. Adolescents often prefer their outside-school literacies over what is expected inside school.

Inside school some individuals excel with print when solving math problems, yet they are at a loss with short stories. Some move efficiently through print associated with technology, yet they stumble with poetry. Making sense of Shakespeare's line "To be, or not to be: that is the question" certainly is challenging in its own right, yet understanding it differs from what is involved with understanding a math sentence such as "Describe the graph of the inequality $|x - 3| < 2$." As noted in the preceding section, the reading demands in science, social studies, mathematics, fine arts, and so on present distinct challenges in school.

Reading magazines with friends is a common outside of school literacy practice.

The reading and writing performed for multiple situations inside and outside school represent an important dimension of literacy among adolescents. Characterizing individuals as illiterate often overgeneralizes their condition and misses their capabilities. Individuals have multiple literacies, often controlling print well in some situations but not well in others. Addressing multiple literacies is important because it calls attention to the complex world of adolescence. Recognizing multiplicity means guarding against lumping adolescents—especially those who struggle with reading in school—into stereotypical categories such as incompetent, immature, or bundles of raging hormones (Finders, 1998/1999). Each adolescent is an individual who functions differently in different situations. Some youth are engaged in history class but disengaged in science; some are adept with friends but awkward with work.

To recapitulate, adolescent literacy is complex. Characterizing someone as illiterate risks oversimplifying the situation and offering short-sighted instruction. Basic literacy, aliteracy, and multiple literacies deserve appropriate attention.

Shouldn't Adolescent Literacy Instruction Concentrate on Remediating Disabilities?

Supporting adolescents who struggle as readers in any situation certainly is essential, but concentrating on remediating disabilities is problematic because of its effect on individuals' identities. Identity—the constellation of attitudes, opinions, and perspectives individuals hold for themselves—influences how individuals approach life. For instance, Deschenes, Cuban, and Tyack

(2001) report the following past and present labels educators have applied to students who experience difficulty completing school tasks:

Backward	Limited
Deprived	Low-division
Disabled	Occupational
Dull	Push-out
Dullard	Remedial
Dunce	Shirker
Handicapped	Sleepy-minded
Immature	Slow
Inferior	Sluggish
Laggard	Stupid

Students labeled negatively according to any of these terms too readily assume the identity of flawed, broken individuals with little control over their plights (Kos, 1991; McCray, Vaughn, & Neal, 2001; Mueller, 2001). A girl might realize she is not expected to excel with math and science, so she adopts a mediocre approach to and proficiency with math and science. A boy might realize that his peers do not value being a proficient, avid reader, so he disengages from print.

Personal identities and resulting actions frequently are shaped by outside influences. For instance, individuals view themselves according to their gender, family income, ethnicity, home language, immigrant status, test proficiency, and career aspiration. Such markers are powerful; they position students to think of themselves and act in certain ways. Influential teachers, parents, and friends who treat adolescent readers as struggling and slow as a result of such markers often produce, or at least reinforce, readers who act accordingly (McDermott & Varenne, 1995).

A positive approach with adolescents who struggle as readers is to continue literacy development for all, making it known that every reader encounters passages he or she finds difficult. Educators with this mindset advocate the goal of everyone learning how to solve reading and writing difficulties. Realizing that literacy is not something mastered once and for all leads to instruction that focuses on extending everyone's awareness of and competencies with whatever reading and writing tasks are at hand.

Acknowledging the influence of adolescents' identities as readers and writers leads to many actions (Rex, 2001). Teachers who contribute to building positive identities recognize learners' difficulties but emphasize what they do well and begin instruction with these capabilities in mind. Such teachers maintain high standards and positive expectations for success. They illuminate proficient readers' roles (e.g., builder, doer, analyzer) and engage students in them. They promote learners' awareness of how literacy fits with life issues such as career goals and personal fulfillment. They invite role models from the community to attest to the value of literacy. Taking personal identity seriously means showing adolescents that literacy counts for something and individuals have the power to control it.

Conclusion

Literacy development proceeds somewhat like physical motor development. Humans increasingly develop control of their bodies, and this development is revealed when, for example, youngsters lift their heads, sit, crawl, and walk. As with physical motor development, humans develop literacy incrementally, building on past accomplishments. Instruction and support throughout the grades is needed for individuals' maximum continued progress.

Too often, students falter with the challenging materials and tasks encountered during adolescence. Simply getting individuals off to a good start in the early grades is insufficient. The International Reading Association's Adolescent Literacy Commission position statement published in 1999 put it this way:

> Public and educational attention long has been focused on the beginnings of literacy, planting seedlings and making sure they take root. But without careful cultivation and nurturing, seedlings may wither and their growth become stunted. (Moore, Bean, Birdyshaw, & Rycik, 1999, p. 9)

CENTRAL QUESTION: THINK BACK

How am I supposed to teach adolescents who can't read?

To answer fully this chapter's central question, build on the following key concepts:

- Provide instructional settings consisting of passion, purpose, partnership, and plans.
- Treat readers and writers as builders in general and as learners, experiencers, doers, and analyzers in particular.
- Teach adolescents as apprentices.
- Acknowledge basic literacy, aliteracy, and multiple literacies as important dimensions of reading and writing development.
- Take personal identity seriously when supporting adolescents' literacy development.

REFERENCES

Abrahamson, R. F. (1997). Collected wisdom: The best articles ever written on young adult literature and teen reading. *English Journal, 86,* 50–54.

Allen, J. (1995). *It's never too late: Leading adolescents to lifelong literacy.* Portsmouth, NH: Heinemann.

Brown, J. S., Collins, A., & Duguid, P. (1989). Situated cognition and the culture of learning. *Educational Researcher, 18,* 32–42.

Campbell, J. R., Hombo, C. M., & Mazzeo, J. (2000). *Trends in academic progress: Three decades of student performance* (NCES Publication No. 2000-469). Washington, DC: U.S. Department of Education, Office of Educational Research and Improvement. National Center for Education Statistics, National Assessment of Educational Progress. Retrieved August 21, 2001, from www.ed.gov/NCES/NAEP.

Cunningham, A. E., & Stanovich, K. (1998). What reading does to the mind. *American Educator, 22*(1), 8–15.

Danielson, C. (1996). *Enhancing professional practice: A framework for teaching.* Alexandria, VA: Association for Supervision and Curriculum Development.

Davidson, J., & Koppenhaver, D. (1993). *Adolescent literacy: What works and why* (2nd ed.). New York: Garland.

Deschenes, S., Cuban, L., & Tyack, D. (2001). Mismatch: Historical perspectives on schools and students who don't fit them. *Teachers College Record, 103,* 525–547.

Finders, M. J. (1998/1999). Raging hormones: Stories of adolescence and implications for teacher preparation. *Journal of Adolescent and Adult Literacy, 42,* 252–263.

Graham, P. A. (1981). Literacy; A goal for secondary schools. *Daedalus, 110*(3), 119–134.

Hiebert, E. H., & Taylor, B. M. (2000). Beginning reading instruction: Research on early interventions. In M. J. Kamil, P. B. Mosenthal, P. D. Pearson, & R. Barr (Eds.), *Handbook of reading research* (Vol. 3, pp. 455–482). Mahwah, NJ: Lawrence Erlbaum.

Keller, H. (1954). *The story of my life.* Garden City, NY: Doubleday.

Kos, R. (1991). Persistence of reading difficulties: The voices of four middle school students. *American Educational Research Journal, 28,* 875–895.

Krogness, M. M. (1995). *Just teach me, Mrs. K: Talking, reading, and writing with resistant adolescent learners.* Portsmouth, NH: Heinemann.

Lakoff, G., & Johnson, M. (1980). *Metaphors we live by.* Chicago: University of Chicago Press.

McCray, A. D., Vaughn, S., & Neal, L. I. (2001). Not all students learn to read by third grade: Middle school students speak out about their reading disabilities. *Journal of Special Education, 35,* 17–30.

McDermott, R., & Varenne, H. (1995). Culture as disability. *Anthropology and Education Quarterly, 26,* 324–348.

McPhee, J. (1990). *Basin and range.* New York: Noonday Press.

Moje, E. (2000). "To be part of the story": The literacy practices of gangsta adolescents. *Teachers College Record, 102,* 651–690.

Moje, E. B., & O'Brien, D. G. (Eds.). (2001). *Constructions of literacy: Studies of teaching and learning in and out of secondary schools.* Mahwah, NJ: Lawrence Erlbaum.

Moore, D. W., Bean, T. W., Birdyshaw, D., & Rycik, J. A. (1999). *Adolescent literacy: A position statement.* Newark, DE: International Reading Association, Commission on Adolescent Literacy.

Moore, D. W., Alvermann, D. E., & Hinchman, K. A. (Eds.). (2000). *Struggling adolescent readers: A collection of teaching strategies.* Newark, DE: International Reading Association.

Mueller, P. M. (2001). *Lifers: Learning from at-risk adolescent readers.* Portsmouth, NH: Heinemann.

Nova Development Corporation. (1996). *Art explosion user manual.* Calabasas, CA: Author.

Pearson, P. D. (1992). Reading. In M. C. Alkin (Ed.), *Encyclopedia of educational research* (6th ed., vol. 3, pp. 1075–1085). New York: Macmillan.

Rex, L. A. (2001). The remaking of a high school reader. *Reading Research Quarterly, 36,* 288–313.

Roeser, R. W., Eccles, J. S., & Sameroff, A. J. (2000). School as a context of early adolescents' academic and social-emotional development: A summary of research. *Elementary School Journal, 100,* 443–462.

Ryan, A. M., & Patrick, H. (2001). The classroom social environment and changes in adolescents' motivation and engagement during middle school. *American Educational Research Journal, 38,* 437–460.

Thorndike, E. L. (1917). Reading as reasoning: A study of mistakes in paragraph reading. *Journal of Educational Psychology, 8,* 276–282.

Wright, R. (1966). *Black boy.* New York: Harper and Row.

CHAPTER

2

Before School Starts

CENTRAL QUESTION: THINK AHEAD

What do I actually need to do in my classroom to start teaching adolescents who struggle as readers?

You might ask this question when you land your first teaching position and truly begin realizing all it entails. You might be committed to passion, purpose, partnership, and plans, but you might be unsure about implementing these principles on a daily basis. If you are like many novice teachers, you are well grounded theoretically but not so well equipped with concrete practices for implementing theories.

In large part, getting started teaching centers about deciding how you and the groups of students entrusted to you will spend time together productively. This means directly addressing your classroom responsibilities. Teaching is an incredibly complex occupation. As one beginning teacher with extensive life experience put it, "I've run a 4,000 person organization—and it's not nearly this intense" (Sturtevant, Duling, & Hall, 2001, p. 77). In the name of promoting literacy and other academic achievement, teachers are responsible for

- Maintaining appropriate learning conditions
- Following mandated instructional guidelines and expectations
- Counseling individuals facing difficult situations
- Serving as a student advocate as well as a judge
- Maintaining accurate records
- Communicating with parents

The time to prepare for your major teaching responsibilities so learners can concentrate on literacy and learning is before school starts. Coming into your classroom the first day well prepared gets momentum moving in the right direction; it gets you started on the right foot. As the saying goes, "You don't get a second chance to make a good first impression." Having a plan before you enter the classroom allows you to jump-start instruction.

Having a plan for general classroom conditions enhances your professional demeanor and increases your confidence. It allows you to move forward purposefully and consistently. It eliminates excessive improvisation, hastily deciding on the fly what to do. Establishing roles right off the bat allows you to be proactive rather than reactive. It helps you prevent negative situations so you do not spend inordinate time and energy remedying them. By envisioning actions, by mentally rehearsing how you will structure classroom instruction successfully from the first day on, you promote your eventual success.

Classroom Culture

Culture encompasses the ways of thinking that classroom members enact. It refers to group members' roles and norms of behavior. Directly planning a positive classroom culture is especially important for adolescents who struggle as readers. Vacca tells of meeting a young man who had been in his high school English class but who dropped out of school. When reading was mentioned, the teen remarked "somewhat wistfully, somewhat defiantly, 'F___ reading. Reading robbed me of my manhood' " (Vacca, 1998, p. 608). Specifics about all the awkward and embarrassing classroom events and personal feelings underlying this comment are left unsaid, but scenes readily come to mind. Frustrating situations with print and negative comments about performance no doubt contributed to this young man's feelings of impotence.

Many adolescents who struggle as readers invent unproductive classroom coping strategies. They might express their resistance to literacy by limiting their participation and by challenging teachers. They might avoid eye contact with the teacher and engage in disruptive behaviors that enable them to avoid reading or being held accountable for it. In the words of Scott:

> Yeah, I'm always scared the teacher is going to call on me. I'll fool around . . . and she tells me to shut up . . . you can do that or act sick or something. Most of the time I just get the answer from Andrea. (Brozo, 1990, p. 324)

Adolescents who have immigrated to the United States often regard themselves as having parents who wrenched them from their homes and friends and brought them to this country against their will (Greenleaf, 1995). This orientation contributes to negative feelings, which interacts with the challenges of reading and writing English.

Adolescents who struggle as readers need classroom cultures that generate encouragement and success, ones that break cycles of failure and enable students to take charge of their learning. They report wanting orderly classrooms that maintain high expectations; they want meaningful assignments and the support needed to accomplish what is expected (Johnson & Farkas, 1997; Wilson & Corbett, 2001). Adolescents who see themselves as academic failures and nonreaders require especially positive classroom cultures to shape productive identities (Gaskins, 1998; Phelan, Yu, & Davidson, 1994).

Naming Classroom Culture

When deciding specifically how you and your students will go about shaping the classroom's culture, a good way to start is by planning what you explicitly will say (Deal & Peterson, 1999). What will you share with students the first few days of school that names and explains the expected culture of the class? What expectations do you have about how students will approach reading and writing? What expectations do you have about how students will interact with you and each other? Moreover, what are your students' expectations along these lines?

During the first few days of school, open lines of communication and get students in on the act of expressing a classroom culture conducive to learning. Consider having students brainstorm individually and in pairs, small groups, or as a whole class their thoughts on the subject.

Literacy Purpose.   Crystallizing expectations goes far in setting the right course when you are before a group. Sharing and explaining expectations the first few days of class alerts everyone to the expected culture. When focusing on literacy, begin by presenting your ultimate purpose, or vision. Classroom literacy purpose statements should engage you and your students with course contents, tap higher-order thinking about many dimensions of course contents, and apply to every unit and lesson presented during the course.

Literacy purpose statements can be expressed through multiple, overlapping expressions. You might use the metaphors presented in Chapter 1 as touchstones for this. Tell students that when they leave your class, you expect them to be able to act like proficient builders, learners, experiencers, and so on. These are the cultural roles they will enact and refine in your class.

Another type of purpose emphasizes what you expect students to achieve. In this situation, tell students that when they leave your class with the literacy proficiencies you will help develop, they will have increased characteristics such as control, insight, opportunities, passport, power, self sufficiency, and voice.

Literacy purpose statements might be displayed—and regularly referenced throughout the course—in the following forms, too:

> *Quotation:* Reading can never be mastered. I have tried all my life, and I have not yet accomplished it. (Goethe)

> *Motto:* "If anything is odd, inappropriate, confusing, or boring, it's probably important." (Rex, 2001, p. 294)

> *Central Question:* How can we build meaning with this passage?

Along with stating overarching literacy purposes to characterize and focus your desired classroom culture, name the norms of behavior associated with them. You might present builder as the role students are expected to enact during the course, then regularly call attention to norms of builders' behaviors: determine importance, use context, be strategic, form images, predict, connect ideas, evaluate, and apply.

If you are implementing a program such as Reciprocal Teaching (Alfassi, 1998; Palincsar & Brown, 1984), you might name expert reader as the role students are expected to enact, and display the expected, associated norms of behavior as follows: summarize, clarify, question, predict, and dialogue.

School Success Expectations.   Other aspects of classroom culture deserving attention involve goals and norms of behavior associated with school success (Jackson & Davis, 2000). These actions are more general than what is involved mainly with reading and writing, but they are especially appropriate with adolescents who struggle as readers. Classrooms devoted to the following school success roles and norms of behavior go far in promoting literacy among those who struggle.

Worker. Engages problems actively; does not procrastinate; manages time productively and responsibly; is punctual; follows directions.

Connector. Defines learning as purposeful acts of integrating personal background with new information and experiences; actively relates school and personal worlds; is not satisfied with rote, superficial understanding.

Listener. Listens attentively when others have the floor; understands and builds on another's perspective; treats others courteously and elicits their input.

Problem solver. Uses multiple strategies and references to solve difficult or ambiguous tasks before asking for help; takes time to think through a problem; creates networks among peers, family members, teachers, and others for feedback and support; is willing to ask for help after initial attempts fail; interacts with others when group dynamics are especially appropriate for learning.

Stabilizer. Tolerates frustration, manages anger, resolves conflicts, negotiates disagreements; manages stress and channels emotions; disagrees without being disagreeable; does not make ugly remarks such as insults, rudeness, put downs, dissing, profanity, and harassment.

Introspector. Demonstrates accurate self-awareness; sets and meets appropriate goals; gives reasons for answers; addresses limitations productively; attributes learning to individual effort rather than to luck.

Classroom Interaction Expectations.   Along with literacy and school success roles and norms of behavior, classroom cultures depend substantially on how people treat each other during face-to-face interactions. Positive interactions in a class make it possible for people to work as partners and achieve common goals. Such classrooms are neither laissez faire with individuals devoted only to what interests them, nor are they overly authoritarian with the teacher always dictating orders. Adolescents who struggle as readers and writers—like most adolescents—typically do best in classrooms that eliminate threats and distractions and support individuals' efforts.

Respect and responsibility are two expectations commonly used to characterize desired classroom cultures. *Respectful person* and *responsible person* are noun forms for expressing these roles, although they are not too elegant or engaging. Some teachers number these 1 and 2, then simply say the number as reminders when needed. Norms of behavior associated with respect and responsibility are as follows:

- Promote everyone's learning—especially your own.
- Participate positively.
- Contribute to a community of learners.
- Support the dignity of yourself and others.

- Honor what others offer.
- Be productive.
- Be courteous.
- Be polite.
- Be responsible.
- Be prepared to learn.
- Make appropriate decisions.
- Promote positive relations.
- Promote a safe and supportive environment.
- Take pride in yourself.

Signaling Expectations for Desired Cultures. Signs and symbols that visually display classroom goals and norms of behavior are helpful in pointing to the desired culture. Put up bulletin boards, posters, and banners communicating where your class is going and some norms of behavior for getting there. Many teachers prominently display a symbol of their desired culture. For instance, one teacher we know keeps in class a hand puppet of a giraffe, representing the land mammal with the largest heart, and another puppet of a jackal, representing an animal that attacks others ruthlessly. This teacher compares the two symbols regularly to help students embrace the idea of respectful civil discourse. Another prominently displays posters of social activists and frequently asks, "What would _____ do?"

General Positives

Doing pleasant things for no apparent reason can contribute to a positive classroom culture. It indicates your intention to make your classroom a good place to be no matter what. Consider actions such as the following:

Academic games: Jeopardy, Trivial Pursuit, Password, Charades, Pictionary, Wheel of Fortune, hangman, baseball, football, Family Feud, Hollywood Squares

General plans: Background music, hold class outside, free social time

Home communications: Notes or phone calls home conveying good news from school

Lottery tickets: Everyone receives a ticket for a Friday drawing with the reward of such things as a snack, front-of-the-line lunch pass, gift certificate, discount card, or free admission to a school function

Passes: Substitutes for student's choice of homework, homework items, tests, test items

Snack for the entire class: Popcorn, candy

Student suggestions: Students brainstorm reasonable and appropriate possibilities for making your class as positive as it can be

General positives along with signs, symbols, and explanations are good first steps for promoting a positive classroom culture, but they go only so far. Daily words and actions carry the most weight in shaping your classroom's culture. Such words and actions are evident in the classroom structure you implement.

Classroom Structure

Think along two dimensions, cultural and structural, when planning how you will carry out your classroom responsibilities. Culture and structure interact, with one reinforcing the other (Newmann, et al., 1996). Whereas the cultural dimension described above is difficult to put your finger on when in a class, the structural dimension is readily apparent.

Structure refers to the concrete practices, resources, and arrangements involved in running your classroom. Emmer, Evertson, and Worsham (2000); MacDonald and Healy (1999); Ryan (1992); Wong and Wong (1998); and Wyatt and White (2001) among others, detail the structural dimension of classrooms for beginning teachers. Next we present three essential structures to plan before school starts: your room arrangement, procedures, and discipline plan.

Room Arrangement

Room arrangement refers to the interior design of your classroom. Plan how you will set up the physical properties of your class to promote literacy and learning. To be sure, your ideal room arrangement might differ from what your actual room allows, but thinking through the possibilities enables you to make the most of whatever situation you inherit.

When deciding the room arrangement that best allows you to fulfill your teaching responsibilities, consider the following items:

Bookcases	Tables
Bulletin boards	Computers
Desks for students	Projectors
Desks for teacher	Television
Displays/Adornments	White boards
Filing cabinets	Wastebaskets
Shelves	

Juggle these classroom items until they are arranged in a way that you foresee promoting literacy and working best for you. The arrangement should be determined mainly by how you intend to conduct business in your classroom; it should expedite the reading and writing you and your class will perform. The following criteria and questions are good touchstones for the decisions you make about your space arrangement:

Compatibility. Does your arrangement fit with your instructional goals and preferred types of activity? For instance, if you plan to emphasize small-group work, does the furniture promote it? If you plan to confer individually with students, do you have a place set aside for such conferences that will not be distracting yet allow you to monitor the class?

Suitability. Does your arrangement invite a positive mindset and inspire literacy? Does it entice adolescents to want to spend time in your room reading, writing, and learning? Does it welcome students with encouraging items such as colorful posters, reading materials, work samples, plants, and photographs of school and outside life? Is a reading or writing space available for free reading? Does the arrangement eliminate distractions such as clutter and congestion?

Proximity. Does your arrangement allow ready access to students? Does it place the least distance and the fewest barriers between you and class members? Does it allow you to move about freely to manage instruction as well as behavior?

Visibility. Does your arrangement allow students to see presentations and displays easily? Are the sight lines appropriate so every student can see you, the projection screen, and white board during class presentations?

Accessibility. Does your arrangement allow you and your students readily to obtain what is needed for class? Can students efficiently pick up books and any necessary folders or resources when entering class? Are high-traffic areas such as the doorway and front of the classroom free of congestion?

Flexibility. Does your arrangement allow different seating configurations? Are students able to move from individual, to paired, to small-group, to whole-class situations with minimal effort?

Security. Is your storage safeguarded? Are unused teaching resources and equipment out of the way? Are any restricted areas of your class clearly identified and out of the traffic flow?

Figure 2.1 portrays a space arrangement plan that acknowledges many of the criteria just presented. In this arrangement, students' desks are compatible with whole-class presentations yet flexible enough to combine readily into pairs. Slanting the outside rows promotes good sight lines for presentations, and it promotes a sense of community. The spaces between the desks and tables provide ready access to individuals and groups. The tables, teacher's desk, and materials are located in back of the room to minimize dis-

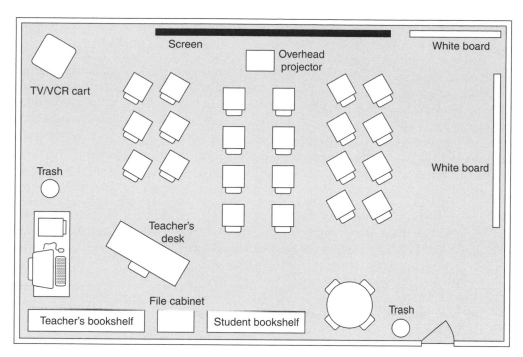

FIGURE 2.1   Sample Classroom Arrangement

tractions. Books and resources are accessible yet secure. Students may read and write at their desks or in the back according to the situation. Literacy-related displays and adornments are not portrayed in this model, but the walls are filled with bulletin boards, posters, and student work samples.

Procedures

Think of the trading floor of the New York Stock Exchange. To the uninitiated, the actions look utterly chaotic, but members follow well-established procedures for buying and selling stock. The underlying pattern of behavior that all members follow provides opportunities to engage in tremendously fast-paced consequential trading.

Classroom procedures are patterned ways of moving through teaching–learning situations. They consist of regular ways of beginning class, distributing paperwork, updating students who missed class, and gaining the floor during class discussions. Establishing a set of routine procedures allows you to use class time efficiently and maximize opportunities to learn. They are important because they free up time and energy for learning. They promote efficiency and reduce disruptions. Adolescents who habitually, easily, and quickly perform some classroom action, such as forming a small group, then are able to apply themselves more fully to the group's project.

All successful classrooms have such procedures to allow class members to handle mundane issues automatically and concentrate on the higher-order aspects. At least three categories of procedures—for instruction, for communicating assignments, and for transitions—enhance the functioning of your classroom.

Instruction.   Instructional routines are a major category of procedures designed to facilitate classroom functioning so you and your students can concentrate on what is important. If you expect students to follow an instructional procedure such as reviewing vocabulary, maintaining notes, or talking about print, show them how to do it and monitor their progress. Following the apprenticeship metaphor presented in Chapter 1, guide students through the mindset and strategies needed for accomplishing each procedure. The following types of instructional procedures set the stage for meaningful teaching and learning to occur.

Bell Work.   Bell work refers to the common practice of engaging students in a brief independent classroom activity as soon as the school bell signals the beginning of class. By involving students academically right from the start, teachers intend to set an academic tone, prevent disruptions, and help students focus themselves on the subject at hand. Bell work often serves as a review of what has been presented and a warm up to what is coming. By providing a brief activity to be accomplished independently, teachers have the time to set out materials, counsel latecomers or those who were absent, and complete clerical administrivia, such as reporting attendance.

For bell work to be effective, structure clear ways for students to respond. Thoroughly teach the procedure when you introduce it, ensuring students' competence. Display the daily bell work assignment, or prompt, in the identical location of the room. Have students maintain their bell work in journals, notebooks, or folders so they can access it readily for each day's addition and so you—or whoever you designate—can access it for accountability purposes. Many teachers count bell work completion as a small proportion (e.g., 5%) of the course grade.

You may provide a new bell work assignment each day (e.g., "Explain the phrase *54–40 or fight!*") or continue with the same task across days (e.g., reading a book related to U.S. expansion into the Pacific northwest). You also may vary the type of bell work assignments on a daily, weekly, or monthly basis. Some types of bell work that tap literacy are as follows:

- Practice test-taking strategies. Complete sample items of mandated assessments.
- Read independently. Students bring their own reading materials or borrow materials from the class and read silently for a designated time.

- Review homework with a partner. Resolve discrepancies.
- Review vocabulary. Study key terms individually or with a partner according to established guidelines (e.g., use in a meaningful sentence, describe any base word or other related words, compare with another listed word).
- Revise the spelling, grammar, and punctuation of intentionally faulty sentences, short paragraphs, or short passages.
- Solve a problem. In math class, students often apply what they are learning to a new word problem at the beginning of class.
- Write in response to a picture, poem, quotation, headline, or political cartoon. Students might respond to two questions: What does it mean? What do I think of what it means?
- Write in response to a specific question or key word derived from what the class is studying (e.g., "Write three questions about yesterday's lesson"; "List the words from the last chapter that are difficult to understand"; "Brainstorm all you can remember about yesterday's lesson.")
- Write independently. Students free write in response to whatever they want (as long as they are willing to have the contents shared with their family members).

During Class.   Think through the nuts-and-bolts practices you intend for your basic instructional organization during class. What patterned ways of teaching and learning will you employ? Present each one as an instructional procedure so students can learn to participate in it automatically, devoting their attention to the academic substance of the lesson. The bell work practices listed above are a special kind of procedure because they commonly are used to open the class period, but you could regularly use any of them during class periods, too. Some common procedures related to literacy that are used during class follow:

Reading aloud.   Either you or someone you designate reads selected passages orally to a group.

Reciprocal teaching.   Students talk about the summaries, clarifications, questions, and predictions they produce in response to what they read.

Taking notes.   In writing students summarize, paraphrase, and react to key ideas while reading or listening.

Talking about print.   In pairs, small groups, or the whole class, students share their understandings of and reactions to what they read.

Think aloud.   You and your students make public how you go about making sense of a passage. Orally think through any mental process such as how to take notes, compare ideas, and form questions.

Vocabulary self-collection.   Students use their interests and talents to generate words to be learned and to explain their meanings.

These practices suggest the vast array that teachers commonly use. Biology teachers can show students how to conduct and report lab experiments; math teachers specify how to write up problem-solving steps for particular operations; and English teachers have students maintain a writing portfolio. Burke (2000); Lenski, Wham, and Johns (1999); and Tierney and Readence (2000) provide handy access to literacy procedures useful during class.

You also might identify a small set of anchor procedures, instructional practices that students accomplish independently during class while you confer with individuals or groups. Like bell work, anchor procedures engage the entire class in an activity so you can interact face to face with individuals. Some types of anchor procedures include reading independently, completing study guides, and writing in response to course topics. Directly teach students how to perform such procedures automatically. Anchor procedures deserve a place in busy classrooms because they enable you to bolster those who struggle with classroom learning, but they can be overdone. A daily diet of anchor procedures soon becomes little more than busy work, so limit them to occasional time slots during each week.

Closure.   Whereas bell work begins class and anchors engage students during class, closure routines end the class. What should be done during the last few minutes of class to review and consolidate ideas? Will students record final thoughts of the class in a notebook or journal? Will they prepare an exit slip reflecting on course contents to hand you as they walk out the door? Will someone orally respond to a general question such as, "What became clear to you today?" or, "What did you learn today?" Will students summarize the class before leaving?

Extra Help.   Procedures benefit students willing and able to avail themselves of extra help. Many teachers make it well known that they are available for extra assistance in their classrooms a certain time before and after school. Some offer sign-up sheets as a way to schedule students for extra assistance. Most teachers circulate regularly during class to monitor who needs help, and some position themselves at a table during class and invite inquiries. Tutoring arrangements with a qualified group such as the school's academic honors society is common. You might publicize your email address.

Communicating Assignments.   Procedures that specify assignments allow students to concentrate on the ideas and skills the assignments tap. Clearly communicating course work expectations allows students to focus on what is important rather than waste time trying to discern what they are supposed to accomplish. Even open-ended assignments (e.g., produce a convincing brochure) benefit from clearly stated deadlines. Think through how you and your students will communicate efficiently about their assignments.

Posting Expectations.   How will you display assignments and their due dates? Many teachers record a weekly, monthly, or term assignment calendar on a white board, poster, or handout. Others produce such a guide for each 2- to 3-week unit of instruction. Many others issue a computer printout that specifies each assignment's objective, description, scoring guide, and due date. We are seeing more and more teachers post assignments on classroom websites, which is especially useful for students absent from class and for parents (of course, this works only when absentees and parents have the technology to access the site!).

Facilitating Make-Ups.   Along with posting expectations clearly, you may want to set aside a special part of your classroom in the back that contains materials absent (and absent-minded!) students need to make up the learning and assignments they missed. Many teachers offer folders for each day of the week, month, or unit containing what they distributed during class. The folders contain handouts, study guides, reprinted materials, and so on. The folders also may contain course notes that the teacher or a designated student produce so those making up the class have access to course contents.

Finally, you may designate individuals for absentee students to consult. These consultants may be teaching assistants, those excelling in the class, or simply friends the absentee selects. To be most efficient, you should not be the first resort when someone says, "I was out the last 3 days of class, did I miss anything?" Once absentees understand expectations at least generally, then intervene instructionally when appropriate.

Handling the Paperload.   Think what happens if you are responsible for 70 or more students each day, and every day a student submits a paper to you. In 1 week you are handling 350 items, and the term *handling* might include actions such as receiving, commenting, grading, recording, and returning in a timely fashion. If you spend 5 minutes with each paper, you will spend 1,750 total minutes—or about 30 hours per week—with this one aspect of teaching. Streamlining this paperwork is essential.

You might initiate paperwork procedures at the beginning of the term by showing your preferred heading, spacing, and any other particular forms to be followed when writing. Tell your students that practically every institution—including your class—uses a common format for paperwork to enhance its handling. Then show how work is to be handed in and how you will return it. For each student, will you use individual folders? For each class, will you use a wire or cardboard container or a filing cabinet drawer? Will students hand in and return paperwork individually, or will a designated person (such as a teaching assistant or an especially energetic student) handle it?

On a more substantive note, will students submit to you everything they write? Will you react to everything students submit? How will you balance encouraging students to write voluminously with closely reading what they produce?

Monitoring Student Performance.   Efficient procedures for students and parents to monitor performance contributes to an effective class. More and more teachers now have access to computer software that is useful for listing assignments, assignment scores, and overall scores that can be distributed daily, if desired. Your school or school district will have a formal plan for reporting grades to parents, with many issuing notices every 3 weeks. How and when will you notify students of their status with assignments within the 3-week periods?

Transitions.   Classroom efficiency is especially vulnerable during student movement from one activity to another. You and your students need to begin the class appropriately, segment activities during the class period, then end the class. Block scheduling, which often configures class periods into more than 80 minutes each, especially calls for you to segment class appropriately. Students might perform a brief activity when they first enter; listen to your greeting, explanations, and directions; work on tasks individually or collaboratively; reassemble as a whole group; then recycle through the pattern. Without procedures, you can waste much time and energy getting everyone to settle down and lock in on the tasks at hand.

Entering Class.   The way students come into your room helps set the tone for how the class will proceed. You may want to develop the following procedures:

> *Greeting at the door.* Speaking individually with each student as he or she comes into class establishes a connection between you two. It is a great time to say something positive. Additionally, you get a good heads up regarding who is having an especially good or bad day and who is within or without dress, gang colors, tattoo, and other limits.
>
> *Class items.* What books, binders, and other academic materials should students bring with them into class? If free reading will occur, should students bring their own reading material?
>
> *Personal items.* What should students do with personal things they bring into class? How should they handle any cell phones, pagers, or personal grooming devices? What about hats and backpacks? If students even show up with food, drink, or gum, what should they do with it?
>
> *Settling in.* What should be done as soon as students step inside your class? Are you simulating an environment found in the workplace, a library, a home, or where? Do you expect students to move directly

to their desks, be seated, and begin working before any school signal sounds off? What level of talk is appropriate? When can students use the pencil sharpener? Is paperwork picked up or dropped off as soon as students come in? Do you have expectations for what is on desktops?

Signals.   You may want to develop gestures or devices informing students that one class segment is ending and a new one is beginning. Having such signals reduces the need for you to request students' attention verbally and possibly raise your voice, which eventually becomes counterproductive. Visual and verbal signals help segment class periods and eliminate the need for you to become overbearing or nagging. Some effective ones we have observed include the following:

- Clap your hands
- Count down (5–4–3–2–1)
- Display an object (social sciences might use a gavel; science might use a bell jar)
- Mimic a claw with your hand
- Raise a finger to your lips
- Extend your arms with palms out
- Raise an outstretched arm
- Say a keyword (*class, learners*)
- Stand at a designated spot (by an overhead projector, in front of a desk)
- Turn on the overhead projector

Leaving the Room during Class.   Having clear procedures for students who must leave during the period is another way to streamline and smooth out classroom operations. Stopping what you are doing and responding to every request to leave is unproductive. If your school has no policy regarding students leaving the room during class, then you should decide the following:

Number. How many students may leave at one time? Most teachers allow one at a time.

Frequency. How many times may a student leave? Will you specify a number? Will you confer individually with anyone who seems to be abusing this privilege? Will you issue coupons for individuals to allocate for themselves during the semester?

Accountability. Will you have students sign out and in so you have their word on when and where they are going? Will you have students carry some artifact in the halls so authorities realize their whereabouts are known?

Exiting Class.   The same manner as the way students enter. You may want to develop procedures for the following:

> *Gathering up.* What should be done during the final few minutes of class? What amount of clean up and what level of talk are appropriate? Are students expected to remain in their seats or may they move about?
>
> *Dismissal.* What counts as your official dismissal—the school's signal or your acknowledgement that it is time to leave?

Discipline Plan

Your discipline plan backs up your classroom culture, space arrangement, procedures, and overall instruction. It is your fall-back position if students begin disrupting their own or others' learning. It is your necessary last resort for maintaining a positive classroom setting.

When designing your discipline plan, follow a common guideline from the insurance industry, "Expect the best, but prepare for the worst." When expecting the best in your class, accentuate the positive. Regularly praise students' productive behaviors. Thank them for being respectful and responsible. Catch troublesome individuals acting appropriately and appreciate their efforts. When preparing for the worst, determine how you will fairly, firmly, and consistently act in students' best interests if they act out.

Norms of Social Behavior.   To begin producing a discipline plan, focus on your expectations for classroom conduct. What acceptable norms of social behavior will you promote? What are the expectations in your classroom for ways of being with others, for classroom protocol, decorum, and etiquette? These expectations commonly emphasize lifelong character traits such as respect and responsibility, previously noted in this chapter's section on Classroom Interaction Expectations, which are applicable inside and outside school now and in the future. They apply to adolescents as individuals, family members, community members, citizens, and employees. They are consistent with school policies and societal laws.

Display the norms of social behavior that trigger consequences if violated. Express these norms as abstract generalizations (e.g., "Respect others") and concrete observable behaviors (e.g., "No insults, rude comments, ugly remarks, or harassment"). Whenever possible, accentuate the positive (e.g., "Contribute to a community of learners") over the negative (e.g., "Do not interfere with the learning of others"). Determine the proportion of teacher-to-student input in defining the expectations. Many teachers name generalizations, then have students brainstorm observable related behaviors. For instance, you might present a generalization such as respecting others, then have students list behaviors that express what this looks like and sounds like in class. What will be seen and heard that indicates respect?

Once you and your class determine the expectations, display them and confidently address them according to the apprenticeship model. Make them public to all concerned at the start of the course and address them frequently. Present lessons on the expectations, explicitly demonstrating what they are and guiding students to the appropriate behaviors so they fully understand what you are talking about. Hold students accountable for the expectations, calmly confronting those who are recalcitrant. Maintain a professional demeanor. Refer students to school authorities only in extreme circumstances or after initial classroom actions and consultations.

The following are some ways to express generalizations regarding classroom norms of social behavior. The first set is samples from the list of classroom interaction expectations previously presented in this chapter. This list is a good beginning for naming what counts as appropriate behavior. When presented as part of a discipline plan, these items resemble commandments more than objectives.

Classroom Interaction Expectations
- Be polite.
- Be prepared to learn.
- Be responsible.
- Contribute to a community of learners.
- Honor what others offer.
- Promote everyone's learning—especially your own.
- Support the dignity of yourself and others.

The following three rules are a bit more straightforward than the expectations listed above.

Rules
- Follow classroom procedures.
- Follow school guidelines.
- Follow district policies.

Some teachers prefer common sayings, often connected with sports or environmentalism, as a general guide to appropriate actions.

Common Sayings
- Be a team player.
- Consider how your actions will affect people seven generations in the future.
- Disagree without being disagreeable.
- Do no harm.
- Have a winning attitude.
- Keep the home court advantage.

- Leave it better than it was found.
- Make a contribution.
- Think globally; act locally.
- Time is precious.
- Treat others the way you want them to treat you.
- We are family.

The next list specifies concrete observable behaviors that exemplify general expectations. It specifies actions deemed appropriate for a classroom. The generalizations above use sweeping language to suggest specific behaviors; the statements below are more blunt. You can select items from the following to exemplify what certain generalizations mean.

Concrete Observable Behaviors
- Be seated when the tardy bell rings.
- Class will be dismissed by the teacher and not the bell.
- Do not interrupt others.
- Do not leave your seat without permission.
- Do not talk while the teacher or another student is talking.
- Follow directions the first time they are given.
- Grooming materials, headphones, pagers, and cell phones may not be used.
- Have materials ready and attention focused when lessons begin.
- Keep hands and feet to yourself.
- Listen attentively when others have the floor.
- No food, gum, or drink are allowed.
- No insults, rude comments, ugly remarks, or harassment are allowed.
- No profanity or obscene gestures are allowed.
- Remove hats upon entering class.

Low Profile Tactics.   Once your expectations for classroom norms of behavior are clear, plan your responses to disruptive situations. Begin by preparing low-profile tactics, ones that encourage students to redirect their behavior with only a little prompting on your part.

A good first step is to be with-it, always aware of what is happening in your class (Jones, 2000). Have eyes in the back of your head, and take action as soon as you sense a disruption emerging. You might move to the area, employing what is called proximity control, or the halo effect. Simply being there often is enough to redirect behavior positively. However, you might need to perform other actions such as making eye contact with the disrupter and frowning, signaling with your palm out, saying the student's name, or issuing a general request for order.

If needed, terminate what you are doing and take a deep breath to relax, center your focus, and oxygenate your bloodstream. Move into the student's

Teachers often circulate during class to provide immediate assistance.

area by placing your hands on his or her desk and request compliance with the relevant behavioral expectation. If still needed, bend down to your elbows to increase eye contact, looking at the desktop if the student stares at you. Move out after the student changes his or her behavior, taking a deep breath and thanking the student for complying.

Consequences.   If any variation of the plan above for resolving minor disruptions is insufficient, move to consequences. Applying consequences invokes your discipline plan somewhat formally and officially. As with all classroom planning, deciding on consequences prior to the beginning of school gets you off on the right foot, enhancing your professional demeanor. It allows you to remain cool during unfortunate situations.

Many teachers prefer the term *intervention* more than *consequence* because intervention implies modifying a situation rather than punishing someone. Most sets of consequences—or interventions—are hierarchical, progressing sequentially from minor to major according to the individual's acting out frequency and severity. If an individual suddenly becomes extremely disorderly, then you may need to invoke a major consequence immediately, bypassing minor ones. Consider the following sequence for your classroom.

Warn.   Issuing a warning means you are implementing your discipline plan as prescribed. When necessary, issue a verbal warning so the individual realizes his or her behavior is unacceptable. State the generalization or concrete observable the individual is offending; you might number the expectations and simply state the number. When designing your plan, decide how you will record warnings. Also decide whether you will give more than one warning before proceeding to the next level of severity.

Confer.   Talking with students as soon as possible about their behavior often goes far in reconciling differences. Schedule a meeting during some mutually free time. You might gain perspective on the student's situation, allowing you to adjust his or her classroom situation. You might establish a caring relationship with the student, letting him or her know you seek to promote their best interests. You might clarify your expectations and reasons for issuing consequences. Some teachers have students write a plan for resolving the acting out behavior, then they react to the plan in writing. This is a more productive use of writing than the traditional one of copying something interminably.

Detain.   The loss of personal time is a common consequence. Many schools hold a common detention so one adult monitors students from more than one class. The time spent in detention may vary. Additionally, you might have a student stay in class after others exit, although you need to ensure that you are not disrupting the next teacher's beginning of class. Some teachers isolate disorderly students in a special classroom space or a neighboring teacher-partner's class.

Contact Family Members.   Involving a family member responsible for the disorderly student can be done earlier, in conjunction with other consequences, or it can stand alone later. You can communicate with the family member through the telephone, a written note, or a face-to-face meeting, but be sure to determine whether you and the family member speak the same language. Your contact may be only to notify the family what has happened, or you might talk through the issue. Have a written record of behaviors so you can be specific, and always emphasize what is in the student's best academic interests. Develop a partnership with the family.

Refer to School Administrators.   Refer to a school administrator those individuals involved in frequent disruptions or in an especially severe one such as physical or verbal abuse. When possible, confer with the administrator prior to any referral, seeking suggestions and notifying him or her of your concerns. The administrator may be a department head, school counselor, social worker, or assistant principal.

Chronic Disruptions.   Students who appear on the way regularly to disrupting their own and others' learning benefit from a special focus (National Research Council, 1993). As soon as you suspect a possible long-term, difficult situation, directly address it with the student. Confer in a neutral part of the class—a place neither you nor the student consider your personal territory—to nip problems in the bud. Document student and your own behaviors, jotting down in a designated folder what is transpiring between you and the student.

As always, work for the individual's best interests. Encourage progress toward high and positive expectations; recognize positive actions and accomplishments. Maintain a positive working relationship with the individual; don't allow your interactions with the student to become adversarial. If your interactions start becoming unfriendly, point it out (e.g., I see that you're becoming upset) so you and the student can chart a different course. Employ active listening and show that you care.

Emphasizing prevention over punishment, determine what might be done to reconcile difficulties. You and the student sit down and explore solutions for the causes of the problem behaviors; seek underlying fundamental roots of the behaviors, and generate possible special accommodations and responsibilities appropriate for your classroom. For instance, one student might benefit from flexible deadlines because he or she is working long hours outside class for family support; another might be allowed into class late with no penalty because she or he has child care responsibilities; still another with impulse control difficulties might do well with personal signals, such as you touching your ear, as a reminder that attentive listening is a behavioral norm in your class. Many times it is appropriate to customize a plan that you and the student sign. Support groups and mentoring relationships also might be appropriate.

Be sure to pinpoint the concrete observable behaviors that indicate students are encountering difficulty. Ensure that you, the student, and others are clear about the issue, repeating it practically verbatim if the student is uncertain or evasive. Involve and notify others of actions throughout this process.

Conclusion

Preparing the cultural and structural aspects of your classroom before school starts promotes what will occur in the classroom. When you and your students are prepared to be good partners, serious attention can be devoted to your purpose for coming together. Everyone can focus on learning in general and literacy learning in particular.

CENTRAL QUESTION: THINK BACK

What do I actually need to do in my classroom to start teaching adolescents who struggle as readers?

To fully answer this chapter's central question, build on the following key concepts:

- Connect classroom cultures with structures.
- Develop cultures relative to literacy, school success, and classroom interaction expectations.

- Plan a room arrangement that best fulfills teaching responsibilities.
- Specify procedures for classroom instruction and transitions.
- Back up instruction with a discipline plan specifying norms of behavior, consequences, and low-profile tactics for handling major and minor disruptions.

REFERENCES

Alfassi, M. (1998). Reading for meaning: The efficacy of reciprocal teaching in fostering reading comprehension in high school students in remedial reading class. *American Educational Research Journal, 35,* 309–332.

Brozo, W. G. (1990). Hiding out in secondary classrooms: Coping strategies of unsuccessful readers. *Journal of Reading, 33*(5), 324–328.

Burke, J. (2000). *Reading reminders: Tools, tips, and techniques.* Portsmouth, NH: Boynton/Cook.

Deal, T. E., & Peterson, K. D. (1999). *Shaping school culture: The heart of leadership.* San Francisco: Jossey-Bass.

Emmer, E. T., Evertson, C. M., & Worsham, M. E. (2000). *Classroom management for secondary teachers* (5th ed.). Boston: Allyn and Bacon.

Gaskins, I. W. (1998). There's more to teaching at-risk and delayed readers than good reading instruction. *The Reading Teacher, 51,* 534–547.

Greenleaf, C. (1995, April). *Sometimes I hate myself: Immigrant teenagers' perspectives on language and learning in San Francisco high schools.* Paper presented at the annual meeting of the American Educational Research Association, San Francisco, CA.

Jackson, A. W., & Davis. G. A. (2000). *Turning points 2000: Educating adolescents in the 21st century.* New York: Teachers College Press.

Johnson, J., & Farkas, S. (1997). *Getting by: What American teenagers really think of their schools.* New York: Public Agenda.

Jones, F. H. (2000). *Tools for teaching.* Santa Cruz, CA: Fredric H. Jones.

Lenski, S. D., Wham, M. A., & Johns, J. J. (1999). *Reading and learning strategies for middle and high school students.* Dubuque, IA: Kendall/Hunt.

MacDonald, R. E., & Healy, S. D. (1999). *A handbook for beginning teachers* (2nd ed.). New York: Longman.

National Research Council. (1993). *Losing generations.* Washington, DC: National Academy of Sciences.

Newmann, F. M., et al. (1996). *Authentic achievement: Restructuring schools for intellectual quality.* San Francisco: Jossey-Bass.

Palincsar, A., & Brown, A. L. (1984). Reciprocal teaching of comprehension-fostering and comprehension-monitoring activities. *Cognition and Instruction, 1,* 117–175.

Phelan, P., Yu, H. C., & Davidson, A. L. (1994). Navigating the psychological pressures of adolescence: The voices and experiences of high school youth. *American Educational Research Journal, 31,* 415–447.

Rex, L. A. (2001). The remaking of a high school reader. *Reading Research Quarterly, 36,* 288–313.

Ryan, K. (Ed.). (1992). *The roller coaster year: Essays by and for beginning teachers.* New York: Harper-Collins.

Sturtevant, E. G., Duling, V. P., & Hall, R. E. (2001). "I've run a 4,000 person organization . . . and it's not nearly this intense . . . ": A three year case study of content literacy in high school mathematics. In E. B. Moje & D. G. O'Brien (Eds.), *Constructions of literacy: Studies of teaching and learning in and out of secondary schools* (pp. 77–103). Mahwah, NJ: Lawrence Erlbaum.

Tierney, R. J., & Readence, J. E. (2000). *Reading strategies and practices: A compendium* (5th ed.). Boston: Allyn and Bacon.

Vacca, R. (1998). Let's not marginalize adolescent literacy. *Journal of Adolescent and Adult Literacy, 41,* 604–609.

Wilson, B. L., & Corbett, H. D. (2001). *Listening to urban kids: School reform and the teachers they want.* Albany, NY: State University Press.

Wong, H. K., & Wong, R. T. (1998). *The first days of school: How to be an effective teacher.* Mountain View, CA: Harry K. Wong Publications.

Wyatt, R. L., & White, J. E. (2001). *Making your first year a success: The secondary teacher's survival guide.* Thousand Oaks, CA: Corwin Press.

CHAPTER

3 Framing and Launching Units of Instruction

CENTRAL QUESTION: THINK AHEAD

How do I start connecting reading and writing with subject matter instruction?

Because secondary school instruction occurs mainly in subject matter classes—social studies, science, English, math, fine arts, vocational arts, physical education, and so on—reading and writing occur mainly there, also. Connecting subject matter instruction with reading and writing instruction, then, is essential. The central question many secondary school teachers ask is how to make this connection.

By moving from general to specific—by first planning the year, then units, then lessons—you are able to concentrate on what is important (Clark & Peterson, 1986). Yearly plans are at the long-term end of instructional decision making. Among other things, yearly plans involve the ultimate purpose of your class. You determine what you want students to accomplish relative to literacy (e.g., becoming self-sufficient) and to classroom interactions (e.g., showing respect).

Lessons are at the short-term end of instructional decision making. Lessons specify day-to-day learning activities; they detail sometimes down to the minute the actions teachers and students will perform. Beginning teachers often write lesson plans that are specific enough for a knowledgeable outsider—such as a substitute teacher—to step into a classroom, read the lesson plan, and instruct the class.

Units are at the middle level of teachers' planning (Gross, 1997). Units indicate how the year's curriculum will be divided among blocks of time lasting from a few days to a few weeks. Science teachers in middle school often divide their courses among astronomy, meteorology, geology, and so on. Senior high language arts teachers might address survival, change, and defining oneself along with literary genres such as short story, drama, and poetry.

Unit planning is a productive time for specifying how reading and writing instruction fit with subject matter instruction. It allows you to set the stage for adolescents—including those who struggle as readers—to engage print. It enables you to structure practices that focus on your subject matter as well as on print. If you are a reading teacher, use unit planning charts for 2- to 3-week periods for clustering reading and writing around a specific focus. Units span enough time for you to incorporate a meaningful series of literacy experiences.

This chapter and the next present unit planning. This chapter describes how to establish unit frames, then how to launch, or kick off, units of study with your students. These actions set the stage for weaving reading and writing through your subject matter instruction, presented next in Chapter 4.

Framing Units

Frames provide structure. They enclose items and mark borders. A picture frame, for instance, holds a picture while setting it off from others, allowing you to concentrate on what is inside. Frames highlight and provide form to their contents.

Especially in response to the state standards mandates of the 1990s, practically every school district in the United States has convened curriculum planning teams to determine what is to be taught in each course at each grade level. When addressing units, curriculum planning teams—and, if necessary, teachers acting individually—frame units most efficiently by connecting topics, standards-based outcomes, central questions, and culminating activities.

Topics

Topics express in one or two words what units are about. They can be considered the titles, or organizing centers, of units. If you ask teachers or students what a class is studying, they generally respond with something like "Graphing," "We're examining electricity," or "We're reading *The Giver.*" Dinosaurs, simple machines, and personal hygiene are topics in countless primary grade units. Transportation, scientific theory, and the 50 United States often appear as middle grades topics. Wave motion, inequalities, and parliamentary procedure are found in the upper grades.

Rather than topics, you might choose themes that are deliberately open ended and invite exploration because they underlie so much. Themes such as identity and strength open the door to much creative thinking and exploring. For instance, strength refers to durable force in a physical as well as a mental sense; people and things manifest strength in countless ways. Complex topics, or themes, such as autonomy, have demonstrated effectiveness because they offer rich possibilities for inquiry.

Teachers of English/language arts or reading often employ topics distinctive to their specialization. They might select topics that revolve around an author (e.g., Jerry Spinelli, Maya Angelou), a genre (e.g., drama, novel), a novel (e.g., *Freak, the Mighty; To Kill a Mockingbird*), or a skill (e.g., following directions, interpreting figurative language). Topics often are sequenced, such as in the history and the algebra topic calendars shown in Figure 3.1, so you know how to pace yourself as you move through the school year (Jacbos, 1997).

Standards-Based Outcomes

Standards-based outcomes designate what students are expected to be able to do following a particular instructional unit. Standards-based outcomes became especially important after the 1994 Goals 2000: Educate America Act prompted virtually every state to establish what educators and students are to accomplish. Most school districts and schools now specify what they expect of students following each unit.

The terminology related to standards and outcomes is confusing. Some educators use the terms *standards* and *outcomes* as synonyms; some use other terms such as *goals, objectives,* and *benchmarks;* some distinguish *content standards* from *performance standards*. Detailed yet accessible explanations of this terminology relative to unit planning are available in Erickson (2001), Mitchell, Willis, and the Chicago Teachers Union Quest Center (1995), and Wiggins and McTighe (1998).

History Topic Calendar

August	September	October	November	December
Precontact America	Worlds meet Colonialism	Revolution Forming a new nation	The nation grows Civil War	Reshaping the nation

Algebra Topic Calendar

August	September	October	November	December
Problem solving Numbers and operations	Exponents and powers Rates and ratios	Equations Tables and graphs	Solving linear equations	Graphing linear equations

FIGURE 3.1   Topic Calendars

When writing this book, we decided to use the term *standards-based outcome* because it is relatively brief, descriptive, and common—but you should realize that it is not universal. In this book, we refer to standards-based outcomes as unit-level academic expectations based on state or school district mandates. The important point here is that educators more and more are expected to align unit plan expectations with external, mandated expectations.

About five standards-based outcomes are appropriate for framing a unit. Going much beyond five outcomes per unit dilutes your teaching and interferes with learning.

Examples of Standards-Based Outcomes. The following adaptations from Kendall and Marzano (2000) represent standards-based outcomes for different content areas:

History: Civil War
- Explains the circumstances that shaped the Civil War and its outcomes
- Portrays how the Civil War influenced Northern and Southern society

Mathematics: Geometry
- Demonstrates how scale in maps and drawings shows relative distance and size
- Compares the basic properties and uses of polar coordinates

Science: Structure and Properties of Matter
- Depicts materials composed of parts that are too small to be seen without magnification
- Reproduces the structure of an atom

Standards-based outcomes for reading at different grade levels often appear this way:

Reading
- Demonstrates that print conveys meaning (grades K–2)
- Adjusts speed of reading to suit purpose and difficulty of the material (grades 3–5)
- Represents abstract information as explicit mental pictures (grades 6–8)
- Identifies and analyzes the philosophical assumptions and basic beliefs underlying an author's work (grades 9–12)

Features of Standards-Based Outcomes. A crucial feature of standards-based outcomes is a plan for observable actions. Each outcome calls for students to do something that can be seen or heard. Strong verbs such as *portray, compare,* and *evaluate* emphasize overt, external responses. They are not entirely covert, internal processes such as *understand, appreciate,* or *learn.* To be sure, understanding, appreciating, and learning are critical, but they are not appropriate terminology for framing units of instruction because they can remain invisible too easily. They leave too much to the imagination. Ask yourself, "What might learners do that demonstrates, or provides evidence of, understanding, appreciating, or learning?"

Effective outcomes are worded concretely and specifically in relation to a particular topic. In a biology unit on cells, the outcome *understanding cell structure* leaves too much to the imagination. How much are students expected to know about the relationships among mitochondria, ribosomes, and the Golgi apparatus? How much are students expected to know of the endoplasmic reticulum? How are students expected to display their knowledge? If expectations are too vague to direct your unit planning, refine them. If you encounter an outcome such as *understands cell structure,* you might reword it: relating the principle structures of cells to their functions.

A second crucial feature of outcomes is a plan for higher-order thinking. Effective standards-based unit outcomes call for students to go beyond the information given—to transform what they encounter. As noted in the Chapter 1 presentation of the reader-as-builder metaphor, students actively construct meaning relative to the topic being studied. Expecting students to accomplish actions such as portraying, comparing, and evaluating what they learn goes beyond recalling or reproducing ideas already stated. Portraying, comparing, and evaluating engage students in higher-order constructive thinking that generates ideas. Moore, Moore, Cunningham, and Cunningham (in press) present the following verbs that are useful when producing standards-based unit outcomes:

Analyze	Debate	Express	Portray
Characterize	Decide	Identify	Produce
Classify	Defend	Interpret	Rate
Compare	Describe	Invent	Recommend
Compose	Design	Judge	Recount
Construct	Develop	Justify	Sequence
Convince	Distinguish	Map	Show
Create	Dramatize	Paraphrase	Solve
Critique	Explain	Persuade	Summarize

Central Questions

Central questions provide students an overarching purpose for examining unit topics and accomplishing unit outcomes. With regard to the Grand Canyon, a productive central question could be, Why is the Grand Canyon considered grand? During practically any middle grade history unit, you might pose a central question such as, How do the actions of these times affect us today?

Central questions turn students into problem solvers. Such questions provoke and sustain students' thinking and learning throughout the unit activities. Central questions connect what students encounter across several days and weeks of instruction. They enable diverse students to form appropriate answers, although the sophistication of the answers may vary (Fogarty, 1997; Jorgensen, 1994–1995).

Similar to the statement of your course vision, or ultimate purpose, unit central questions help students grasp the numerous facts associated with topics, but these facts become the building blocks of thinking. With central questions in mind, students treat potentially inert ideas and facts as ideas in action and facts in action. Students use facts and ideas to construct personal insights into the topic. Five lists of examples and a sixth list of central questions follow (Moore, Moore, Cunningham, & Cunningham, in press):

History/Social studies
Is the United States today more like Athens or Sparta?

What are appropriate limits to freedom of speech?

How does the Civil War affect the United States today?

What happens when you judge a group of people according to the actions on one member of the group?

How can a political leader win a war yet lose a peace?

Literature
What makes a short story outstanding?
What does it take to be a hero?
Why is Shakespeare considered such an outstanding writer?
What is the "heart of darkness"?
When should you follow others?

Mathematics
Do the advantages of the metric system outweigh the disadvantages?

How economical is it to buy food from a convenience store compared to a full-service grocery store?

You see a highway sign that contains the message: "Caution 6% grade." How can you determine this figure by yourself?

How can statements such as "The lake has an average depth of 3 feet" and "The region has an average temperature of 70 degrees" mislead people?

Is a straight line always the shortest possible distance?

Science
How is food digested?

What factors most influence plant development?

Why does printing "no cholesterol" on food packages not protect people from increasing their cholesterol after eating the food?

How are mountains formed?

Why is the weather difficult to predict?

Interdisciplinary
What new city in our state would be ideal?

How can we stop violence?

How can we handle our pollution problem?

What new invention might be most beneficial?

How can our community be better prepared for natural disasters that probably will occur?

Nonexamples of Central Questions
What are mammals?
What do living things need for survival?
Who are the major characters in this story?
What types of spiders are there?
How do you divide fractions?

Central questions need to be general enough to provoke thinking, yet specific enough to guide it. They need to allow multiple responses and have no single, obviously correct answer, yet they need to elicit answers that are supportable. To produce central questions, begin by using the common question words—(*who, what when, where, why,* and *how*)—to blend the unit outcomes into a question. Search for a commonality underlying the outcomes. For instance, answers to the question, Why do people drink alcohol? can touch on physical effects of alcohol, psychological mechanisms, social pressure, and advertising techniques.

Posting central questions on a bulletin board and on unit handouts reinforces learners' attention to them. At the end of each class, you might direct students to the central question with the following inquiries: How does what you learned today help you answer the central question? Given what we've studied today, why do you think people drink alcohol? Now that we know more about the westward expansion of the late 1800s, how do those actions affect us today? Students use their minds fully to solve the problem, combining factual information to construct ideas.

Culminations

Like topics, standards-based outcomes, and central questions, culminations help frame units. Culminations do so by structuring closure to units of instruction. Taking place at the end of a unit—although highlighted at the beginning—they give form to what is being taught and learned.

Culminations specify how learners are to express their responses to central questions such as those already described: Why is the Grand Canyon considered grand? Why do people drink alcohol? How does the westward expansion of the late 1800s affect us today? They typically consist of students' written, spoken, or artistic work produced during the unit. Students might present their answers to these questions either through performance or product. If through performance, students may choose debate, interview, panel discussion, persuasive speech, or role play. If through product, students may choose art display, demonstration or experiment, multimedia production, newspaper report, pamphlet, picture book, poster talk, song, videotape, or website construction. Culminating activities can be somewhat open ended, such as a debate, as well as more closed, such as a newspaper report. Culminating activities can capitalize on creative outlets such as role plays and art displays as well as on traditional pencil-and-paper assignments.

Learners often publicly exhibit what they accomplish during culminating activities. For instance, they might share what they learned with an audience, such as classmates, younger or older students, or adults including parents, teachers, school administrators, governmental office holders, or community members. Public exhibitions offer students a chance to refine their presentation abilities; they also tend to stimulate effort by providing an authentic, external audience.

Units of instruction involve much reading and writing.

Along with exhibitions, culminations often occur as unit exams. Students who know they eventually will encounter an essay test item such as, Why do people drink alcohol? or, How does the westward expansion of the late 1800s affect us today? have an opportunity to focus their attention productively during instruction. To be sure, unit exams commonly serve as culminating activities and they certainly have a place in instruction. Yet, you might supplement exams with the exhibitions just noted, and you might display the essay test item when you first introduce the unit topic as a means of framing the unit for your class.

Finally, culminations can be enrichments, recreational activities that recognize what has been accomplished. Students might tour a museum, a historical site, or a business or manufacturing center. You might schedule a guest speaker or a video presentation. You might play a board game or participate in a simulation based on the unit. You might serve refreshments as students look over their peers' exhibitions, celebrating what others have produced. Such activities end the unit on a high note with or without an accompanying assignment and with or without being graded.

Framing Units Coherently

Topics, standards-based outcomes, central questions, and culminating activities work best when they fit together as a coherent frame—when they correspond with each other. In effective units one part of a frame leads to another; each is consistent with each other. For instance, a standards-based outcome calling for students to read like analyzers corresponds with a central question asking about the decade in which people were better off. Students analyze the different decades. Both of these components relate well with a culminating activity calling for a persuasive pamphlet. The parts fully connect with one another.

When you have drafted the components of your unit frame, revisit them and assess their coherence. Does one flow from the other? Do the parts fit logically? If necessary, revise what is needed, smoothing over the parts so the frame holds. Additionally, keep in mind that assessing student performance, which Chapter 8 presents, can be considered part of the unit frame. Determining how you will assess student performance relative to each unit goes far in structuring and highlighting what you will teach and what students will learn.

Launching Units

Framing a unit topic provides structure and direction so you know what to highlight during instruction. Launching units then begins the journey for the class. Unit launches focus students' attention and arouse curiosity. They prime students for reading, writing, and learning, engaging students with upcoming contents.

Launching units occurs the first day or two of a new unit. When beginning study of the Holocaust, for example, you might spend the first 20 minutes displaying and talking about pictures of concentration camps, orally reading brief excerpts from survivors' accounts, and brainstorming ideas about how such an event could occur. Such introductions go far in setting the stage for instruction.

You can launch units in numerous ways. Five unit launch practices that you can blend into countless combinations are real-world observing/participating, reading aloud, previewing passages, brainstorming, and writing (Moore, Moore, Cunningham, & Cunningham, in press).

Real-World Observing/Participating

Real-world objects, media, skits, and guest speakers connect students with abstract ideas (Guthrie, McGough, Bennett, & Rice, 1996). For instance, you might launch units with the following real-world observations and participations:

Mathematics: Graphing
- Display magazine or newspaper graphs.
- Portray measures of height in relation to shoe size.

Language Arts: The Novel Downriver
- Display photos of the Grand Canyon.
- Invite guest speaker to share firsthand experiences of the southwest U.S. outdoors.

Science: Food for Growth and Energy
- Preview enlarged displays of nutrition facts for various snack foods and staples.
- Trace the digestive system on a chart.

Social Studies: Urbanization
- Discuss maps showing population densities.
- Compare photos taken of land in the past and in the present.

Reading Aloud

Reading aloud passages that introduce a unit topic and engage students is a good launch practice (Richardson, 2000). Hearing vivid presentations of personal experiences and exciting or unusual events arouses interest. For instance, accounts of the medical practices of the Middle Ages, such as the actions taken to combat the Black Plague, are fascinating.

When hearing someone read aloud, students can access ideas they might miss due to the difficulty of a passage. Students also can access the structure of complex written language, which differs from that of spoken language. Suggestions for reading aloud follow:

1. Select only compelling pieces that are reasonably certain to engage your listeners. Keep the reading brief (under 15 minutes), and use pictures and props when appropriate.
2. The piece might be from nonfiction, short story, or a novel. The piece can be read in its entirety, its first chapter, or a particularly exciting or relevant portion.
3. Rehearse the entire piece, making sure you can produce a vivid rendition in public.
4. Use the read aloud as a springboard, talking about how the passage will connect with the upcoming unit.

Previewing Passages

Previewing passages involves skimming and scanning reading materials before studying them (Readence, Moore, & Rickelman, 2000). After leading your students through a number of passage previews, they can do so with any material on their own. Suggestions for previewing passages follow:

1. Display library and classroom materials related to unit contents. Set aside a table or display case to hold these materials and allow student access to them during the unit.
2. Show the cover of some reading material related to the unit. Have students describe what they see in the cover and predict upcoming contents.

3. Have students examine interior pages with an open discussion of what they encounter. Direct attention to pictorial displays such as illustrations, photographs, maps, diagrams, tables, and graphs as well as the text notes about these displays. Also examine the materials' titles, section headings, and bold face print.

4. Have students scan a passage for unfamiliar terms they believe essential for understanding what is coming. Talk about the terms as you create a group list.

Brainstorming

Brainstorming is a flexible and popular way to introduce units. Brainstorming occurs best in a freewheeling atmosphere with just enough structure to maintain focus. First, stimulate students' brainstorms with real-world observations and participations, reading aloud, or previewing passages as just suggested. Then have students generate knowledge about a topic. Devices such as KWL and list-group-label are helpful when recording what students first have to say about a topic.

KWL. KWL abbreviates the three steps of a well-known procedure: what we *know,* what we *want* to learn, and what we *learned* (Carr & Ogle, 1987). Adding *focus questions* to KWL, as shown in the chart in Figure 3.2, promotes inquiry into subject matter (Huffman, 2000).

When launching a unit, have students complete the first two blank rows of the chart. Then during the unit have them return to the chart and revise What We Want to Learn and complete What We Learned. If the unit topic is the Grand Canyon, a KWL chart with the focus questions found in Figure 3.2 might be used. When using KWL as a unit launch activity throughout the year, consider including other rows with appropriate questions: How will we find out? What do we still need to learn? and, What do we think about what we're learning? Additionally, consider using webs, or concept maps, such as the one depicted in Figure 3.3 to establish relationships among ideas.

List–Group–Label. Much like KWL, students use list–group–label to organize the words they brainstorm in response to a topic. This practice also builds on prior knowledge and elicits categorization. Again, stimulate students' brainstorming with real-world observations and participations, reading aloud, or previewing passages. Then follow three basic steps:

1. *List.* Record words the students associate with the topic. For example, the Grand Canyon may be associated with deep, beautiful, fossils, mining, mule rides, old rocks, dry, and river rafting.

The Grand Canyon

	How was it formed?	What does it portray about the Earth?	What are its major features?
What We *Know*			
What We *Want* to Learn			
What We *Learned*			

FIGURE 3.2   **KWL Chart for Grand Canyon Unit Topic**

2. *Group.* Categorize words initially listed. For example, three categories may be created to contain (1) deep, beautiful, and dry; (2) fossils, and old rocks; and (3) river rafting and mule rides.
3. *Label.* Name the categories. For example, the first category containing deep, beautiful, and dry may be called *physical description;* the second category containing fossils and old rocks may be called *geology;* and the third category containing river rafting and mule rides may be called *recreation.*

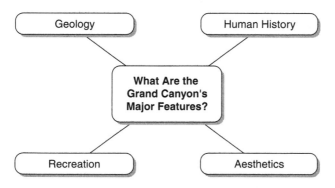

FIGURE 3.3   **Web of Grand Canyon's Major Features**

You might post on a bulletin board the word groups and their labels as a reference throughout the unit. Then you can use certain words from the brainstormed list to introduce lessons, talk about what has been learned, add new words, and revise the categories.

Writing

Writing as a way to launch units is especially appropriate because it helps crystallize and clarify thinking about a topic. Two writing practices useful for unit launches are quick writes and extended personal writes.

Quick Writes.   Quick writes are the least formal kind of writing and in some ways the easiest to fit into a crowded curriculum. Two examples follow for what you might say to initiate quick writes.

> Look at these pictures representing aspects of the Roman Empire. Then write down all that you think of when you think of the Roman Empire. You have 3 minutes.

> Draw as many different types of triangles as you can. Then jot down what the differences are.

The following are suggestions for using quick writes to launch units:

- Emphasize the speed of this practice. Students have a very brief time to blast down what they are thinking in first-draft, rough fashion.
- Occasionally have students tell what they have written down as you list it on the board. Point out that this is the starting point for future learning, the what-we-know phase of a KWL-type event.
- Occasionally use small index cards for recording the quick writes and have students hand them to you as their tickets for exiting class.

Extended Personal Write.   Extended personal writes take longer than quick writes, but they are intended to produce deeper, longer-lasting knowledge. This writing encourage students to connect with subject matter at a somewhat personal, emotional level. Two examples follow that illustrate how to initiate extended personal writes.

> Pretend you are your current age in the Roman Empire, marching with Caesar toward Gaul. Based on what you know of this period, write a letter home describing your experiences and feelings.

> You are a raptor who is able to keep a journal. Based on what you know of these animals, describe an hour in your life.

When using extended personal writes to launch units, consider the following:

- Have students maintain the writing in a journal.
- Redirect students to the compositions for revision as the unit progresses.
- Have students read their compositions in groups or to the class.

Conclusion

Preparing units of instruction allows you to set the stage for teaching and learning. Framing units structures and highlights learning expectations for students. When your unit is framed appropriately, you establish a purpose that shapes your classroom for a few weeks. Launching units then clarifies the purpose and promotes the desire to learn. Launching a unit stimulates meaningful classroom activity.

CENTRAL QUESTION: THINK BACK

How do I start connecting reading and writing with subject matter instruction?

To answer fully this chapter's central question, build on the following key concepts:

- Concentrate on units of instruction when planning how to connect reading, writing, and subject matter.
- Frame units by designing topics, standards-based outcomes, essential questions, and culminations.
- Launch units through real-world observing/participating, reading aloud, previewing passages, brainstorming, and writing.

REFERENCES

Carr, E., & Ogle, D. (1987). K-W-L plus: A strategy for comprehension and summarization. *Journal of Reading, 30,* 626–631.

Clark, C. M., & Peterson, P. L. (1986). Teachers' thought processes. In M. C. Wittrock (Ed.), *Handbook of research on teaching* (3rd ed., pp. 255–296). New York: Macmillan.

Erickson, H. L. (2001). *Stirring the head, heart, and soul: Redefining curriculum and instruction* (2nd ed.). Thousand Oaks, CA: Corwin Press.

Fogarty, R. (1997). *Problem-based learning and other curriculum models for the multiple intelligences classroom.* Arlington Heights, IL: Skylight.

Gross, P. A. (1997). *Joint curriculum design.* Mahwah, NJ: Erlbaum.

Guthrie, J. T., McGough, K., Bennett, L., & Rice, M. E. (1996). Concept-oriented reading instruction: An integrated curriculum to develop motivations and strategies for reading. In L. Baker, P. Afflerbach, & D. Reinking (Eds.), *Developing engaged readers in school and home communities* (pp. 165–190). Mahwah, NJ: Erlbaum.

Huffman, L. E. (2000). Spotlighting specifics by combining focus questions with K-W-L. In D. W. Moore, D. E. Alvermann, & K. A. Hinchman (Eds.), *Struggling adolescent readers: A collection of teaching strategies* (pp. 220–222). Newark, DE: International Reading Association.

Jacobs, H. H. (1997). *Mapping the big picture: Integrating curriculum and assessment K–12.* Alexandria,

VA: Association for Supervision and Curriculum Development.

Jorgensen, C. M. (1994–1995). Essential questions— inclusive answers. *Educational Leadership, 52* (4), 52–55.

Kendall, J. S., & Marzano, R. J. (2000). *Content knowledge: A compendium of standards and benchmarks for K–12 education* (3rd ed.). Aurora, CO: Mid-Continent Regional Educational Laboratory. Retrieved August 8, 2001, from www.mcre.org/standards-benchmarks/.

Mitchell, R., Willis, M., & Chicago Teachers Union Quest Center. (1995). *Learning in overdrive: Designing curriculum, instruction, and standards, a manual for teachers.* Golden, CO: North American Press.

Moore, D. W., Moore, S. A., Cunningham, P. M., & Cunningham, J. W. (in press). Developing readers and writers in the content areas, K–12 (4th ed.). New York: Allyn and Bacon.

Readence, J. E., Moore, D. W., & Rickelman, R. J. (2000). *Prereading activities for content area reading and learning* (3rd ed.). Newark, DE: International Reading Association.

Richardson, J. S. (2000). *Read it aloud! Using literature in the secondary content classroom.* Newark, DE: International Reading Association.

Wiggins, G., & McTighe, J. (1998). *Understanding by design.* Alexandria, VA: Association for Supervision and Curriculum Development.

CHAPTER

4 Weaving Literacy through Units of Instruction

CENTRAL QUESTION: THINK AHEAD

How do I specify ways for students to improve their reading and writing during units?

Having a plan for framing and launching units helps focus instruction, as shown in Chapter 3. Such a plan structures and highlights what to teach and gets learning off to a good start. However, framing and launching units go only so far toward literacy. Weaving literacy through units is the next step.

Weaving literacy through units of instruction is a good way of explicitly linking reading and writing with subject matter. Weavers crisscross, or interlace, pieces to form a whole. For instance, when using a loom, rug weavers splice lengthwise vertical strands with crosswise horizontal strands. Interlinking the strands this way produces a unified piece.

When weaving literacy through units of instruction, think of unit topics as the lengthwise vertical strands on a loom. Then think of literacy as the crosswise horizontal strands you use for holding unit topics together and forming a complete design. You weave literacy within and among the topics you cover during the year. For instance, reciprocal teaching (RT) (Palincsar & Brown, 1984) is a common literacy strand that calls for students to summarize, clarify, question, and predict what they read. A reciprocal teaching strand might be woven among U.S. history topics incrementally as shown Figure 4.1.

As the calendar in Figure 4.1 suggests, you begin with summarizing in August. In September you continue with summarizing and introduce clarifying. By October you have introduced all four competencies, having students apply them to unit reading materials for the rest of the semester or year. RT instruction should extend over an entire semester or year because summarizing, clarifying, questioning, and predicting are complex processes and cannot be mastered quickly. Reading and writing strands are braided into more than one unit because students require multiple opportunities to become proficient.

Selecting Literacy Strands

By planning and implementing literacy strands, you demystify reading and writing and focus classroom teaching and learning. You have a systematic way to apprentice students into the reading and writing of your discipline.

U.S. History Calendar

August	September	October	November	December
Precontact America	Worlds meet Colonialism	Revolution Forming a new nation	The nation grows Civil War	Reshaping the nation
• Summarize	• Summarize and clarify	• Summarize, clarify, question, and predict	• Summarize, clarify, question, and predict	• Summarize, clarify, question, and predict

FIGURE 4.1   Sample Calendar for Using Reciprocal Teaching

In many cases, curriculum planning teams will have determined the reading and writing strands to be presented in each course at each grade level of your school. Just as they do with unit frames, the teams usually calendar the strands across the semester and the school year. In many other cases, schools will have no plan for weaving literacy through subject matter units of instruction. If you are in this situation, you might advocate a team or departmental approach to deciding what is to be done. This is a long-term, but potentially powerful, way to connect literacy and subject matter instruction. If you are going it alone, select the reading and writing competencies that you understand and are committed to and that you foresee integrating into your course.

When considering literacy strands to incorporate within and among your units, consult the standards your state mandates for adolescent reading. Your school district, school, or department already might have distributed these standards in the form of a curriculum guide. Additionally, the research-based literature (e.g., Flood & Lapp, 2000; Kamil, Mosenthal, Pearson, & Barr, 2000; Mastropieri & Scruggs, 1997) offers insight into possible strands. Professional texts that array recommended practices also are helpful (e.g., Buehl, 2001; Burke, 2000; Readence, Moore, & Rickelman, 2000; Tovani, 2000). Finally, the ancillary materials in the main textbook for your subject typically describe appropriate literacy strands.

To synthesize possible literacy strands into a meaningful and manageable set, we use the metaphors for readers presented in Chapter 1. They are the roles good readers perform. Table 4.1 presents major reading competencies associated with each metaphor. These metaphors and competencies suggest how proficient readers act, what good readers do when they read. To be sure, the categories in Table 4.1 overlap; they are not airtight. The metaphors and accompanying competencies in Table 4.1 are meant to be entry points for deciding what literacy strands to weave through your instructional units.

Isolating and Integrating Literacy Strands

Weaving literacy through subject matter units calls for you to teach students how to read and write subject matter material. A tension exists when deciding how to focus students' attention on reading and writing as well as on subject matter. Educators have recognized this tension for many years, as the following quote indicates:

> The difficulty which constantly confronts the teacher is to keep the reading skills sufficiently in the foreground that they may be improved and refined, yet at the same time make them subservient to the real interests and larger purposes for which pupils read. (Whipple, 1925, p. 140)

TABLE 4.1   Reading Competencies by Metaphors

Metaphor	Examples of Reading Competencies
Builder	Interpreting unfamiliar word meanings: using surrounding words in the text and examining meaningful word parts (prefixes, bases, suffixes) to determine the meanings of apparently important yet unfamiliar terms.
	Fluency: processing print smoothly, flexibly, and efficiently
	Determining importance of ideas: reading selectively
	Discerning the organization of text and using that organization as a tool for understanding
	Questioning: asking self-questions about text ideas
	Being strategic: monitoring, reviewing, and repairing one's comprehension performance; clarifying what is unclear; planning future actions
	Summarizing: condensing ideas and information; paraphrasing
	Formal visual, auditory, and other sensory images
	Predicting: anticipating upcoming information and ideas; skimming passages before reading them closely
	Grasping explicitly stated literal information: nothing what's stated right there on the page
	Connecting author's ideas across different parts of a passage: thinking and searching to get it all together
	Relating authors' ideas with the ones already in mind: associating what authors say with what is known
	Interpreting visual displays of information and ideas ·
Learner	Writing down ideas to crystallize the message and access it in the future
	Graphically organizing information through a device such as an outline, web, table, flowchart, diagram, or illustration
	Creating mnemonic devices
	Talking about ideas with others to test oneself, clarify misconceptions, and seek new insights
	Reviewing information and ideas
	Inquiring further into a topic
Experiencer	Sharing personal reactions
	Connecting personally with authors, story characters, and other readers
	Deriving pleasure, entertainment, comfort, and delight through print
	Reading widely for reaction and enrichment
	Reacting intellectually, emotionally, and viscerally to literature
	Monitoring reading preferences, interests, habits, and options
	Setting goals for reading engagement and development
	Increasing confidence and risk taking when reading

TABLE 4.1 *(continued)*

Metaphor	Examples of Reading Competencies
Doer	Taking tests strategically and confidently
	Following directions
	Assembling products
	Contributing to collective actions
	Locating and accessing information for appropriate sources
	Synthesizing information from various sources
Analyzer	Recognizing the writing characteristics expected of particular disciplines, genres, and authors
	Monitoring how authors and publishers attempt to influence their readers
	Evaluating: judging the quality of authors' writings, the trustworthiness of authors' messages, and the appropriateness of ideas
	Applying: thinking about how to use the text in the future; using the passage as a springboard to new ideas
	Weighing alternative points of view

A convincing answer to this tension comes from a study of 10 schools that are beating the odds (Langer, 1999). *Beating the odds* means that students in these schools are reading better than demographically similar student populations in other schools.

Schools that beat the odds in terms of adolescent literacy mix isolated and integrated instruction. To illustrate, a school might name summarizing as a literacy strand. Effective teachers initially would demonstrate and have students practice summarizing in isolation, with materials unrelated to unit topics. They would set aside brief portions of class time devoted only to this competency. They might use short, skill-building, commercial reading materials unrelated to the particular unit topic. They would demonstrate and explain how to go about summarizing passages. Such an introduction is a way of separating a particular competency, for example, summarizing, from the ongoing flow of class life, and highlighting it for students' undivided attention. Separating instruction from ongoing unit activities marks the competency for future use and signals its importance.

As students become proficient at summarizing, effective teachers ensure that it is soon integrated into instructional units with the actual tasks at hand. For instance, in U.S. history class, students initially might summarize materials unrelated to precontact America, but, as their proficiencies increase, they would summarize materials when reading about colonialism, revolution, and forming a new nation. Students might record summaries in journals or notebooks, then use the summaries during inquiry projects, culminating activities, or when preparing for a test. They might report their summaries in a class newspaper or include them in posters.

Weaving literacy through units of instruction calls for students to take competencies presented in isolation and integrate them with purposeful work. Competencies presented out of the context of unit topics are put to real use when students apply them to meaningful unit assignments. Teachers remind the class of the reading and writing competencies learned previously, then have students apply these competencies in relevant situations. Such weaving combines isolated and integrated teaching practices throughout the school year.

Examples of Literacy Strands

The remainder of this chapter illustrates teaching practices and competencies appropriate as literacy strands to be woven through subject matter units. These practices sometimes would be isolated when first introduced so students could focus attention on them, but they would be integrated with ongoing units of instruction most of the time. These examples are presented according to the different metaphors for readers discussed in Chapter 1. Again, the practices and competencies are categorized by metaphor so you can gain a better understanding of them; they are readily mixed and matched according to your local literacy plan.

Builder

As Chapter 1 explained, readers as builders construct meaning. They do not simply listen to themselves read silently or orally, then grasp the message. They actively select what is important, connect what they already know with what they are reading, anticipate what is coming up, figure out what is confusing, and so on.

The following two practices illustrate how to go about instructing students in the competencies associated with the reader-as-builder metaphor. The first, constructing main idea statements, addresses a highly visible competency especially helpful for success in school reading assessments. The second, reciprocal teaching, has potential benefits for practically any reading inside or outside school.

Constructing Main Idea Statements for Informational Passages (**About, And**).   Students often find it difficult to state concisely the most important contents of informational text in a main idea format. Proficient reading certainly has more to it than constructing main idea statements, but we begin with it here because it is commonly taught and assessed.

A productive practice for constructing main idea statements focuses on key words. This practice often is modeled for students in a listening mode and then transferred to reading by students. Consider the following steps:

1. Select a short informational piece to read aloud to students.
2. Tell students that stating the main idea is easy with the help of two questions containing two powerful words: *about* plus *and*. Write these words on the board or overhead.
3. Read a selection and demonstrate how to ask and answer two questions as follows:

   Q: In one word, what is this selection *about*?

   A: Birds.

   Q: Adding the word *and*, what is this selection *about*?

   A: Birds and how they fly.

4. Think through this procedure aloud, displaying your decision making for students (e.g., "Is this passage about mammals? No, it's more specific than that." "Is it about birds and how they eat? No.").
5. As students become adept at asking and answering these two questions, continue creating sentences that are more elegant (e.g., "This passage explains how birds fly.").
6. Integrate main idea statement construction with reading materials encountered throughout the remaining units.

Reciprocal Teaching.   Reciprocal teaching (RT) is a popular practice that has rather convincing research supporting its effectiveness with upper-grade readers (Alfassi, 1998; King & Johnson, 1999; Rosenshine & Meister, 1994). It is a way to teach four competencies: summarizing, predicting, questioning, and clarifying. Although it originated with expository text, RT fits narrative, too (Grimes, 1996). It is termed *reciprocal* because it emphasizes reciprocity, a give-and-take, a back-and-forth dialogue among teachers and students and among students and students. The following fictional account portrays how one English teacher isolates then integrates reciprocal teaching with units of instruction.

> *A Case of RT*
> During the second week of school, as we were beginning our unit "Fables and Tales," I introduced reciprocal teaching (RT). One day after going through our procedures for opening class, I told the students that I was going to present this system and that in a few weeks I expected them to be able to perform it with any passage they could read fluently. I also told them RT would help them

better understand any passage they read this semester and in the future. I compared RT to a tool box, saying that it consisted of several devices useful for constructing meaning about texts.

Next, with no reference to our unit on fables and tales, I explained the four specific RT competencies: summarizing, questioning, clarifying, and predicting. I placed cards containing these words on a bulletin board. Then I talked through how to use each strategy with the following short passage:

> A woman is sitting in her old, shuttered house. She knows that she is alone in the whole world; every other thing is dead.
> The doorbell rings.

I selected this passage because it was sure to be easy for the class; I wanted everyone to concentrate on RT—not on the intricacies of a complex piece. I summarized it aloud, reported the questions I had, thought through what needed clarification, and shared my predictions of what was coming.

The whole class then read a picture book of the *Tortoise and the Hare*. Next, in conversation-like language, several students and I jointly produced summaries, questions, clarifications, and predictions for this fable by Aesop. After this, students read another short fable and volunteered summaries, questions, clarifications, and predictions. Classmates contributed to each others' comments; I praised effort and especially apt statements. During this time, I focused on the RT strategies rather than on the literacy characteristics of fables and tales.

During the next few days we began integrating RT into our study of fables and tales. I showed students how to set aside parts of their notebooks for recording their RT responses as we moved through stories, poetry, drama, and so on. I paired individuals to help each other by discussing their summaries, questions, clarifications, and predictions. On several occasions I had RT pairs write their summaries on an overhead transparency, then the class talked about what they liked about each summary and inquired about unclear ideas.

After a few days I noticed that the pairs were having trouble with the questioning portion of RT; they were asking low-level unproductive questions such as, "What was the girl's brother's name?" So I took about 15 minutes out of each of the next few days to isolate RT again. We revisited questioning with short easy passages, concentrating on higher-order meaningful questions.

After a few more days, I varied the RT procedures so that sometimes students thought through their responses as a whole class, sometimes they wrote responses as a pair, and sometimes they worked individually and wrote their responses to the short stories being read. Students also began assessing their performance with RT. I gave them criteria sheets (e.g., summary expresses important ideas in a few words; questions focus on reading between the lines), and students applied these to their RT responses for the fables and tales.

When we began our next unit, "Short Stories," I varied students' reading materials while using RT. I raided the school resource center for short story anthologies so students could find passages that fit their interests and abilities. I brought in assorted stories written at different levels of difficulty and had individuals choose one. Individuals were to divide their passages into fifths and write summaries, questions, clarifications, and predictions for each in their notebooks. I went from person to person and had them explain their responses, and I commented in writing after they submitted their notebooks to me. This was in addition to our examination of short story elements.

At the end of the short story unit, I formally assessed individuals' competence with RT. I read aloud a short passage while the class followed along. The students then recorded their RT responses on a separate paper. I collected the papers and determined how well they had summarized, questioned, clarified, and predicted in response to the passage. Most students indicated they were catching on. In fact, I was so impressed with their responses that I brought in some treats the next day as a special reward. I think they liked the food as well as their proficiency with this new comprehension tool! We planned how to apply it to the next unit on poetry.

As can be seen, this teacher wove four reading competencies into his instructional units while maintaining his focus on his English curriculum. The practice of reciprocal teaching allowed him to isolate specific reading competencies then integrate them when reading fables, tales, and short stories.

This example suggests how you can weave any competency (e.g., using context, analyzing word structures, forming images, interpreting visual displays of data) into any instructional unit (e.g., westward expansion, photosynthesis, personal finance). You can blend isolated and integrated instruction when weaving into your units anything associated with the reader-as-builder metaphor.

Learner

Readers as learners actively manipulate ideas not only to understand them, but to remember them. Have you ever heard a joke, laughed at it whole-heartedly, then been unable to retell it to friends later? You clearly under-stood the joke—you constructed meaning for it—but you did not perform the actions needed to store it in memory and recall it when appropriate. You did not learn the joke well.

Practices such as the following enable you—and your students!—to learn. Like the ones in the preceding section, you can weave any of these practices into your units of instruction. In a manner similar to the RT exam-ple above, present the following through isolated and integrated instruction.

Graphically Organizing Information.   Just as maps portray the layout of a certain territory, graphic organizers depict where ideas are in relation to each other. Representing ideas graphically through devices such as outlines and timelines enhances learners' grasp of the ideas.

Data Charts.   Data charts enable students to categorize important informa-tion (McKenzie, 1978). The charts support students in synthesizing informa-tion from multiple sources and constructing multiparagraph reports. They offer a specific cell-like structure for recording thoughts.

Tribe	History	Housing	Lifestyle	Interesting Information
Apache				
Hopi				
Navajo				

Timeline.   Students mark and date important events on a line. Comments and illustrations about the events may be included.

Venn Diagram.   Students write similarities in the overlapping section and differences in the outer sections.

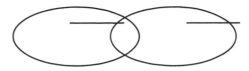

Flowchart.   Flowcharts depict cause–effect as well as sequential patterns of text.

T-Chart.   T-charts represent the letter *T*. They are useful for noting ideas on one side and attaching comments or related information on the other.

Story Frames.   Story frames support students' initial attempts at structuring retellings (Oja, 1996). Students should use their own wording and structure as they become proficient with their retellings.

Story Summary with One Character
This story is about _____. _____
_____ is an important character in our story. _____
_____ tried to _____. The story ends when _____.

Important Idea or Plot
In this story, the problem starts when _____.
After that, _____. Next, _____
_____. Then _____. The problem is finally solved when _____. The story ends when _____.

Character Analysis
_____ is an important character in this story.
_____ is important because _____

_____. Once he/she _____.
Another time, _____. I think [*character's*
name]_____ is [*character's trait*]_____ because
_____.

Note Taking. Writing down ideas when reading or listening is a time-honored way to learn. The process of writing leads learners to crystallize the message, and writing stores personal messages for later review. Teachers recognize the power of writing as a mode of learning by having students maintain learning logs, notebooks, and journals.

As usual, the note-taking practice we describe here begins by isolating it for students' undivided attention, then having students integrate it with the subject matter they encounter in later units of instruction. You will need quantities of acetate—blank overhead transparencies—for you and your students to write on as you use the light-on/light-off approach (Moore, Moore, Cunningham, & Cunningham, in press):

1. Prior to class, record section headings from the student text on an overhead transparency. List three to five key words or phrases from the text under the first heading.
2. List other section headings from the text with three to five numbered spaces underneath each on the overhead. Write key words/phrases for these headings on a separate sheet.
3. Direct students to open their texts and list the first heading and the number of listed spaces. Show this on the overhead with your words covered. Have students read the first section.
4. Reveal the selected key words/phrases and tell why you selected each. Think through the decisions you made, explaining as fully as possible your reasons for them. Have students write these words/phrases on their papers.
5. Direct students to write the headings for the remaining sections to be examined with the numbered spaces underneath. Turn off the overhead projector.
6. Students read the next section. You list the words previously selected for this section on the transparency while students read. Students write their own choices on their papers.
7. Ask a volunteer to present the words/phrases he or she selected. Other students might share their selections. Show the words you selected and compare your words and reasons for selecting them with the students'. Justify any differences; honor logical choices that differ from yours as well as good effort.
8. Eventually have students record their notes individually or in groups on acetate to be displayed and discussed. Also, have students act as the teacher, guiding the class through this practice. Use note taking in

future sessions until students can independently list key words and phrases from their reading.

9. As students become proficient with note taking, have them apply it to the materials they are reading during your ongoing units of instruction.

Experiencer

Readers who experience books get something other than new ideas. They are engaged in the moment, experiencing the pleasure and wonder of stepping into text worlds. Setting the stage for this to happen is especially important for adolescents who tend toward aliteracy. As noted in Chapter 1, encouraging students to experience reading positively provides worthwhile recreational and aesthetic experiences; it also promotes volume of reading, which indirectly results in achievement test gains.

The practices associated with the metaphor of reader as experiencer differ somewhat from those associated with the other metaphors. Instructional emphases are on integrating books into units of study. Little isolation occurs because experience addresses emotions, dispositions, and responses more than technical competencies. This metaphor points to individuals forming personal identities more than to acquiring skills. To paraphrase a common expression, experiencing books is something that is *caught* rather than *taught*. The following practices weave attention to readers as experiencers throughout units of study.

Literacy Autobiographies.   Highlighting the reading adolescents have found worthwhile in the past is especially appropriate during the beginning of your course (Myers, 1997). It signals the importance you place on reading, and it accentuates the positive. You can have students recall early enjoyable memories of reading and writing. The memories may include inside- or outside-of-school experiences. You can have students form pairs to share memories and decide which is the best one to express publicly. Individuals might combine several memories that link conceptually and portray a common message. You can also have students share the memories either in writing or orally with the class. Call attention to how the memories enable students to think about themselves as readers and writers and what they might do to promote their future reading and writing.

Guest Book Talks.   Role models play a significant part in adolescents' lives. Having someone to emulate, especially when youth come from communities that de-emphasize academic literacy, offers important alternatives. Partnerships with other educators as well as community and business groups to present role models interacting with literacy might center on guest book talks (Morley, 1996).

Schedule a regular specified time (e.g., 15 minutes every other Monday) for guests (e.g., teachers, administrators, staff, older students, parents, business representatives, community members) to visit your class. Guests then share a favorite book or set of books with the class. They might (1) tell why they brought the particular book(s) to share, (2) share favorite portions of the book(s), (3) describe what else they read and why they read, (4) explain how reading fits into their lives, and/or (5) answer questions and interact with class members

You can talk about your favorite books with your classes, too. Post a record with photographs and illustrations of who talked about what books to be used for reminders and motivation. You might present live or audio- or videotape guest book talks for airing on school or community-access stations.

Quick Book Share.   As noted in Chapter 1, students have multiple literacies. They might read and write poorly in one situation, yet excel in another. They might disdain the authors and books that schools offer, preferring to read what they, their friends, and family value. Adolescents who categorize themselves as nonreaders because they scorn academic discourse severely limit their options. Conducting quick book shares (Eldridge, 1998) every 4 to 6 weeks is a way to counter this situation.

As usual, when first introducing this practice, model it before having the class perform it. Bring in books you recommend, display prompts (e.g., "Why do you like this book?" "What part really captured your attention?"), and demonstrate responses to them. Set criteria for what is appropriate to share in class (e.g., material students are willing for the teacher to show their mother). Consider the following additional steps:

1. Form groups of about three students in each.
2. Designate a recorder, who writes down each student's name and material that is recommended.
3. Using a timer, give individuals specified amounts of time to talk about their material and answer questions or respond to comments.
4. Circulate among the groups to maintain activity flow, but do not add to the talk.
5. Collect the recorders' sheets and read the materials to the class.
6. Display the top 25 recommendations.

Literature Discussion Groups.   In literature discussion groups, students participate in authentic book club situations like the ones churches, community agencies, and Oprah Winfrey's television program hold. Students gather in groups to talk about what they are reading. The emphasis is on readers sharing what they are experiencing through books, what they are learning, and what they find vague or unknown. Ideal literature discussions are respectful and engage conversations. Indeed, some adolescents we know have reported valuing discussions that enable them to hear others' insights and trigger new ideas (Alvermann, et al., 1996).

Subject matter teachers who integrate literature discussion groups into units of instruction establish clear expectations. Begin by demonstrating and having students practice how to think and talk about books, displaying the kinds of questions you want students to be able to ask and answer. For instance, you might have students select items for self-questioning like the ones Moore, Moore, Cunningham, and Cunningham (in press) suggest in Table 4.2. Self-questions are ones individuals can ask of themselves, with no

TABLE 4.2   Self-Questions

Developing Knowledge

What information did the passage contain that you did not already know?

What became clear to you while reading this?

What ideas did you gain from reading?

What will you remember most about the passage?

If you were to tell another person what this passage was about but could use only a few sentences, what would you say?

Forming Sensory Images

While reading this, what pictures did you see, what sounds did you hear, what tastes and smells did you detect, and what sensations did you feel?

Determining Importance

What is the most important word (sentence/ section)?

Do you think the title is the best one for this? Why? If not, what would be better? Why?

What parts of this are more important than others?

Connecting

What have your read that is similar? Explain the similarities.

What does this remind you of that you already know about? Explain the similarities.

How are you (or someone you know) like a character in the passage?

What did you already know that helps you understand this book?

Self-Monitoring

What were you thinking while reading?

What difficulties did you have with this? What did you do?

How far did you go before knowing you would finish this?

What parts made you feel the strongest?

What part of the book do you wonder about or question?

Accessing Author's Craft

How might you write differently after reading this?

How does this begin? Why do you suppose the author began this way?

How might you change the ending of this?

How did the author hold your attention?

How did the author let you know what was important?

Evaluating

Why did you choose this book?

What did you like best about this?

Do you like this more or less than the last book you read?

Should this receive a literary award? Why?

If you had the chance, what would you tell the author about this book?

Why would you like or not like to read other books by this author (and illustrator)?

If you rewrote this passage, what would you change?

teacher or partner prompting them. They apply to any piece of literature that is read during your course, in other courses, or after graduation. Show students how you think through such questions in response to a book.

Also demonstrate and practice the individual roles and group processes students will need. When beginning this practice, isolate a few group literature discussions so class members focus their attention on appropriate roles to play. Different authorities recommend different discussion roles, as the following lists illustrate:

Cooperative Learning Roles (Kagan, 1992)	*Literature Circle Roles (Daniels, 2001)*
Active participant	Content connector
Encourager	Discussion director
Mayor	Passage presider
Record keeper	Summary spokesperson
Time keeper	Vocabulary virtuoso

Along with teaching literature discussion roles, present general expectations for productive interactions. Highlight the social skills needed for the groups to be effective. You might have students brainstorm the interactions that characterize effective small groups, displaying their responses in a chart like the one in Figure 4.2. After conducting group discussions, have students reflect on their group participation in a written or oral note to you, themselves, or their teammates.

When you are ready to integrate literature discussion groups with units, form groups of students, match groups with materials, and schedule the week (Daniels, 2001; Gambrel & Almasi, 1996). The group time might consist of 20 minutes during each class, and be allocated as shown in Figure 4.3.

Doer

Adolescents who read and write can accomplish specific tasks. They can use reading and writing as tools for composing and replying to email messages,

Look Like	*Sound Like*	*Feel Like*
People face each other	One person at a time talks	My ideas are being taken seriously
Everyone concentrates on what each person is saying	Remain on task	
	Give and take of ideas	I'm confident that I will learn from others and they will learn from me
Friendly faces		

FIGURE 4.2   Effective Group Social Skills

Group	Monday	Tuesday	Wednesday	Thursday	Friday
A	Whole-class activity	Silent reading	Response writing	Group sharing	Teacher conference
B	Whole-class activity	Response writing	Group sharing	Teacher conference	Silent reading
C	Whole-class activity	Group sharing	Teacher conference	Silent reading	Response writing
D	Whole-class activity	Teacher conference	Silent reading	Response writing	Group sharing

FIGURE 4.3   Weekly Schedule for Literature Discussion Group

accessing information from various sources, and completing projects, among other things. Readers as doers intend to get a job done more than commit ideas to long-term memory or vicariously experience a text world. The following practices suggest instruction associated with the reader-as-doer metaphor. The first is a somewhat straightforward practice devoted to gathering information. The next practice describes how to take tests strategically and confidently. The other practices elicit somewhat creative expressions of what has been gathered. Again, effective teachers isolate such practices for initial student attention, then integrate them with instructional materials and tasks.

Information Chart.   Information charts structure inquiry tasks, helping students remain focused while sifting through massive amounts of material (Randall, 1996). Information charts extend the data charts previously presented in this chapter by highlighting research components such as topics, prior knowledge, references, findings, and new questions (see Figure 4.4). Students may complete such charts individually or collaboratively.

Taking Tests Strategically and Confidently.   The following guidelines apply to all types of tests. Posting them in the classroom allows ready reference and practice.

1. Think like a test maker.
2. Survey the test; plan your time accordingly.
3. Skim the passage along with the questions and answers. Shuttle among the passage and the questions when marking your choices.
4. Highlight the important words in each question; be especially alert for qualifying terms such as *always, never,* and *most.*
5. Do not spend too much time on any one question; move along.

Name: Topic:

Subtopic:

What I already know:

Bibliography:

_____   _____

_____   _____

Interesting related facts:

Key words:

New questions to research:

FIGURE 4.4   Sample Information Chart

6. Answer the easy questions first. Mark the ones you skip and go back to them when you are ready. Remember that information contained in later items can help you answer previous items.

7. Answer every question as long as there is no penalty for guessing.

8. Narrow possible answers to two, then make your choice based on the most correct answer.
9. Rephrase questions, when possible.
10. Answer questions in your head before studying the choices, when possible.
11. Change your answers only if you misunderstood the question the first time or if you are absolutely sure your first response is wrong.
12. Stay hydrated and energized. Drink water and eat a nutritious snack as needed.
13. Avoid anxiety. Take a deep breath or perform some other relaxation technique if you are becoming anxious.

Pantomime. Pantomime has a place in the upper grades as much as the lower ones partly because it taps multiple intellectual and expressive aspects at any level of sophistication (Douville & Finke, 2000). Students invent physical movement to represent a procedure, event, or concept nonverbally. Selections from nonfiction, fiction, drama, and poetry can be pantomimed.

Typically, one person orally reads a passage while student actors use gesture and movement to represent what is being said. As class members become adept with this, they can pantomime subject matter with no accompanying reading. Upper-grade topics such as the following are pantomimed readily:

Photosynthesis. Students can portray carbon dioxide, water, the sun, and a plant.

Viral infections. Students can act out viruses entering, multiplying, and exiting cells.

The French Revolution. Students can depict Louis XVI, members of the second estate, Robespierre, national assembly members, and Napoleon Bonaparte.

Paul Revere's ride and the battles of Lexington and Concord. Students can portray Paul Revere, colonists and the minutemen, and the British military.

Role-Play Monologues and Interviews. Interviewing individuals or having them present a monologue in role-play situations promotes inquiry (Smith, 1997; Smith & Herring, 2001). For instance, investigative reporters may interview important figures from science, social studies, literature, or mathematics. The questioning might occur during a fictional news conference, talk show, or on-the-scene report.

As always, when initiating role-play monologues or interviews, demonstrate them before students perform them. Encourage students to dress and talk (as much as possible) in the manner of the participants—you might be pleasantly surprised at the creativity and effort this elicits. After the interview, discuss the individuals' accomplishments and the audience's thoughts.

When studying the ancient world, for example, famous individuals can be interviewed, such as Alexander the Great, Confucius, Siddharta Guatama, Iceman of the Alps, Liu Bang, Menes, Paul, Socrates, and Thutmose III. Interviews also can be conducted with unnamed individuals who represent groups, such as archaeologists, artisans, barbarians, caravan riders, disciples, martyrs, patricians, plebians, and regents. As students become adept with role-play interviews, they can include multiple reporters or figures during one interview session (e.g., bring together and interview Confucius, Siddharta Gautama, and Paul).

Patterned Poetry.   Poetic response encourages students to engage subject matter at more than a coldly conceptual level. Poetry encourages visceral aesthetic connections with topics, helping students get personal with what they are examining (Dunning & Stafford, 1992; McWorter & Bullion-Mears, 1997). Patterned poetry is a practice that provides relatively easy entry to this way of thinking and writing (Hise, 1982). Many adolescents prefer a clear structure to initiate their writing—combining and extending the patterns as they become comfortable and proficient with them.

The patterned poems described next fit a unit on the geology of the Grand Canyon. You may find these patterns suitable during some of your units of instruction.

Acrostics.   Spell the topic vertically, then use words, phrases, or sentences to describe the subject:

Great	Coursing through
River carved	And
Astonishing	Navigating rocky
Natural	Years
Delight	Of
	Nature's erosion

Copy Changes (Found Poems).   Select words, phrases, and sentences from passages, change what you want, and arrange them in a poem. The following is from prose passages in Whitney (1996):

Kaibab limestone
at the top
from the Permian Period, before dinosaurs lived.
Vishnu schist
at the bottom
extending to unknown depths.

List Poems. Present a list of key words from a unit of study. Students rearrange words and phrases, add to them, and produce a poem:

Key Word List

Kaibab	Hermit	Bright Angel	shale
Coconino	Redwall	sandstone	limestone

Poem

Kaibab limestone
The top canyon strata.
Coconino sandstone
Looking like a bathtub ring.
Hermit shale
Where low tides flowed in and out.
Redwall limestone
Hikers beware!
Bright Angel shale
Going easy.

Repetitions. Like much popular music, repeat selected terms as a refrain. Add information to the refrain as the poem progresses:

What natural wonder is in northern Arizona?
The Grand Canyon

What natural wonder in northern Arizona is 1 mile deep, 10 miles wide, and 271 miles long?
The Grand Canyon

What natural wonder in northern Arizona uncovered rocks 1,200 million years old?
The Grand Canyon

What natural wonder in northern Arizona has four life zones?
The Grand Canyon

Cinquain. This popular form of poetry consists of five lines with specified numbers and types of of words per line:

Line 1   One word—a noun that names the topic of the poem
Line 2   Two words—a description of the topic
Line 3   Three words—*ing* words that convey the action of the topic
Line 4   Four-word phrase—a description of the topic that shows feeling
Line 5:   One word—expresses the essence of the topic

Canyon
grand magnificence
moving challenging climbing
natural deep Earth wonder
sacred

Haiku.   Haiku is another common yet powerful type of poem with an established pattern. It consists of three lines, each with a predetermined number of
syllables—5, 7, 5—to total 17.

> *Wondrous Grand Canyon*
> *esplanade precambrian*
> *geology now*

Question–Answer Poems.   The title of this pattern reveals its structure, first a
question and then an answer. Repeat until done.

> *Where is the Grand Canyon?*
> *the soul of Gaia*
> *What's so grand about the canyon?*
> *mass, mystery, adventure, color*
> *What will you learn?*
> *layer-cake geology*
> *ecology*
> *and wonder*

Wh- Poems.   Like question–answer poems, asking about the topic jump-
starts this pattern. At least five *wh-* words can be used to launch questions.
They might be arranged as follows, although no particular order is required.

> Line 1   Who?
> Line 2   What?
> Line 3   When?
> Line 4   Where?
> Line 5   Why?

> *Naturalists, tourists, adventurers*
> *Studying, experiencing, challenging*
> *Some return often*
> *Where the river cuts the rock*
> *There's no comparable experience*

or

> *Where the river cuts the rock*
> *There is no comparable experience*
> *Studying, experiencing, challenging*

Understandings.   The beginning of the poem expresses what students understand about a topic; the ending states what they find confusing, ambiguous,
or unstated that they hope to learn eventually.

I understand
　　how the rock strata were deposited
And I understand
　　how the river cut the rock
But I don't understand
　　why the river didn't just run somewhere else

Permissions.　　Students complete two stems. The first addresses factual, exact descriptions; the second concludes with a personal statement about the topic (e.g., what it makes you think, how you feel about it, an insight).

Permit me to tell you about the Grand Canyon
　　It is 1 mile deep
　　10 miles wide
　　271 miles long.
　　The Colorado River carved it
　　through the Kaibab Plateau.
　　Water and wind deposited
　　what became the layers of rocks we see.
But what you should remember about the Grand Canyon
　　Is that natural forces made it
　　But people might destroy it

Comparisons.　　Compare the topic with another in a four-line pattern:

Line 1　Form an image of the topic and briefly describe it.
Line 2　Describe what this image reminds you of.
Line 3　Explain the comparison by stating how the two are alike.
Line 4　Close with a question or personal statement.

A river at the bottom of 6.5 million years of geological formations
Like a knife cutting through the Earth's epidermis
Deep and open
And I'm ready to explore

To a Topic.　　Directly address the topic with factual, exact information, then conclude with a question or personal statement.

You are a natural wonder
That displays 1,200 million years of geography
And provides recreation to river runners, hikers, and tourists
You blocked north-south travel and early empire building
I know why they call you Grand

Analyzer

Readers as analyzers don a critical hat. Like all critical thinkers, they are skeptical about what is presented in a text. They know that the contents of books are ideas composed by another human being—not by some deity. They realize that writers, editors, and publishers are fallible. They understand that some messages are expressed more clearly and completely than others, so they need to determine what is needed to fill in writers' gaps.

Readers as analyzers also realize that writers, editors, and publishers have conscious and subconscious predispositions, biases, and agendas. This realization leads readers to interrogate passages for hidden messages. The following practices accentuate a critical, analytical stance toward print.

Questioning the Author. Like the self-questions contained in Table 4.2, questioning the author (QtA) inquiries are productive tools for examining print (Beck, McKeown, Hamilton, & Kucan, 1997). QtA fosters students' capacity to step back from what they are reading and gain some perspective on it by asking and answering pertinent questions about the author. Emphasizing questions about authors—rather than about passages, classmates, or readers (themselves)—promotes readers' control of print. Three types of questions (called queries by the QtA originators) are recommended: initiating queries, which are most appropriate early in a passage; follow-up queries, which are most appropriate later in a passage; and narrative queries.

Initiating Queries
What is the author trying to say here?
What is the author's message?
What is the author talking about?

Follow-Up Queries
Does this make sense with what the author told us before?
How does this connect with what the author has told us before?
Does the author tell us why?
Why do you think the author tells us this now?

Narrative Queries
How do things look for the character now?

How has the author let you know that something has changed?

How has the author settled this for us?

Given what the author has already told us about this character, what do you think he's/she's up to?

When first planning to use these queries, insert passage language into them. For instance, with a passage about the movement of glaciers, initiating queries might be recast as the following:

What is the author trying to say here about the movement of glaciers?

What is the author's message about the movement of glaciers?

What is the author talking about with regard to the movement of glaciers?

Interrogating Texts.   Interrogations are somewhat formal attempts to uncover layers of meaning. Those who conduct interrogations know that texts are not neutral, that they favor particular points of view at the expense of others. Interrogating texts is a general mindset as much as a specific practice for critiquing the ways authors and publishers influence their readers. It capitalizes on a skeptical perspective when evaluating print and accompanying pictorial support. Like all proficient scientists and critical thinkers, interrogaters habitually question generally accepted matters.

Unlike the QtA queries just delineated, which focus on authors' and publishers' craftsmanship, text interrogations address intentions. A good way to initiate text interrogations is with the following questions adapted from Werner (2000):

What is the author claiming to depict?

What is the author's attitude toward the subject (e.g., [un]sympathetic, [dis]approving, [non]supportive, [dis]respectful)?

What do you think the author wants us to value or celebrate through this depiction?

What does this text say about the status (i.e., occupation, social rank, vested interest) of the author?

How might this text be partial (i.e., incomplete, biased, not telling the whole story)?

What is your personal opinion of the text?

What might someone different than you think of the text?

If the text were rewritten by someone different, how might the message be different?

Conclusion

Addressing the literacy of adolescents through units of subject matter instruction involves weaving. Throughout your course you enmesh unit topics with reading and writing. Teaching practices such as reciprocal teaching, graphically organizing information, and questioning the author serve as crosswise horizontal strands. Teachers interlace these crosswise strands through unit topics such as short stories, constitutional governments, acids and bases, and statistics. Teachers who isolate and integrate these literacy strands during the school year promote maximum literacy learning.

CENTRAL QUESTION: THINK BACK

How do I specify ways for students to improve their reading and writing during units?

To answer fully this chapter's central question, build on the following key concepts:

- Select literacy competencies to link with subject matter instruction.
- Mix isolated and integrated literacy instruction.
- Teach adolescents as builders through (1) constructing main idea statements for informational passages (*about, and*) and (2) reciprocal teaching.
- Teach adolescents as learners through (1) graphically organizing information and (2) note taking.
- Teach adolescents as experiencers through (1) literacy autobiographies, (2) guest book talks, (3) quick book shares, and (4) literature discussion groups.
- Teach adolescents as doers through (1) information charts, (2) taking tests strategically and confidently, (3) pantomime, (4) role-play monologues and interviews, and (5) patterned poetry.
- Teach adolescents as analyzers through (1) questioning the author and (2) interrogating texts.

REFERENCES

Alfassi, M. (1998). Reading for meaning: The efficacy of reciprocal teaching in fostering reading comprehension in high school students in remedial reading classes. *American Educational Research Journal, 35*(2), 309–332.

Alvermann, D. E., Young, J. P., Weaver, D., Hinchman, K. A., Moore, D. W., Phelps, S. F., et al. (1996). Middle and high school students' perceptions of how they experience text-based discussion: A multicase study. *Reading Research Quarterly, 31*, 244–267.

Beck, I. L., McKeown, M. C., Hamilton, R. L., & Kucan, L. (1997). *Questioning the author: An approach for enhancing student engagement with text.* Newark, DE: International Reading Association.

Buehl, D. (2001). *Classroom strategies for interactive learning* (2nd ed.). Newark, DE: International Reading Association.

Burke, J. (2000). *Reading reminders: Tools, tips, and techniques.* Portsmouth, NH: Boynton/Cook.

Daniels, H. (2001). *Literature circles: Voice and choice in book clubs and reading groups* (2nd ed.). York, ME: Stenhouse.

Douville, P., & Finke, J. (2000). Literacy as performance: The power of creative drama in the classroom. In K. D. Wood & T. S. Dickinson (Eds.), *Promoting literacy in grades 4–8: A handbook for teachers and administrators.* Boston: Allyn and Bacon.

Dunning, S., & Stafford, W. (1992). *Getting the knack: 20 poetry writing exercises.* Urbana, IL: National Council of Teachers of English.

Eldridge, B. H. (1998). The quick book share. *Journal of Adolescent and Adult Literacy, 41*(6), 473–474.

Flood, J., & Lapp, D. (2000). Reading comprehension instruction for at-risk students: Research-based practices that can make a difference. In D. W. Moore, D. E. Alvermann, & K. A. Hinchman (Eds.), *Struggling adolescent readers: A collection of teaching strategies* (pp. 138–147). Newark, DE: International Reading Association.

Gambrel, L., & Almasi, J. (Eds.). (1996). *Lively discussions! Creating classroom cultures that foster discussion, interpretation, and comprehension of text*. Newark, DE: International Reading Association.

Grimes, P. (1996). Reciprocal teaching in literature study groups. *Social Studies Review, 36*(1), 37–42.

Hise, J. (1982). *Patterns in poetry*. Lakeside, CA: Interaction Publishers.

Kagan, S. (1992). *Cooperative learning*. San Juan Capistrano, CA: Resources for Teachers.

Kamil, M. J., Mosenthal, P. B., Pearson, P. D., & Barr, R. (Eds.). (2000). *Handbook of reading research* (vol. 3). Mahwah, NJ: Lawrence Erlbaum.

King, C., & Johnson, L. (1999). Constructing meaning via reciprocal teaching. *Reading Research and Instruction, 38*(3), 169–186.

Langer, J. (1999). *Beating the odds: Teaching middle and high school students to read and write well*. (CELA Research Report No. 12014). Albany: State University of New York, National Research Center on English Learning and Achievement. Retrieved July 9, 2001, from http://cela.albany.edu/eie2/index.html.

Mastropieri, M. A., & Scruggs, T. E. (1997). Best practices in promoting reading comprehension in students with learning disabilities. *Remedial and Special Education, 18*(4), 197–213.

McKenzie, G. R. (1978). Data charts: A crutch for helping pupils organize reports. *Language Arts, 56*(7), 784–788.

McWorter, J. Y., & Bullion-Mears, A. T. (1997). Writing poetry in content classrooms. *Middle School Journal, 29*(2), 46–50.

Moore, D. W., Moore, S. A., Cunningham, P. M., & Cunningham, J. W. (in press). *Developing readers and writers in the content areas, K–12* (4th ed.). New York: Allyn and Bacon.

Morley, S. (1996). Faculty book talks. *Journal of Adolescent and Adult Literacy, 40*(2), 130–132.

Myers, E. L. (1997). Beginning the semester with literacy introductions. *Journal of Adolescent and Adult Literacy, 40*(8), 644.

Oja, L. A. (1996). Using story frames to develop reading comprehension. *Journal of Adolescent and Adult Literacy, 40*, 129–130.

Palincsar, A., & Brown, A. L. (1984). Reciprocal teaching of comprehension-fostering and comprehension-monitoring activities. *Cognition and Instruction, 1*, 117–175.

Randall, S. N. (1996). Information charts: A strategy for organizing student research. *Journal of Adolescent and Adult Literacy, 39*(7), 536–542.

Readence, J. E., Moore, D. W., & Rickelman, R. J. (2000). *Prereading activities for content area reading and learning* (3rd ed.). Newark, DE: International Reading Association.

Rosenshine, B., & Meister, C. (1994). Reciprocal teaching: A review of the research. *Review of Educational Research, 66*, 181–221.

Smith, C. R. (1997). Using student monologues to integrate language arts and social studies. *Journal of Adolescent and Adult Literacy, 40*(7), 563–564.

Smith, J. L., & Herring, J. D. (2001). *Dramatic literacy: Using drama and literature to teach middle-level content*. Portsmouth, NH: Heinemann.

Tovani, C. (2000). *I read it, but I don't get it: Comprehension strategies for adolescent readers*. Portland, ME: Stenhouse.

Werner, W. (2000). Reading authorship into texts. *Theory and Research in Social Education, 28*(2), 193–219.

Whipple, G. M. (1925). *Report of the National Committee on Reading*. In *24th Yearbook of the National Society for the Study of Education* (Pt. II). Bloomington, IL: Public School Publishing Company.

Whitney, S. (1996). *A field guide to the Grand Canyon*. Seattle, WA: The Mountaineers.

CHAPTER

5 Moving toward Differentiation

CENTRAL QUESTION: THINK AHEAD

How do I reach individual readers and writers when my classes are so diverse?

In terms of instruction, effective teachers realize that one size does not fit all. These teachers understand that habitual teaching practices and ways of interacting affect different students differently. They also know that adolescents who struggle as readers do best when they are personally involved with school work.

Educators have acknowledged numerous factors influencing student learning, and they have institutionalized numerous approaches to accommodating the factors. Special education programs are available for students demonstrating overall cognitive exceptionalities as well as emotional difficulties, physical impairments, and specific learning disabilities (Masters, Mori, & Mori, 1999). Bilingual education and sheltered English programs are available for language minority students whose families recently have immigrated to the United States (Gonzalez, Brusca-Vega, & Yawkey, 1997).

Culturally responsive education bridges academic settings with students' ethnic heritages (Shade, Kelly, & Oberg, 1997). Educators also adapt instruction according to students' socioeconomic class, gender, and religious principles. They address individuals' preferred learning styles (e.g., mastery, interpersonal, self-expressive) and intelligences (e.g., visual/spatial, verbal/linguistic, intrapersonal) (Silver, Strong, & Perini, 2000).

Regular classroom teachers who accommodate the factors affecting learning (such as the ones just enumerated) assume that each individual follows a different path to learning (Tomlinson, 1999). These teachers realize that one student might do best with a methodical approach that includes answering questions about expository writing and deferring to an answer key, whereas another might excel when negotiating possible answers through highly creative, open-ended responses to imaginative literature. One student might do well in free-flowing discussions with students interrupting each other to produce ideas jointly, whereas another might prefer silently recording ideas in a journal for personal reflection. One might benefit from graphically organizing ideas prior to writing, and another might write best in stream-of-consciousness fashion. Consequently, teachers move toward differentiating instruction.

An important first step in moving toward differentiation is to address diversity directly. Through open dialogue in class, teachers acknowledge diversity and express plans to differentiate instruction. They are explicit about developing a classroom climate of inclusion, one that embraces all individuals. They affirm the values of diversity, describing the inherent dignity of individuals as well as the collective attributes of multiple perspectives and relative strengths. They explain how everyone will be treated as part of the club, how no one will be marginalized. They praise and reprimand students equitably, not treating any individual or group preferentially. They hold high expectations for all.

Teachers who differentiate instruction insist upon respect—expecting everyone to act courteously and to honor what others offer. They set out to eliminate threats and distractions by not tolerating rudeness or insults. Asserting everyone's right to be heard, these teachers regularly provide each student opportunities to express himself or herself during whole-class, group, paired, and individual situations.

When assigning membership for projects and other group activities, they integrate students. Positive inclusive images adorn the walls. Role models from various sectors of the community regularly speak about their successes, emphasizing their uses of literacy. Students relate experiences connecting their personal and home lives with school and business spheres.

Additionally, teachers who accommodate individuals regularly vary classroom activities amid whole-class, small-group, and individual configurations, and they pace activities briskly to accommodate students' various attention spans and learning preferences. When presenting information, they often provide lecture notes so students have a listening guide to follow. They might display the identical notes on an overhead and emphasize what is especially important to know about selected items.

Teachers begin their move toward differentiation by initially foregrounding themselves in highly visible roles, then moving to the background as students assume more and more control of their learning. Educators refer to this process with terms such as *gradual release of responsibility* and *fading*. The process moves from teacher-directed to student-directed instruction throughout the year. Thoroughly planning how to initiate group instruction and how to accommodate individuals promotes this process.

Initiating Group Instruction

Beginning teachers often report great anxiety and exhilaration associated with the first day of teaching (Dollase, 1992). First contacts typically produce nervousness, but tremendous joy and stimulation follow when the experience goes well. By the end of the first week of school, we hope that your class members share thoughts such as the following:

- "This teacher seems to know where we're going and how we're going to get there."
- "I think I'm going to learn something worthwhile in here."
- "I can live with these class rules and expectations."
- "This teacher seems to care whether or not everybody learns."

Getting the whole class off to a good start and establishing ground rules the very first day of a new school year sets the stage for what follows (Atwell, 1998; Tomlinson, 1999). The classroom culture and structure that will persist the rest of the year is shaped during the first few minutes of the first day when you first meet your students. Your demeanor, expectations, and explanations influence how the rest of the year will progress.

Begin the school year by setting a positive tone right away, getting momentum moving in the right direction, and laying the foundation for what follows. Being especially well planned for the first few days of teaching pays off many times over during the year.

New Beginnings

The following describes the school opening of a hypothetical reading teacher's class. We present this description as if a teacher entered it in a personal journal, so we use the first person, *I*. These entries present concrete examples of how to get started in a realistic classroom situation.

Boy, am I nervous! I feel prepared for my ninth-grade class, *Reading for Today and Tomorrow,* but what about the students? Will they respect me? Will they try to improve their reading and writing? I know this class enrolls students with a mix of reading competencies, some reading at about the 20th percentile and some at about the 60th, and I am especially concerned about those who struggle as readers. I intend to make sure they don't give up on school, reading, or me!

The physical part of my classroom is arranged pretty well. Since I inherited individual student desks, I placed them in columns and rows, planning to have students move them as needed. The desks easily can be placed side by side when students work in paired situations; they also can be grouped into foursomes. My desk and a small table are in back of the class to minimize disruptions while I confer with individuals and groups. I placed a stool and audiovisual cart containing an overhead projector and storage space in front of the class for whole-group presentations.

Books, magazines, and other reading material surround the classroom. I modeled this like a youth-friendly library as much as possible, wanting to invite students into reading. Posters promoting reading as well as popular culture icons adorn the walls. One bulletin board displays key terms for the first unit we will study, another holds the calendar of daily class events, and a third holds photographs of past students involved with in-school and out-of-school activities. Three computers are in one corner, and a second conference table for small group work is in another. My philodendron plant by the north-facing windows continues to thrive.

Day 1

Well, we had a great day! I dressed as professionally as possible, arrived at school early, and had everything prepared. I stationed myself just outside the classroom door to greet my students. Wearing a (hopefully) confident and friendly smile, I greeted each individual, speaking briefly with those I knew already and simply welcoming those who were unfamiliar to me. I ensured that each student was coming to the right room and handed each a large 6-by 8-inch numbered card.

The numbered cards directed students to assigned seats in the classroom. I purposely separated students who entered as groups, hoping to avoid a ring of friends luring each other into troublesome behavior. I told students to begin filling out the information requested on the back of the card as soon as they found their seats.

The back of the cards contained a questionnaire entitled Getting to Know You. The headings asked for each student's name, address, telephone number, and other ways to be contacted (email, pager, cell phone). Another heading asked for the name of someone at home or work for me to contact in case of emergency. (I didn't initiate discussion of what constituted an emergency, but, if asked, I would have said something like, "When something suddenly interferes with your learning.") The remaining items required responses longer than the initial one- and two-word response items:

- How do you feel about reading?
- What have you enjoyed reading in the past?
- What does someone have to do to be a good reader?
- What are you involved in before or after school that might affect your class performance?
- What can I do to help you improve your reading the most?

When the bell rang to begin class, I welcomed everyone, introduced myself briefly, and congratulated them for just accomplishing the first class procedure: "Thank you for moving directly to your seats and beginning work," I said. "This is how we will begin class every day. The difference is that from now on the opening task, which we'll call bell work, will be listed here on the white board, rather than me handing it to you when you enter."

Next, I explained more about completing the cards, giving special attention to what the last item meant about how I can help. I explained that I intended to fit what we do in class with each individuals' interests and goals, so each person should tell me about himself or herself. I asked the students to complete all items fully to help me get to know them better. "To connect the course with your interests, I need to know more about you," I said.

I circulated throughout the room as students completed the cards. This got me closer to the class, allowing me to intervene if anyone needed my attention. As students completed the cards, I handed them a printed course introduction. Immediately providing them something to read accommodated the ragged ending—students finishing at different times—that always happens when students write. It also allowed me a quick personal interaction with each student.

The last person completed the card after about 15 minutes. This offers good information about students' academics; right away I begin learning the rates at which individuals work. Additionally, the cards offer valuable early insights into individuals' literacy attitudes and competencies.

I sat on my stool at the front of the class, clapped my hands a few times, and told the group that this was my signal for requesting everyone's attention. Holding up a file folder, I explained that these would be used like envelopes for us to mail course work back and forth. They would store completed assignments on their own. Then I distributed file folders and asked everyone to write their names on the tabs, saying that they could decorate the folders later—of course, using only school-appropriate words, drawings, and symbols. The students inserted their Getting to Know You cards into the folders and passed them to the front of the class. Again, I explained that this would be the procedure for submitting regular course work throughout the year.

Then I drew attention to the handout containing my course introduction. This introduction contained what I figured students and parents needed to know initially to make sense of the course. I made it as friendly and informative as possible, fitting it on the front and back of a single sheet of paper. Knowing that I would distribute copies of this to parents during the open house/curriculum night scheduled for the next week, I had a Spanish language version available and was ready to request other translations if needed. My course introduction contained nine parts:

- *Upbeat opening.* "Welcome to *Reading for Today and Tomorrow!* This course will benefit you now and in the future."
- *Course outcomes.* "The goal of this class is to speed up your development as independent lifelong readers."
- *Overview of course contents.* "It promotes your abilities to build understandings of challenging passages, remember what you have read, experience the joy of reading, accomplish tasks using literacy, and examine how reading fits your life."
- *How people at home might help students.* "People at home can promote reading by talking about what is being accomplished in school and by providing time, space, and materials for reading. I will notify your home when special projects are due."

- *Noteworthy behavioral expectations.* "Every day bring to class a pen or pencil and a book for self-selected reading. Respect for ourselves, others, and the classroom governs how we act in here."
- *When I will communicate with parents.* "According to school policy, I will send home grades every 3 weeks. Additionally, I will contact your home personally if there is a reason for special concern or celebration. Grades are based on self-selected reading journals (30%), unit projects and assignments (40%), and tests and quizzes (30%)."
- *How parents can contact me.* "Open communication is very important. I am available in my classroom 1 hour before and after school every day; please let me know to expect you if you plan to come. My telephone number and email address are listed below."
- *Upbeat closing.* "Together we can make this a great year! I am looking forward to every student improving his or her reading!"
- *Confirmation of receipt of this information.* "Please sign and return the attached confirmation that you have received this course introduction."

I moved briskly through the description, taking about 15 minutes to highlight the main points. Not wanting to drag out the introduction, my main emphasis was on the course outcome: *independent lifelong reading.* I showed pictures and graphs depicting the dramatic social and occupational changes occurring during our lifetimes, and explained how reading was crucial for maintaining pace with future changes.

While accentuating the positive, I pointed out that every reader—like every athlete—has room to grow. I mentioned all-time sport greats such as Michael Jordan, Tiger Woods, and Wayne Gretzky, athletes without peer, and explained that none of them reached mastery. "Even Michael, Tiger, and Wayne constantly worked to improve themselves. We all can improve our athletic performance—and our reading," I said. "Everyone in here is on the path toward reading development; my goal is to promote it."

Next, to preview expectations for self-selected reading, which is a big part of my class, I had the group look around the room at all the reading materials. "Beginning the day after tomorrow," I said, "you should have a book to read on your own. Just as athletes continually are involved with their sport—even in the off-season—great readers need to read. And some truly wonderful titles are available here for you!" I picked up and described a few of the more compelling books, such as *Into Thin Air, Maus: A*

Survivor's Tale, and *Jacob Have I Loved.* Showing the covers—and the interior graphics of *Maus*—I promoted each book, reading excerpts from each. Then I explained my self-selected reading plan.

Next, I told them that we needed to begin the year with a test that mainly was a warm-up for the more challenging work to follow. My test called for students to count the number of times the letter *F* appeared in a quotation. I told them that we needed to move quickly, so they would have only 15 seconds to count the letters I would display. I projected the following sentence onto the overhead screen:

FINISHED FILES ARE THE RESULT OF YEARS
OF SCIENTIFIC STUDY COMBINED WITH THE
EXPERIENCE OF MANY YEARS.

Switching the projector light off after 15 seconds, I recorded on the white board responses to the following series of questions:

How many of you saw 0 letters F?
How many saw 1—and only 1—letter F?
How many saw 2—and only 2—letters F?
How many saw 3—and only 3—letters F?
How many saw 4—and only 4—letters F?
How many saw 5—and only 5—letters F?
How many saw 6—and only 6—letters F?
How many saw 7—and only 7—letters F?

As always happens, practically all students reported seeing three Fs, when, in fact, six Fs are in the sentence. We talked about reasons for this, and I explained that I liked this demonstration because it highlighted the value and necessity of reading long words proficiently.

Then I projected onto the overhead screen what probably still is the single longest word in the English language:

pneumonultramicroscopicsilicavolcanoconiosis

I pronounced it several times and informed the group that they were going to learn its meaning and spelling today. Amid a few groans and protests, I also informed them that they needed to trust me to show them how to go about learning its meaning and spelling. Then I guided the class through a process of morphemic analysis—identifying prefixes, bases, and suffixes—to grasp this seemingly impossible word. I could see that this was having the desired effect, students were intent on accomplishing a clear and vivid task that would pay off in the future. We were establishing a productive learning trajectory.

With about 5 minutes remaining in the period, I reviewed what we accomplished. I specified the procedures they had followed: (a) entering the class quietly, (b) moving directly to seats, (c) beginning work on a task, (d) starting another task immediately upon finishing the first, (e) giving me their full attention when I sat on the stool, especially if I clapped my hands, (f) using their folders when submitting work, and (g) having a book available for self-selected reading.

Then I probed and commented on their understandings of the course outcome, becoming independent lifelong readers, and asked for any questions regarding the rest of the information on the course introduction. I had each student write the longest English word on a prepared strip of paper and asked them to remain in their desks until the end-of-period bell sounded and I excused them. Finally, I stood by the door, collecting the word strips as an exit slip when they left class.

Day 2

Just as on the first day, I greeted students at my classroom door. Maintaining a friendly yet firm demeanor, I reminded them to take their seats right away and look at the white board for the bell work. The task was to divide each of 15 words into prefixes, roots, and suffixes. This followed what we had done yesterday with the word *pneumonultramicroscopicsilicavolcanoconiosis* so they knew how to go about accomplishing the task. I presented words with fairly recognizable morphemes (e.g., *agreeable, uncomplaining, replay*) to maintain the momentum from our previous good experience.

When the bell rang, I sat on my stool, expecting the class to recall my signal for their attention. I thanked them for giving it to me and welcomed everyone back to day 2 of *Reading for Today and Tomorrow*. I briefly reviewed what we accomplished yesterday, and explained that from now on my teaching assistant would distribute their folders when they entered.

Next, I called attention to the bell work begun this day, saying, "You should be pretty far along with these terms, so please take a few more minutes and finish them up." I circulated again, then sat on my stool, got everyone's attention, and introduced a major procedure I intended to use—study partners. "I believe in the old saying that two heads are better than one, so we'll frequently work with partners in here," I said. Then I explained why partnerships were valuable and what was needed to benefit the most from them, emphasizing school success skills I had posted, such as *drawing on resources* and *controlling emotions.*

Two volunteers came to the front of the class and, with my prompting, demonstrated how to reach consensus on their first five responses to the bell work just completed. Following this fishbowl exercise, we brainstormed what such a productive partnership looked like and sounded like (e.g., doing your fair share of the work; disagreeing without being disagreeable). I recorded these actions, planning to recopy and post them later. I explained to the class how to form pairs and move desks together. Then the newly formed partners reviewed their bell work. After about 5 minutes I called time, everyone placed their work in their individual folders, and returned to single-file formation.

To help me and everyone in the class learn each other's names, we played a brief bean-bag toss where the tosser (not *thrower*) called out someone's name then tossed him or her the bag. I demonstrated how to say a name then toss—not throw—the bag, and away we went.

After about 5 minutes with the bean bag, I demonstrated how to locate yesterday's course materials, information, and directions if they were to need it. I showed the weekly calendar of activities posted on a bulletin board and each day's handouts and course notes filed in an open-topped plastic filing box. "This is how you catch up on your schoolwork if you have been absent," I said. (And thank goodness for my ever-helpful teaching assistants each hour maintaining these files!)

My next class segment formally began the 2-week unit I planned for the beginning of this course, which was connected with the Getting to Know You cards completed yesterday. I had framed the unit as follows:

Topic: Reading Self-Awareness

Unit outcomes: Students will be able to (a) analyze their reading strengths and limitations, (b) describe the learning environment most effective for them, and (c) identify promising recreational readings.

Essential question: "How can I develop myself as a reader?"

Culminating activity: Following a corporation's action plan format, explain how you can develop yourself as a reader.

"All right, group," I began, "yesterday you reported some very good information that will help me get to know you and your reading. You told me what improved your reading in the past and how you feel about reading, and this is good information for me to have. Today we're going to begin a project that will help you know about your reading even better."

I returned to my sports analogy of Jordan, Woods, and Gretzky, this time displaying pictures of these stars in various poses and action shots. I asked for the names of other superstars, men and women who truly excelled in sports, entertainment, and other fields. Then I showed pictures of young unknowns involved in the same fields as Jordan, Woods, and Gretzky, and I asked what the unknowns needed to do to be like the superstars. The class brainstormed pertinent ideas related to commitment, desire, resources, and talent, to name a few.

Then I showed some of my favorite books, selected John McPhee's *Basin and Range* (1990), read some brief difficult excerpts ("There are basalt flows in the Basin and Range that are also post-Miocene—lavas that poured out on the surface well after the block faulting had begun, like the Watchungs of New Jersey" [p. 61]), and explained how I couldn't or didn't read them when I was younger but grew into them as I developed. I emphasized my point here that people develop as athletes and as readers—often at different paces and in different ways. I solicited comments from students about them developing their proficiencies in any area outside school, accentuating the idea of growth and incremental improvement.

I stated, "So the question we'll be pursuing for the next 2 weeks in this class is this: How can I develop myself as a reader? Given where we are, how can we continue growing? So tell me, how can you develop yourselves as readers?" I asked. We brainstormed some valid suggestions for future reference. I pointed out how the responses could fall into three categories: (a) reading strengths and limitations, (b) learning environment, and (c) recreational reading. These were the three areas we would explore in this unit. Then I displayed different action plans I gathered over the years from the world of work to exemplify the culminating activity. The action plan write-ups all contained objectives, methods for achieving them, timelines, and evaluation plans. This unit kick-off lasted about 20 minutes.

To culminate the class, I asked what new classroom procedures had been introduced (obtaining folders, locating make-up work, and forming partnerships). I asked for reasons for examining prefixes, bases, and suffixes in long words. Then we reviewed plans for the upcoming unit. "Tomorrow we begin self-selected reading," I informed everyone. "Bring your own books."

Day 3
Again I was at the door confidently and cheerfully greeting students to class. Another set of 15 words clearly composed of pre-

fixes, roots, and suffixes awaited division. Most of the class got right to work, although one individual was having trouble settling down, so I stood nearby.

After the bell rang, I directed class members to form pairs and reach agreement on the words' morphemes. We moved right through this practice as I circulated about the classroom; the students placed the word study sheets in their folders when finished. I explained again how these bell work tasks formed the basis for powerful independent reading strategies: "You won't encounter bell work like this outside school, but you will encounter long, unfamiliar words. When you meet long, unfamiliar words when you read, look for their parts. We'll be analyzing words in here all yearlong, so you eventually will be superstars at it."

"A topic we must cover today involves the classroom discipline plan," I said. "Let me be brief: I expect no behavior problems. We've got too much to do, and reading is too important. I expect the best, but I am planned for the worst. If individuals choose to act out in here, then I do have a plan. As I said the first day, respect is the key word. Respect for yourselves, others, and the classroom is the expectation in here. But let's take this a step further: what does respect look like and sound like in these three areas? Please remain with your partner and generate lists for these areas."

After 5 minutes I collected the pairs' lists, intending to display the most informative items on a master. "All right, everyone seems on track regarding what respect looks and sounds like. We'll talk about some of these examples tomorrow. Now let's go over the consequences for disrespect." At this point I drew attention to my hierarchy of consequences:

- Warning
- Second warning
- Conference with student, and contact with home
- Detention, and conference with home
- Assign to front office

"Before we move on, let's take a little more time to learn everyone's name," I said while holding up the bean bag. "Victor," I called, before tossing him the bag, and away it went.

Following this activity, I picked up where we left off yesterday. "OK, group, remember the action plans from yesterday? At the end of this 2 weeks you will have produced an action plan for developing yourself as a reader. The idea is for you to understand how you go about reading so you can continue doing what you do well and pay some attention to what could be improved."

I connected a reading action plan to dietary guidelines. "It's clear that a healthy diet emphasizes bread, cereal, rice, and pasta, but you still have lots of choices within this category. Knowing that you should select much from bread, cereal, rice, and pasta, you still get to select the specific brands and types that you prefer. Part of my job is to help you understand the established guidelines for improving reading so you can make the choices best for yourself."

Then I distributed a brief article, gave the students 5 minutes to read, collected the articles, and had the students individually record everything they remembered. After a few minutes, I asked, "What did you do to understand and remember the article? How did you determine what to write down?" We brainstormed a few strategies, then I distributed a rating scale for students to complete.

I reminded them that healthy reading—like healthy eating— had room for personal preference within established guidelines, and now was the time to think these through. I explained some of the less-familiar strategies on the rating scale, such as forming mental images and monitoring performance. The scale called for students to check the following items according to "very useful to me," "somewhat useful to me," "not useful to me," and "distracting to me":

- Analyzing the parts of long, unfamiliar words
- Asking myself questions about the passage
- Clarifying what is unclear
- Connecting author's ideas across different parts of a passage
- Connecting author's ideas with the ones already in mind
- Determining the meanings of unfamiliar words by using the surrounding words
- Forming mental images
- Judging the value of what the author is saying
- Monitoring performance
- Predicting what is coming
- Previewing the passage before reading
- Rereading confusing parts
- Summarizing
- Thinking about how to use the text ideas in the future
- Writing notes

I collected the rating scales, saying that I would tally the responses for discussion tomorrow. I planned then to explore individuals' reasons for their choices, the similarities and differences among the choices, what other strategies are possible, and when some strategies are more appropriate than others.

As students completed the rating scales, I directed them to their self-selected reading books. They knew to bring a book to class today or select one from the available materials. I had explained that time spent reading was the outcome here. They were to involve themselves in sustained silent reading. Later we would form small groups and share what we were reading as well as our responses to the materials. I played some light rock music as background to set an appropriate mood. No one complained about the music selection.

We closed the class by returning books to their shelves and gathering as a group. A few students shared their reactions to what they were reading. Then I reminded the group of the procedure for and value of bell work and partner formation. Next, I asked about the purpose for the reading strategy rating scale. Finally, I informed the class, "Tomorrow we continue examining our diet of reading strategies, and we will continue with self-selected reading. See you then!"

Features of the Course Opening

Thinking of the Four Ps presented in Chapter 1 highlights much of what occurred in the first days of school just presented. The Four Ps help unpack some of the teacher's actions, explaining how she is moving toward differentiation.

Passion.　　This teacher's passion for reading is evident in her comments and actions. She shares *Basin and Range,* acknowledging it as a personal favorite that she grew into. She extols the qualities of *Into Thin Air, Maus,* and *Jacob Have I Loved.* She promotes the value of self-selected reading and independent lifelong learning right off the bat.

This teacher also demonstrates passion for her students' well-being. She immediately begins efforts to connect with them personally. She explains how reading links with individuals' well-being, affirms her belief that everyone in class will accelerate their reading development, and labels no one as a failure in the past or potentially in the future. Meeting students at the door indicates her caring attitude toward them. Such passion goes far in promoting a climate where individuals are willing and able to exert themselves, take risks, and learn.

Purpose.　　This teacher immediately shares the goal of this class (i.e., to speed up students' development as independent lifelong readers) so she and the students are clear about where they are going. This teacher also calls attention to the lofty nature of the purpose, explaining that even sports and entertainment superstars continually strive for increased levels of proficiency.

The reading materials and posters throughout her room signal the class purpose. She expresses it frequently and structures the word study activity (with *pneumonultramicroscopicsilicavolcanoconiosis*) to guide students toward this the first day. Additionally, she makes sure learning occurs right off the bat so students sense some accomplishment and expect more. Right away they feel they are making progress. This is aligned with suggestions by Alatorre-Parks (2000), Huffman (1996), Kessler (1999), and Schanker (1995) for initiating vivid and direct expectations for future learning.

At the level of specific teaching practices, she clearly specifies what is to be accomplished through the bell work, self-selected reading, and "Reading Self-Awareness" unit. Such direction allows learners eventually to take control of their own learning and chart their own courses.

Partnership.   The teacher right away begins linking students with course work, each other, herself, and the community. The reading strategy rating scale enlists student engagement with their own reading development. Guiding students through self-assessment of their own reading competencies and preferences is consistent with offerings by Archambeault (1992), Pearson and Santa (1995), and Schoenbach, Greenleaf, Cziko, and Hurwitz (1999). Self-rating and self-selected reading gets students in on the act of directing their own reading growth.

Several activities described in the preceding scenario lead toward partnerships. The Getting to Know You cards help the teacher link with individuals. The study partner formation used the second day with the bell work clearly exemplifies a classroom partnership. Whole-class brainstorming practices accomplished in a respectful manner are another example of students collaborating. She invites student input into describing what respect looks like relative to self, others, and the environment. She conducts the bean-bag toss so she and the group can learn each others' names quickly and build community. When students are writing, she circulates about the classroom and moves quickly to students' sides when necessary. The course introduction prepared with the students' homes in mind indicates partnering outside the classroom.

Plans.   Extensive planning is evident during this course opening. Right from the start this teacher addressed plans for reading. Introducing required class reading materials, initially directing students through them, and teaching students how to use them independently is a well-validated practice (Davis, 1993; Gee & Rakow, 1990).

This teacher clearly planned classroom instruction and management, enabling her to guide students appropriately. She followed several classroom procedures that authorities such as Emmer, Evertson, and Worsham (2000) recommend for opening the school year. For instance, she immediately brings order to the class by greeting students at the door and assigning seats. She hands each student a card, involving them right from the start in an activity, and has the course description ready to go as soon as students complete the cards.

Additionally, she has arranged the physical aspects of the classroom to suit her teaching style, planned bell work, produced a course description, decided how grades would be determined, and formulated a discipline plan. She teaches students procedures such as how to enter class, submit assignments in folders, and form study partners as the need for them arises. She readily and confidently begins self-selected reading; the unit on individuals learning about their reading is centered on the essential question, How can I develop myself as a reader?

Final Word

The reading teacher's first few days described in the preceding scenario is an example of one approach. Other decisions and preparations certainly are proper. The important point is that this school opening set a positive tone, high expectations, and clear procedures. It got momentum moving in an appropriate direction.

Accommodating Individuals

As soon as students collectively begin advancing through a course, begin fading your presence out and the students' presence in. Plan modifications in your instructional practices so individuals have a voice and a choice in their education. Opportunities for self-selection help students connect with academics in ways that are personally and culturally appropriate. Two major ways to accommodate individuals center on instructional choices and partner choices.

Instructional Choices

Instructional choices offer leeway during units of study. Teachers direct everyone in the class toward central questions, as presented in Chapter 3, yet they accommodate individuals by offering multiple avenues and supports (Jorgensen, 1994–1995). Teachers weave literacy through units, as presented in Chapter 4, yet they accommodate individuals' literacy proficiencies and preferences through choices.

Table 5.1 illustrates how a unit on the Grand Canyon might offer choices relative to print materials, forms of expression, and sequence. With such a unit, teachers typically establish overall expectations (e.g., "At the end of 3 weeks, explain what makes the Grand Canyon grand") as well as possible choices.

As Table 5.1 shows, teachers offer multilevel print materials (in this case, books and a website) so that students will find some materials more challenging than others. Along with these multilevel reading materials,

TABLE 5.1   Possible Grand Canyon Unit Accommodations

Print Materials	Forms of Expression	Sequence
Very Accessible Price, L. G. (1999). *An Introduction to Grand Canyon Geology.* Grand Canyon, AZ: Grand Canyon Association. www.grandcanyon.org	ads biographies brochures commercials debates diaries	The order of completing unit activities; the succession in which tasks are completed **Student Choice** Individuals follow the sequence presented by the teacher or set their own.
Moderately Difficult Collier, M. (1985). *Grand Canyon Geology.* Grand Canyon, AZ: Grand Canyon Association. Stegner, P. (1995). *Grand Canyon: The Great Abyss.* New York: Tehabi Books.	encyclopedia entries interviews journals magazine memoirs myths	
Difficult Ghiglieri, M. P. (1992). *Canyon.* Tucson: University of Arizona Press.	newspapers observational notes poems scripts skit	
Student Choice Individuals select print materials from above or locate their own.	**Student Choice** Individuals select forms of expression from above or design their own.	

teachers might contribute audiotaped recordings of passages, opportunities to read passages orally, and multimedia CDs containing encyclopedias or simulations. They might offer pamphlets, brochures, paper editions of encyclopedias, periodicals, and alternative textbooks. Library books consisting of nonfiction accounts of the Grand Canyon as well as stories set amid the Grand Canyon setting certainly are appropriate. Culturally relevant materials such as ones presenting Native American or Hispanic experiences with and perceptions of the canyon add to the choices. Students might select the material they wish to read from those provided, or they might locate their own, typically with teacher input and required approval before use.

Multiple forms of expression also appear. Students select the way(s) they will express themselves from the choices provided, or they design their own way(s) to express themselves. They use study guides and notes to gather what they will put into their final form. Working with teachers, bilingual students strike a balance between use of their first and second languages when expressing themselves (Echavarria & Goldenberg, 1999). For instance, they might produce forms that are translations of one another, paying special attention to terms that are cognates of each other (e.g., *canyon/canon*).

To be sure, teachers generally limit the possible forms of expression to ones students already know or soon will learn; they also determine whether appropriate scoring guides will be available. An extensive list of forms such as the one presented in Table 5.1 would be best offered to classes that already have experienced them.

Finally, the sequence choices (i.e., students deciding the order in which they will complete tasks) depend on pertinent due dates and what students know how to perform. The sequence options, like the other options, maintain attention to essential unit understandings while contributing to students' voice and choice in their learning.

Partners

As Chapter 1 declared, partners accomplish things by working together. They help each other out, supporting one another's efforts. Partners lend a hand when it is needed. When completing a unit on a topic such as the Grand Canyon, students might work in cooperative learning groups to promote academic and social outcomes (Lord, 2001). Partners can collaborate when gathering information about the Grand Canyon, planning how they will express themselves, and revising and polishing their final products. The opportunity to work alone is frequently an option, too. Of course, teachers frequently intervene in the membership of pairings and groupings to ensure cooperation and productivity (Sharan, 1994).

Multiple partnerships come from within-school quarters. Classroom teachers position themselves as partners by setting aside time for one-to-one conferences during class and being available before and after school for special help. Teaching paraprofessionals, aides, and older students might be available for supporting and monitoring unit efforts. Teachers in support classes such as special education, reading, or second language learning might help guide individuals as they determine and report what makes the Grand Canyon so grand.

Partners outside the school certainly are appropriate. Send home unit expectations, suggestions for support, and notes of praise for academic achievement and effort whenever appropriate. Consider agencies such as public libraries, the YMCA, and Boys and Girls Clubs that offer after-school tutoring and homework assistance. Community college and university students frequently offer intern assistance, tapping another available partnership.

Conclusion

Differentiating instruction is a way of thinking as much as it is a set of teaching practices. When you plan how to enable success for all students, including those adolescents who struggle as readers, you enact basic beliefs about individuals' inherent worth and dignity. You address justice and fairness. You endorse equal opportunity amid a world of inequality. Clearly and passionately adhering to such thinking validly guides your plans to initiate group instruction and accommodate individuals.

CENTRAL QUESTION: THINK BACK

How do I reach individual readers and writers when my classes are so diverse?

To answer fully this chapter's central question, build on the following key concepts:

- Directly address diversity with the classes.
- Foreground yourself visibly when initiating group instruction, then fade to the background when students begin assuming responsibility for their learning.
- Offer choices in print materials, forms of expression, and sequence.
- Facilitate partnerships.

REFERENCES

Alatorre-Parks, L. (2000). Aligning student interest with district mandates. *Journal of Adolescent and Adult Literacy, 44,* 330–332.

Archambeault, B. (1992). Personalizing study skills in secondary students. *Journal of Reading, 35,* 468–472.

Atwell, N. (1998). *In the middle: New understandings about writing, reading, and learning* (2nd ed.). Portsmouth, NH: Heinemann.

Davis, E. D. (1993). Teacher perceptions of the reading and study skills needed in middle and junior high school social studies classes. *American Secondary Education, 22,* 26–29.

Dollase, R. H. (1992). *Voices of beginning teachers: Visions and realities.* New York: Teachers College Press.

Echavarria, J., & Goldenberg, C. (1999). *Teaching secondary language minority students* (Research Brief #4). Santa Cruz, CA: Center for Research on Education, Diversity and Excellence. Retrieved July 12, 2001, from www.crede.ucsc.edu.

Emmer, E. T., Evertson, C. M., & Worsham, M. E. (2000). *Classroom management for secondary teachers* (5th ed.). Boston: Allyn and Bacon.

Gee, T. C., & Rakow, S. J. (1990). Helping students learn by reading: What experienced social studies teachers have learned. *Social Education, 54,* 398–401.

Gonzalez, G., Brusca-Vega, R., & Yawkey, T. (1997). *Assessment and instruction of culturally and linguistically diverse students with or at-risk of learning problems: From research to practice.* Boston: Allyn and Bacon.

Huffman, L. E. (1996). What's in it for you? A student-directed text preview. *Journal of Adolescent and Adult Literacy, 40,* 56–57.

Jorgensen, C. M. (1994–1995). Essential questions—inclusive answers. *Educational Leadership, 52* (4), 52–55.

Kessler, J. W. (1999). An alternative approach to teaching biology terminology. *The American Biology Teacher, 61,* 688–690.

Lord, T. R. (2001). 101 reasons for using cooperative learning in biology teaching. *The American Biology Teacher, 63,* 30–38.

Masters, L. F., Mori, B. A., & Mori, A. A. (1999). *Teaching secondary students with mild learning and behavior problems: Methods, material, strategies* (3rd ed.). Austin, TX: Pro-Ed.

McPhee, J. (1990). *Basin and range.* New York: Noonday Press.

Pearson, J. W., & Santa, C. M. (1995). Students as researchers of their own learning. *Journal of Reading, 38,* 462–469.

Schanker, N. B. (1995). Biology questionnaires: Grabbing student interest the first week! *The American Biology Teacher, 57,* 286–287.

Schoenbach, R., Greenleaf, C., Cziko, C., & Hurwitz, L. (1999). *Reading for understanding: A guide to improving reading in middle and high school classrooms.* San Francisco: Jossey-Bass.

Shade, B. J., Kelly, C., & Oberg, M. (1997). *Creating culturally responsive classrooms.* Washington, DC: American Psychological Association.

Sharan, S. (Ed.). (1994). *Handbook of cooperative learning methods.* Westport, CT: Greenwood Press.

Silver, F., Strong, M. J., & Perini, M. J. (2000). *So each may learn: Integrating learning styles and multiple intelligences.* Alexandria, VA: Association for Supervision and Curriculum Development.

Tomlinson, C. A. (1999). *The differentiated classroom: Responding to the needs of all learners.* Alexandria, VA: Association for Supervision and Curriculum Development.

6 Interventions in Special Classes

CENTRAL QUESTION: THINK AHEAD

What can be done to help adolescents who are not fully served by literacy instruction across the curriculum?

We hear this question often, especially lately, as authorities have begun to require high-stakes test performance for high school graduation. Teachers and administrators who ask this question understand that adolescents who struggle with school literacy tasks may need specialized help—intervention—beyond what is usually possible in a content-focused class. Such help needs to be directed toward helping adolescents develop understandings of literacy that will add to their success in and beyond school.

Specialized reading programming in secondary schools has not been a funding priority since the 1970s, which, notably, is the last time significant improvements in adolescents' performance occurred across ethnic groups on the National Assessment of Educational Progress (Campbell, Hombo, & Mazzeo, 1999). But such improvements were not well correlated to specific features of secondary school programs, and critiques of the observed weaknesses of such programs proliferated (Allington, 1994).

One common criticism was that such support was typically provided apart from content study and, thus, was difficult for students to transfer. Another critique was that adolescents who were targeted for such instruction could come to feel stigmatized because they were separated from peers. In addition, teachers in such programs could spend several months each year on diagnostic testing instead of on instruction, creating suspicion and resentment among instructional staff. Secondary school curriculum left little time during the day for services that seemed "extra," so resources were poured, instead, into interventions in earlier grades that had more direct empirical support (Klenk & Kibby, 2000). Programs to support adolescents who struggled with literacy development gradually disappeared from the secondary school landscape (Vacca, 1998).

Fortunately, pressures wrought by today's increased literacy requirements for graduation mean that schools have begun to free up resources that can be used to provide extra support for adolescents who struggle with school literacy tasks, especially reading and writing. Unfortunately, knee-jerk uses of these resources is sometimes ill advised, replicating the worst of the 1970s and ranging from whole-cloth implementation of prepackaged skills programs not suited to students' needs to large special classes with poorly trained teachers who contradict other classroom instruction. In our experience, adolescents have difficulty drawing helpful generalizations about literacy practices in and out of school from such interventions. Teenagers who are already frustrated with school literacy tasks can become even more confused or angered by such disjointed approaches, making them more likely to act out their frustrations in the classroom or to drop out of school (Jackson & Davis, 2000).

We begin this chapter with the assumption that even the most responsive efforts to weave literacy across subject matter units of study might not be enough to address the literacy needs of some adolescents, especially the needs of those who struggle as readers and writers. In these cases, special small classes are required, with interventions providing students with instruction that is negotiated according to young adults' interests, needs, goals, and strengths.

In this chapter we explain dimensions of secondary school literacy interventions, and we present ways to modify them given individual adolescents' needs. We emphasize pedagogy that invites adolescents to connect their existing literacies to school literacies—to see themselves as readers and writers who can use their competencies to position themselves in various settings.

Dimensions of Responsive Interventions

When adolescents struggle as readers and writers in significant enough ways to need interventions, we can be certain that they have begun to construct identities for themselves that are, at best, equivocal. Thus, it is important that any attempt to intervene grow out of sensitivity to this issue. You can build such an intervention if you establish positive relationships, negotiate a shared agenda, plan instruction that begins with existing literacies, provide models of proficient performance, and foster extended, engaged reading and writing.

Positive Relationships

"Some teachers just stand up in front and teach. They don't know anything about you, and they don't care if you understand," complained a high school student recently to Kathy. This is a sad comment, yet our suspicion is that it is typical of students' experiences in many secondary schools. Conversely, relationships between teachers and students are critical to the success of literacy interventions (Hinchman, 1999), especially when the targeted students are adolescents. An important dimension of responsive intervention is that it is set within a context of a listening, observing, respectful relationship (Ladson-Billings, 1997; Noddings, 1992).

When we work with adolescents who struggle as readers and writers, we try to learn as much about them as we can. We are respectful of what we learn about them, even when what we hear does not match our own life choices. We get to know our students, learning to care about and respect each one. Not only does this give us good information about their competencies and interests for instruction, it makes it a lot easier to work with them each day.

Teachers who are charged with intervention can and should make a particular point to talk with students about their lives outside school. They should make sure to learn about what goes on between classes and during extracurricular activities, to understand current influences from the popular culture, to appreciate day-to-day hardships and joys, and to learn about interests and abilities. Teachers can also make sure that instructional activities include regular opportunities for adolescents to talk about their interests and concerns (Moore, Bean, Birdyshaw, & Rycik, 1999).

Unit launch activities, as introduced in Chapter 3, can cast an especially wide net (Clay, 1993). Invite students to jot notes, talk, and solve problems so that strategies and passions related to a unit of study can be observed more closely and the unit designed to suit them more directly. You can invite students to read silently and aloud, individually, in pairs, or in small groups, so that their oral reading fluency, response, and comprehension of texts can be observed and, eventually, mediated without embarrassment.

A Shared Agenda

Adolescents become used to subject-matter classes that teachers plan in advance, leaving little room for voice and choice that follow interest but deviate from the plan. Detail-thick requirements in classes focused on biology and geometry leave little time for individual accommodations. Students are expected to contribute to the gradual accumulation of content information by taking coherent lecture notes, keeping up with textbook reading, looking up information in outside resources, or doing a certain number of practice exercises each evening for homework. Students who struggle with the pace of such classes often cut compromises in their conceptualizations. As Keisha, a 16-year-old young woman Kathy met during one study, noted, "I like it when I understand. I just don't always have time" (Hinchman & Zalewski, 1996, p. 91).

Contrary to the preceding example, an effective intervention reflects an agenda that is constructed and shared by the teacher and adolescent. Teachers who form such partnerships are, in effect, designing a third space, not wholly teacher or student centered, for integrating the insights of both (Gutierrez & Baquelao-Lopez, 1997). When interventions meant to support particular adolescents' literacy development are negotiated in such a space, adolescents are more likely to perceive such interventions as in their best interests. They respond favorably, adding productive ideas of their own. Results can mean that struggling readers and writers are invited to make academic literacies their own, sometimes in ways that neither they nor their teachers had thought possible (Gee, 1996, 2000).

Talk with students about their goals and their conceptualizations of content and literacy processes. Offer multiple avenues of completion so that students can extend existing competencies in varying ways, suited to their needs. Make a point to follow up on individuals' insights. Modify text length, tasks, explanations, participation, or even expectations in ways that are pertinent to particular adolescents' interests, strengths, and needs.

The more choices adolescents have about the directions and tasks of instructional units—thereby demonstrating their interests and inclinations—the more they are likely to maintain their interest throughout a course of study (Allen, 2000). In judiciously planned units, adolescents may be able to choose, alternatively, the manner of investigation, groups within which to work, texts to read, perspectives to explore, written pieces to produce, or projects to complete. When you know your students well, you can entice particular teenagers to work in venues that might be most interesting to them. You also learn to revise the way they think from soliciting students' insights.

Adolescents' Existing Literacies

When David was teaching reading at a Tucson, Arizona, high school, he explained standardized test scores so students knew where they stood according to these assessments. After one such session, a young man who scored above the 50th percentile was so ecstatic that he called out to the class, "Hey! I'm not as dumb as I thought!" This statement came from a person who saw himself as not quite measuring up, suggesting the personal and emotional dimensions of reading difficulties. When addressing this same issue, Meek (1983) put it this way:

> Readers in secondary school who want to learn to read have to subject themselves to a particular kind of metaphysical distress. Nothing written about it can fully convey the strain of what, hitherto, has been superficially described as "reluctance," "failure," "poor motivation." The real condition of these pupils was not lack of desire to learn, or poor basic skills, but absolute conviction that they could not be successful no matter what they did. (p. 214)

As we noted in Chapter 1, literacy development is entwined with the ways adolescents identify themselves as individuals and learners (Alvermann, Hinchman, Moore, Phelps, & Waff, 1998; Colvin & Schlosser, 1997). Our own work with teenagers has taught us that the same students who struggle with or resist school literacy have knowledge of other literacy practices. Virtually all the hundreds of students with whom we have worked demonstrate some reading and writing competence—no matter how much they struggle with school literacy.

Adolescents can develop real expertise suited to the contexts in which they are inspired to participate. Researchers have begun to find many such examples, such as students reading and responding to teen zines, noted by Finders (1996), gangsta notations described by Moje (2000b), or computer literacies observed by Fabos (2000). Such competencies are often far more extensive than one might predict from observing these same students in school, within the context of academic tasks and testing situations (Hagood, 2000). If accepted by others, such competencies can provide entrée into the culture of reading in a way that invites them to "get reading right" based on what they know rather than dismissing this knowledge altogether (Alvermann, 2001).

Thus, another dimension that is important to providing special interventions is that they begin with what students bring to the table. This is important in any instructional design, but is especially so for those who are already in the margins because they struggle as readers and writers. It is important that interventions enlist adolescents' complicity and consider their existing literacies as a basis for introducing school literacies. No quick fix, that is, published program, can serve this function (Allington & Walmsley, 1995). Instead, particular teens should be helped to use what they know to generate academic engagement and success, to break cycles of failure, and to take charge of their learning and literacy.

For instance, students can begin participation in an intervention by keeping a reading/writing journal to record the reading and writing they do each day. They can be encouraged to share their journal and materials with their intervention teacher. This teacher can, in turn, help the student find similar material by searching the Internet and local libraries and judiciously build lessons in decoding, fluency, and comprehension around them. "Judiciously" means not basaling readings around students' favorite topics but, instead, engaging in relevant, brief discussions about single readings and then moving on to others. Students can also develop online or pencil-and-paper dialogue journals with other students who share their interests.

Models of Proficient Performance

Reading and writing are, in a manner of speaking, invisible. We can see their products, that is, listen to a student read or describe a just-read story. We can read student-composed essays or poems. But the actual processes by which these products are produced are not observable. We use hidden activities that must be made explicit for struggling readers and writers (e.g., Keene & Zimmerman, 1997).

In response to this observation, Gallagher and Pearson (1983) described their gradual release of responsibility model. According to this model, teachers should be encouraged to invite students to experiment with literacy processes through use of an instructional model that includes three steps. For the first step, the teacher should use exposition and modeling, asking students: What is the strategy I am using, and how does it enhance comprehension? In the second step, teachers should provide students with an opportunity for guided practice. Finally, students should have the chance to try the strategy on their own, and to reflect on their successes or their need for more coaching.

Because this process depends on the student hearing and understanding the advice the teacher is giving, it is not an easy process to implement. You must understand processes well enough to give clear, brief, understandable explanations. You must know your students well enough to be able to identify their understandings of that which is being recommended. You must also be able to change your explanations in response to students' spoken and unspoken queries.

Trickier still is that you will not usually be working with students in a one-to-one tutorial, although, of course, this would be an optimum situation deserved by those who reach adolescence in need of significant intervention. Thus, you must be able to provide such scaffolds to groups of students who have varying insights about how the process works, and to keep all engaged while addressing the specific needs of one or two at a time.

Engaged, Extended Reading and Writing

Many well-intentioned teachers want to help struggling adolescent readers cover required content by having them read assigned texts aloud, one paragraph at a time, until a section of reading is completed. In our experience, few students in these settings actually read the passage in its entirety, instead determining in advance which paragraph they will be assigned and practicing until their turn. Concerned teachers may also share important information in a lecture and, then, assign reading and question answering on the same content for homework (Cazden, 1988). Resource teachers and reading specialists who work with students who struggle as readers sometimes help them in a kind of translation process, telling students the content of reading materials and then colluding on the construction of answers rather than spending time teaching students strategies for independent reading.

The end result is that many teenagers never get a chance to engage in extended school-assigned reading. Many of these students also do not choose to engage in reading as a free-time activity. Their reading cannot get any better because they never really read in any extensive way. Conversely, when adolescents can already read and write, even a bit, one of the clearest routes to developing their competence is to entice them to read and write in greater quantities (Anderson, Hiebert, & Scott, 1985). Struggling readers and writers can enhance their understanding of new words, their fluency, and their ability to construct meaning with such practice. Interventions that are going to make a real difference in reading and writing abilities are those that entice adolescents to extended, engaged reading and writing. A critical dimension of special class interventions is that they should encourage adolescents to do some extended reading and writing each day.

Texts for such extended reading can come from anywhere. Trade books, magazines, and the Internet are all good sources. They may be tied to school requirements, or they may be texts selected for pleasure reading. E-sources, found on the Internet and on CD-ROMs, can provide especially useful information in subject-area study (e.g., Leu & Leu, 1998). Such sources can contain quite readable, visually oriented, smaller chunks of text that are appealing to struggling readers. Such sources are especially helpful for adolescents' inquiry because they provide good access to readable information about issues that are current in popular culture.

Students should learn to select wisely, identifying the level of difficulty and choosing texts that are neither too easy nor too challenging. Teens can be taught to preview texts, scanning sections to judge whether they are in a position to read the text with some fluency and comprehension. A good rule of thumb may be that used in the Betts formula: when texts can be read with greater than 90 percent accuracy and understood, readers are in a better position to develop fluency, new concepts, and word and discourse knowledge as they read. Of course, exceptions can be made in this selection process if students have enough motivation, prior knowledge, or other support by which they can glean needed insights.

Journals are a good choice for extended writing. Students can keep dialogue journals, writing to peers about things that happen to them each day or about texts they are reading. They may even choose to engage in email correspondences with buddies in other locations. The point is that, just as it helps young children develop fluency as beginning writers, such writing is a good way for adolescents to write to think, and to explore ways of expressing their thoughts about the varieties of things that are important to them in a non-threatening context.

Planning Interventions with Balance and Breadth

Given the preceding, it seems obvious that, the more you know about language and literacy and the smaller the group with which you work, the more likely a responsive and productive pedagogical relationship can be orchestrated. In addition, many who have recommended instructional frameworks for preadolescent youngsters have suggested balanced approaches that involve students in some reading, some writing, and some skill work each day. For instance, Marie Clay's Reading Recovery lesson framework (1993) begins with rereading previously read texts, continues with introducing new texts, involves eliciting some writing, and includes participating in some word work each day. Patricia Cunningham's Four Blocks program suggests that some guided reading, independent reading, writing, and word work take place each day during a 90- to 120-minute language arts instructional block (Cunningham & Allington, 1999). These frameworks make sense as reminders that readers and writers need to engage continually in reading and writing to improve. They also remind teachers that readers and writers who are concerned with development need some explanation and guided support as they attempt certain aspects of reading and writing processes (Snow, Burns, & Griffin, 1998).

Yet such approaches do not acknowledge the complexities of literacy in ways that might be most appreciated by and useful to adolescents. The goals for adolescents are quite complex: we want nothing less than to invite them to develop existing literacies in ways that will give them access to a portfolio of the competencies most necessary for them to be successful in our increasingly technological society (Gee, 2000). Because of its emphasis on "flexible and sustainable mastery" and "repertoire of practices" (Luke & Freebody, 2000, p. 22), we prefer the literacy framework developed by Allan Luke and Peter Freebody for the Department of Education in Queensland, Australia, as a framework for adolescent interventions (Freebody & Luke, 1990; Luke & Freebody, 1997, 1999). Called the *four resources model for literacy*, this framework is organized to account for two aspects of literacy: media of communi-

Media of Communication

Roles of the Literate	Oral	Print	Multimedia
Code Breaker			
Meaning Maker			
Text User			
Text Analyst			

FIGURE 6.1   Four Resources Model for Literacy

Source: From Luke & Freebody, 2000.

cation and roles of the literate (see Figure 6.1). More specifically, to become literate members of information societies, students must master at least three overlapping media of communication:

1. *Oral communication.* The systems of spoken language. This may be the lingua franca of spoken English but also includes, for many children, other community languages spoken by their families and peers. Attention to various systems of oral language gives a teacher a chance to help students find connections between the language(s) used at home or in peer groups and the language used in school.

2. *Written communication.* The systems of alphabetic writing and print culture. This includes traditional "basics" of reading and writing—handwriting and spelling. It also includes other formalized codes that have developed in parallel to spoken and written language, such as Braille and sign language.

3. *Multimediated communication.* The blended systems of linguistic and non-linguistic sounds, and visual representations of digital and electronic media. These require "multiliteracies" that entail processing, interpretation, and critical analysis of online and on-screen sources of information that blend the printed word with visual, audio, and other forms of expression (New London Group, 1996). This includes what have variously been called "media literacy" and "computer literacy" during the past decade. Attention to such literacies gives a teacher a way to capitalize on students' observed strengths and a way to help them develop those skills they feel an urgent need to continue developing, because of the directions they see for the world of their generation.

In a manner similar to the metaphors presented in Chapter 1, this framework divides the repertoire of practices students must master into the following four roles:

- Code Breaker: The practices required to "crack" the codes and systems of written and spoken language and visual images

- Meaning Maker: The practices required to build and construct cultural meanings from texts
- Text User: The practices required to use texts effectively in everyday, face-to-face situations
- Text Analyst: The practices required to analyze, critique, and second-guess texts (Luke & Freebody, 2000, 22–23)

Interventions Using the Four Resources Model

The four resources model invites you to attend to multiple practices as you invite adolescents to expand their literacies, rather than simply focusing on one type of reading competence over another. It provides categories of practices to consider as you assess adolescents' current practices and inclinations. It provides categories of practices to plan for in instruction. Moreover, the four resources model provides a way to help adolescents understand various aspects of literacy, what it can do for them, and how they can expand their own repertoire of practices to become better suited to their changing society. Lessons should be planned to build on and to continue to develop students' oral language and multimediated skills as they maintain attention to written language development.

When planning lessons, each of the four resources should be kept in mind. Too much emphasis on one over the others gives students a misleading sense of literacy overall. For instance, too much attention during instruction on developing someone's competence as a text analyst may leave that person unable to handle new vocabulary words encountered while reading unfamiliar texts. On the other hand, too much attention to code breaking could leave a student unaware of the very real purposes of literacy in today's society. If a teacher and student decide to focus more on one area or another for a specific time period, they should pay careful attention to maintaining a sense of the four resources in their overall approach.

A workshop approach is a good way to structure adolescent literacy interventions (Williams, 2001). Consistent with the reader-as-apprentice metaphor from Chapter 1, workshops point toward master–apprentice relationships. Teachers support learners' efforts as they are involved with valued projects such as reading independently and conducting inquiries. The supports are offered relative to readers as code breakers, meaning makers, text users, and text analyzers.

Code Breaker

When you see adolescents who struggle with the fundamental features and architecture of written texts, you can help them understand how to use these aspects of written texts more efficiently. These aspects can include attention to the alphabet, sounds in words, spelling, and conventions and patterns of sentence structure and text. Particular difficulties with fluent code use can be observed by listening to individuals read aloud—either words on lists or words in passages—or by asking them to write without benefit of a spell checker. Such observations should be made in a nonpublic setting when it is likely that teenagers will be embarrassed by their competence.

Finding Words for Beginning Code Study.   In our experience, only on rare occasions do teachers find adolescents who do not have awareness of letters and their sounds. Such information can be picked up from instruction, environmental print, or cultural experiences. When individuals do seem to be just beginning to have an understanding of the workings of letter–sound relationships, we have found it beneficial to begin with words taken from texts that they find most interesting or necessary to read. These may be texts they want to read for pleasure or because they have an interest in learning about something. Or texts may be their own, dictated language experience stories (Ashton-Warner, 1963).

Teachers can initiate the language experience approach by discussing a shared experience with students. They then elicit a short—one- or two-sentence—story from the students about this experience, printing the story on paper so that students can note spelling and word formation, as well as sentence structure. Once a satisfactory story has been composed, the teacher can read it back to students, asking for corrections or rewordings.

Then the teacher can reread the story, inviting students to pick one or two words to learn from the story and printing these on cards for later study and review. Students can also engage in repeated reading of such texts (Samuels, 1972), either as they work with a teacher or participate in a readers' theater (Allen, 2000), to practice fluent reading (Cheatham, Colvin, & Laminack, 1995).

With adolescents who especially struggle as readers and writers, teachers may choose to begin instruction with texts students bring in that represent their interests and skills with regard to the popular culture. Pop culture texts can include greeting cards, comic books, music lyrics, poetry, movie reviews, a driver's manual, and teen magazines (Alvermann, Moon, & Hagood, 1999). Indeed, we should note that we have known many teenagers and adults who have learned to read using a driver's manual.

When these texts are too difficult for students to read fluently, teachers should read these texts to students, inviting them to join in on shared reading of certain segments. They can even be invited to listen to the books on audiotape as they follow the print with their eyes (Allen, 2000). They then can be invited to join in on rereadings of segments of these same texts.

A good deal of shared reading may have to take place before struggling adolescent readers and writers will be ready to attend to the details of print. If years of attempted learning have failed to result in such understandings already, these teens have quite likely begun to construct identities that do not see the value of developing competence in this area. It is critical to make the move to word study with adolescents' full complicity, and to adjust such study to suit attention, motivation, and interest. Anyone who has worked with teenagers knows that demands for rote completion of drill-and-practice sheets is a sure way to drive many of these students out of school. On the other hand, experiencing success with word study may be just the thing to motivate a reluctant adolescent. One can never really tell until one is in a relationship with the student!

For more in-depth study adolescents can be asked to choose a few words from the texts they encounter during shared reading. Such words can then be printed on index cards with drawn illustrations and used in student-dictated sentences written on the back for repeated review and reinforcement. Initially, such words may simply be those students think they will most likely need. After a time, such words can be selected because they represent a particular spelling pattern (Bear, Invernizzi, Templeton, & Johnston, 1999) and categorized on a word wall (Cunningham, 1999) for future reference.

Strategic Code Breaking.   In those rare instances when adolescents have difficulty remembering letters and their sounds, it is best to use an approach that assumes they need assistance for remembering these cues. Thus, we have found it beneficial to start with teaching whole words taken from stories in which the adolescents are interested and that represent some sort of generalization useful in breaking the codes of other words.

Initially, we have found it helpful to introduce some sort of key word to help students remember the sounds of consonants (e.g., this is a *b* as in *bear*), writing the letter, key word, and several example words on an index card for later review. Such an approach has long been recommended in a variety of contexts, but especially in the recommendations for older readers by Literacy Volunteers (Biasotto, 1993; Cheatham, et al., 1995; Wilson, Hall, Leu, & Kinzer, 2000).

Once students have a good sense of initial consonants, we favor moving to teaching common word families. Thus, students can be taught to read a particular word, then shown how to replace the initial consonant to make a new, rhyming word (e.g., *c-at*, to *h-at*, to *m-at; c-ane*, to *m-ane*, to *l-ane*) (Cunningham, 1999; Wilson, et al., 2000). This can be done by printing on paper, using letter tiles, or using a three-pocket chart known as a sound board (Blachman, Tangel, Ball, Black, & McGraw, 1999). Such instruction becomes strategic when students review and read many members of the same word family, decoding by analogy, and discuss the similarities and differences in the words with teachers as they work.

Dealing with Multisyllabic Words.   It is more usual to find adolescents who have gaps in an already existing, extensive repertoire of code-breaking skills. Often they can decode single-syllable words but have difficulty with multisyllabic ones. Such teens need ways to strategize, to generalize from what they already know to words they cannot recognize. In this case, we have found it useful to begin, again, with words that teens select from pop culture texts they want to read or from content-area texts they need to read. We teach them to roughly syllabicate and to decode by analogy, talking with them about the patterns across words, thinking with the students of other examples of particular usages, rather than simply telling about them (Ehri & Robbins, 1992; Gaskins, Gaskins, & Gaskins, 1991).

Kathy has found particular success in her literacy clinic when teachers teach older students to categorize syllables via six syllable types (Blachman, et al., 1999; Moats, 2000). These include closed syllables, such as *pot* and *slat* (e.g., consonant–vowel–consonant); final-*e* syllables, such as *pane* and *bike* (e.g., consonant–vowel–consonant–silent e); open syllables, such as *my* and *be* (e.g., consonant–vowel); vowel team syllables, such as *rain* and *peach*, vowel + *r* syllables, such as *car* and *her*; and consonant + *le* syllables, such as *maple* and *bottle*. To teach the syllable types, teachers focus instruction on one syllable type at a time, spending several days reviewing the workings of each syllable type and thinking of examples of single-syllable words that fit each category. These are posted on a word wall (Cunningham, 1999) or other visible word list, organized by syllable type.

Once adolescents can read words and recite some form of the rule governing pronunciation of each syllable type, they are taught to roughly syllabicate words. If they cannot pronounce any part of the word as a way to guess at syllable types, they are asked to place a dot under each vowel to roughly mark each syllable. Then they are asked to identify what syllable types might be represented by the letter combinations surrounding each vowel, and to categorize the syllable by syllable type on the word wall.

Meaning Makers

A few years ago, in the midst of reciprocal teaching, a student in Kathy's college class on learning strategies exclaimed, "I didn't know you were supposed to stop reading when you didn't understand!" The exclamation caught Kathy by surprise because it revealed something she thought was obvious. This student viewed reading as pronouncing the words, not as making meaning, a problematic position for a young man beginning life as a college student. Adolescents who struggle as readers can develop a sense for meaning making by reading a lot in texts related to their interests, but it may also be important for them to participate in opportunities for guided reading and writing with a wider variety of texts. Such activities provide a context within which teachers explain those strategies good readers use to comprehend what they read (Allen, 2000; Fountas & Pinnell, 2000).

Introductory Activities Begin with Adolescents' Concerns.   When working with adolescents who struggle as readers and writers, it is especially important that the central questions and introductory grabbers for guided reading activities be developed with special concern for heightening students' interest and curiosity. As already noted, looking for connections to popular culture and other aspects of day-to-day life is a way to invite even the most reluctant student to read and write (Alvermann, Moon, et al., 1999). Like all of us, when adolescents are intrigued by a topic, they are much more willing to try activities in which they might not otherwise engage.

Alvermann (2001) recently described a project in which a teenager named Grady was observed reading and writing in ways that demonstrated dramatically previously undiscovered competence. Teachers can call on music, movies, sports, reading, writing, and other interests to form the basis for exploring and representing insights about responses to the central questions of a unit—the Internet provides a great source of texts related to this rapidly changing scene. They can also invite adolescents to develop projects that demonstrate their insights about central questions through community service, drama, or other public demonstrations (Moje, 2000a).

Introductory activities for struggling readers and writers should also help students understand that good readers make predictions when they read based on their prior knowledge of texts and passage content (Gallagher & Pearson, 1983; Keene & Zimmerman, 1997). Talking with students about the value to be found in prediction helps them add an important comprehension strategy to their repertoire. For instance, prior to reading a passage about the recent Super Bowl winner, one might ask students to discuss what they already know about the team, its members, its other games, and other Super Bowls and then explain that activating such insights can help build bridges between the new information found in the text and that which is already known.

Giving students a chance to talk with each other in pairs or cooperative groups as they solve problems posed in introductory activities allows them a chance to explore new concepts and words in less threatening environments. But again, students and teacher should also talk about the value of such prediction in a way that is followed with reminders and requests for reflections in later guided reading lessons.

Vocabulary Instruction Models Independent Word Learning.   Much new learning in subject-area study is concerned with the technical language pertinent to study of the content. Vocabulary instruction can introduce students to the words they need to understand key ideas pertaining to a central question and, at the same time, model generative vocabulary development techniques by referring to context, reference tools, and structural analysis as words are reviewed (Allen, 1999; Bear, et al., 1999). Categorizing activities that involve adolescents in paired or grouped discussion of the similarities and differences of words can be very helpful for expanding students' banks of known words. List–group–label activities described in Chapter 3 can invite adolescents with varied vocabulary expertise to share words and insights with one another. Such strategies are especially helpful to struggling readers and writers who may not come to school with the same bank of academic words as other students.

Adolescents who struggle as readers and writers need to be taught to scan the text for context clues that help them determine the meaning of unknown words. They must also be taught how to use their textbooks, dictionaries, thesauruses, encyclopedias, and other reference tools to determine the meanings of unknown words. Teacher minilessons can remind students of general practices that help with using such tools (e.g., organization within and across entries). More detailed instruction in the nuances of such entries can be even more beneficial (e.g., pronunciation and usage guides).

In our experience, homework assignments that require looking up and writing definitions and sentences for 10 to 20 nuanced technical vocabulary words are probably more tedious than beneficial, especially for struggling readers. An easy and less time-consuming alternative could involve pairs of students looking up 2 to 3 words each, finding examples of words in multiple texts, and teaching the words to the rest of the class, which could be more engaging and beneficial.

Another way for teachers to help struggling readers and writers is to assist in reading words they find difficult in a particular text selection. As anyone who has tackled reading unfamiliar content knows, it is not easy to engage in fluent, comprehensible reading when one must keep a dictionary or glossary on hand to help with pronunciation and meaning of many words. A quick way to support fluent reading of a particular text is to scan the text before reading and discuss the pronunciation and meaning of difficult words found during the scan. We have adapted a version of Clay's (1993) "debugging" technique for use with older readers. This generative strategy involves a teacher showing a student how to scan for such words prior to reading. The student runs a finger along the lines of print in a section of text, looking for hard words and marking them with a note or writing them down. Then the student can use other strategies to discern pronunciation and meaning for the noted words, including, possibly, looking them up. Finally, students can read the section of text without the necessity of struggling with words.

Supporting Reading.   Struggling students' reading may be supported in class. This may be paced by asking students to read silently or quietly aloud in pairs, small segments of text progressively, then discussing the segments in a think–pair–share format either with each other and, potentially, with the larger group. Such reading of common texts can also include brief periods of instruction in studying segments of text, which can be beneficial for an entire class regardless of individuals' reading fluency.

Students can together discuss the meaning of the text, mark portions of text that need clarification, underline main ideas, and compose summaries. As described elsewhere in this text, techniques such as reciprocal teaching (Brown & Palincsar, 1985) and ReQuest (Manzo, Estes, & Manzo, 2000) involve a teacher modeling appropriate predicting, reading, questioning, clarifying, and summarizing strategies section by section, followed by students imitating the meaning making of a proficient reader. Such instruction best occurs on a one-on-one basis or with small groups of students so that the teacher can be responsive to students' particular insights and understandings.

You should observe struggling readers and writers as they engage in such activities. You may decide that it is important to some students to explain the various aspects of proficient reading previously mentioned in this text. Such explanation should be provided with the benefit of careful modeling by you, followed by giving the student a chance to try what was recommended so that you can help him or her alter the approach as it is being learned (Keene & Zimmerman, 1997). In addition to prediction, aspects of proficient reading include the following:

1. Determining importance: reading selectively
2. Discerning the organization of text and using that organization as a tool for understanding
3. Being strategic: monitoring, reviewing, and repairing one's comprehension performance; clarifying what is unclear; planning future actions
4. Summarizing: condensing ideas and information into usable form
5. Forming visual, auditory, and other sensory images
6. Grasping explicitly stated literal information: noting what's stated right on the page
7. Connecting author's ideas across different parts of a passage: thinking and searching to get it all together

Writing Together.   Completed within the context of a workshop, writing activities in varied forms can provide a context within which struggling adolescent readers and writers can choose how to represent their understandings and insights. When students are primarily engaged in writing that which they have chosen to write and in helping each other with such writing, teachers can provide minilessons on brainstorming, webbing, writing mechanics, and content development suited to some students' needs, by grouping students workshop style in room corners for brief explanations and discussions.

In such settings, students can use scoring rubrics akin to those used for scoring unit tests and statewide tests to help each other with individual pieces of writing and to internalize the outcomes suggested by the rubrics. They can see and model writing as they look at each other's writing. Students can also complete paired or cooperative writing activities that allow them to talk through together mechanics and content development techniques.

Text User

Many adolescents seem to operate on the assumption that if it's in print, it must be true, a misconception that does not readily allow them to synthesize across texts with competing perspectives. Conversely, adolescents learn to be text users when they read with teachers in pursuit of a central question, as in the unit design previously described. Such pursuits send students the message that making meaning is central—telling them that reading is about learning and understanding that which you may not have understood in the same way prior to interacting with a particular text. Content may be something that is tied to the requirements of one course or another, or it may be something particular to the interests of an adolescent or of a group of adolescents.

Struggling readers may especially need support for their content-area reading assignments as they participate in intervention. Although the teacher providing the intervention wants to avoid the trap of reading the text to the student, this teacher can work with the content-area teacher to make the assignments as doable as possible, and then work with the student to develop strategies for doing this. Struggling adolescent readers can and should be asked to read assigned texts for homework, but with appropriate preteaching and supports so that parents are not left alone with a nightly battle. Students should be asked to judge how various perspectives are represented in the text, and invited to discuss this with peers and teachers. Throughout all, teachers model and students try, with teachers mediating and helping students to adjust their attempts.

Identifying Important Ideas.   Marginal glosses—adjunct aids that note key terms and concepts as students read with a study guide that follows the pages of a text—can help students organize their thinking as they read as well as invite them to note alternative perspectives. We have also had some success with teaching students to highlight key ideas, and to make notes and draw graphic representations in the margins to organize their understanding section by section. (Photocopies suffice when students cannot write in textbooks that must serve more than one group of students.)

Modifying Assignments.   Assignments can be modified with consideration for the time it takes students to complete them. Some students benefit most from reading selected sections whereas others appreciate reading introductions, conclusions, and scanning headings and pictures. Taped texts can be made available for those who especially struggle with fluency; volunteer groups and parent–teacher associations can be recruited as readers. Students are helped to get over the hump provided by the difficult texts so that they can use the information in the text for the rest of their content-area study. A caveat is in order here: even students who may benefit from using taped texts to complete content reading assignments still need to engage in extended reading of other texts to improve their reading fluency and comprehension. Ideally at least some of these texts can represent varying perspectives toward a central idea.

In some cases, you may want to read in pairs with a particular student, and to take turns reading sections and thinking aloud about how texts are connected to one another, or about how they may be applied. It is important for you to observe students carefully as they engage in and talk about extended reading and writing to discern the need for instruction in competencies that will help the student to be a better text user. You should find ways to talk with students about the ways in which they make connections across segments of text when they read and use the subsequent information.

Other competencies, mentioned elsewhere in this text, are important to attend to and include the following:

- Relating authors' ideas with the ones already in mind: associating what authors say with what is known; paraphrasing
- Applying: thinking about how to use text ideas in the future; using the passage as a springboard to new ideas
- Synthesizing information from various sources

Text Analyzer

Kist (2000) suggests several characteristics of instruction that promote readers as text analyzers. First, teachers encourage ongoing use of multiple forms of representation. Second, teachers support explicit discussions of symbol usage, past and present. Third, students engage in ongoing metadialogues about the workings of texts and their points of view in an atmosphere of cognitive pluralism. Fourth, instruction presents a balance of individual and collaborative activities. Fifth, instruction shows evidence that students are engaged. Finally, teachers invite diversified expression in the classroom.

So, for example, in completing an inquiry-based poetry unit, students can be encouraged to read to each other in pairs, in student collaborative groups, or in guided reading groups, multileveled stacks of published and found poetry, discussing their responses and performing favorite pieces at class end each day. They can read both contemporary work and pieces representing a variety of time periods. They can be invited to discuss how these varying styles of poetry are accessible to them or addressed to them or not and why. In like fashion, students can also read varying levels of literary criticism that discusses the "meaning" of particular poems or of poetry in general, also sharing at class end. Students can keep notes about their thoughts and opinions in dialogue journals shared with other students, or in personal journals, within which they also record their own efforts to write poetry.

Critical Questions.   When adolescents agree that a central question is worth studying, they can be encouraged to read to find answers. Materials can include multileveled texts that students with varying competence can use to search for and comprehend answers to central questions. Teens can share insights gained from their varied sources to sort through multiple perspectives about a central question. Such multidimensional study leaves them in a better position to critique and recognize political positions of text messages. It encourages them to evaluate and to judge the quality of authors' writings, the trustworthiness of authors' messages, and alternatives, as described in Chapter 4. It is the kind of study that especially appeals to naturally critical adolescents and encourages them to ask, "Who wants me to read this text and why?"

What Counts as Reading.   Alvermann (2001) suggests that adolescents who are text analyzers can be invited to discern how they are being constructed as readers. These readers can be encouraged to wonder how they are the same readers, as well as how they differ, when they read texts for pleasure as when they read an assignment for a teacher. They can be asked to consider whether and which of their teachers consider their pleasure reading to be "real" reading, what would happen were such reading included in their assignments, and why they feel the way they do about such issues. They might poll classmates to ask what counts as reading when reading really counts, and for whom. Other texts with information about promoting critical literacy that makes someone a competent text analyzer include those by Fehring and Green (2001), Cope and Kalantzis (2000), and Muspratt, Luke, and Freebody (1997).

Assessment Literacy.   In this age of high-stakes testing, students can be invited to become scholars of such tests—"developing assessment literacy"—as a teacher at one of Kathy's recent presentations coined. Struggling readers in particular are text analyzers if they understand the arguments for and against such tests, as well as how such tests position them and their schools. They can learn the foibles of such tests by reading any of the numerous series that have appeared in media around the country and talking about the implications of these criticisms. They can also discuss the structure and content of the tests that are used in their schools, including completing practice exercises that mimic those on the tests. As Alvermann (2001) suggested with regard to the reading of other texts, just explained, adolescents can talk about their perception of what the tests represent as well as what they do not represent about them.

Conclusion

No quick-to-use phonics programs, no content-area required activities, and no assignment of extra time on task can solve the difficulties of adolescents who find themselves lacking some aspect or another of basic literacy. When adolescents struggle with reading or other literacy practices, such difficulties are unique to the tapestry of background experiences adolescents have woven into the fabric they present in school. Teachers who attempt to address students' needs in such a situation must know a lot about language and literacy, and should lobby as much as they can for the smallest groups possible so that they can respond efficiently and effectively to adolescents' initiations.

Teachers can orchestrate interventions best if they establish positive relationships, negotiate a shared agenda, plan instruction that begins with existing literacies, provide models of proficient performance, and foster extended, engaged reading and writing. Luke and Freebody's (1998, 1999) along with Luke, Freebody, and Land (2000) four resources model for literacy provides a framework for such interventions. This framework reminds us of oral, written, and multimediated communication and that, to be literate, students must master four roles, that of code breaker, meaning maker, text user, and text analyzer.

As discussed in this chapter and throughout this text, those charged with intervention must be passionate advocates for students, aiming for whatever is in individuals' best interests. Their purpose must clear and shared with students. At the schoolwide level, counselors, librarians, and other resource personnel can assist with planning. Attention to a combination of modeling and experience within a context built around the uniqueness of each teenager's identity construction helps guarantee the success of our efforts to intervene.

CENTRAL QUESTION: THINK BACK

What can be done to help adolescents who are not fully served by literacy instruction across the curriculum?

To answer fully this chapter's central question, build on the following key concepts:

- Plan responsive interventions characterized by positive relationships, a shared agenda, instruction that begins with existing literacies, models of proficiency, and extended, engaged reading and writing.
- Teach adolescents as code breakers through (1) finding words for beginning code study, (2) strategic code breaking, (3) dealing with multisyllabic words.
- Teach adolescents as meaning makers through (1) introductory activities beginning with their concerns, (2) vocabulary instruction that models independent word learning, (3) supported reading, and (4) writing together.

- Teach adolescents as text users through (1) identifying important ideas and (2) modifying assignments.
- Teach adolescents as text analyzers through (1) critical questions, (2) what counts as reading, and (3) assessment literacy.

REFERENCES

Allen, J. (1999). *Words, words, words: Teaching vocabulary in grades 4–12.* York, ME: Stenhouse.

Allen, J. (2000). *Yellow brick roads: Shared and guided paths to independent reading 4–12.* Portland, ME: Stenhouse.

Allington, R. (1994). What's special about special programs for children who find learning to read difficult? *Journal of Reading Behavior, 26,* 95–115.

Allington, R., & Walmsley, S. (1995). *No quick fix: Rethinking literacy programs in America's elementary schools.* New York: Teachers College Press.

Alvermann, D. E. (2001). Reading adolescents' reading identities: Looking back to see ahead. *Journal of Adolescent and Adult Literacy, 44,* 676–690.

Alvermann, D. E., Hinchman, K. A., Moore, D. W., Phelps, S. F., & Waff, D. R. (Eds.). (1998). *Reconceptualizing the literacies in adolescents' lives.* Mahwah, NJ: Lawrence Erlbaum.

Alvermann, D. E., Moon, J., & Hagood, M. (1999). *Popular culture in the classroom: Teaching and researching critical media literacy.* Newark, DE: International Reading Association.

Anderson, R. C., Hiebert, E., & Scott, J. (1985). *Becoming a nation of readers: The report of the Commission on Reading.* Urbana: University of Illinois, Center for the Study of Reading.

Ashton-Warner, S. (1963). *Teacher.* New York: Bantam Books.

Bear, D., Invernizzi, M., Templeton, S., & Johnston, F. (1999). *Words their way: Word study for phonics, vocabulary, and spelling instruction.* Englewood Cliffs, NJ: Prentice-Hall.

Biasotto, V. L. (1993). Project ASSIST Institute: An Orton-Gillingham/Spalding based curriculum for teachers and volunteers. *Annals of Dyslexia, 43,* 260–270.

Blachman, B., Tangel, D., Ball, E. W., Black, R., & McGraw, C. K. (1999). Developing phonological awareness and word recognition skills: A two-year intervention with low-income, inner-city children. *Reading and Writing: An Interdisciplinary Journal, 11,* 239–273.

Brown, A. L., & Palinscar, A. S. (1985). *Reciprocal teaching of comprehension strategies: A natural history of one program to enhance learning* (Technical Report No. 334). Urbana: University of Illinois, Center for the Study of Reading.

Campbell, J. R., Hombo, C. M., & Mazzeo, J. (1999). *Trends in academic progress: Three decades of student performance* (NCES No. 2000–469). Washington, DC: U.S. Department of Education, Office of Educational Research and Improvement, National Center for Education Statistics. Retrieved August 21, 2001, from www.ed. gov/NCES/NAEP.

Cazden, C. (1988). *Classroom discourse: The language of teaching and learning.* Portsmouth, NH: Heinemann.

Cheatham, J., Colvin, R., & Laminack, L. (1995). *Tutor* (7th ed.). Syracuse, NY: Literacy Volunteers of America.

Clay, M. (1993). *Reading recovery: A guidebook for teachers in training.* Portsmouth, NH: Heinemann.

Colvin, C., & Schlosser, L. K. (1997). Developing academic confidence to build literacy: What teachers can do. *Journal of Adolescent and Adult Literacy, 41*(4), 272–281.

Cope, B., & Kalantzis, M. (Eds.). (2000). *Multiliteracies: Literacy learning and the design of social futures.* New York: Routledge.

Cunningham, P. M. (1999). *Phonics they use: Words for reading and writing* (2nd ed.). New York: HarperCollins.

Cunningham, P., & Allington, R. (1999). *Classrooms that work: They can all read and write* (2nd ed.). New York: Addison-Wesley.

Ehri, L., & Robbins, C. (1992). Beginners need some decoding skill to read words by analogy. *Reading Research Quarterly, 27,* 12–26.

Fabos, B. (2000). Zap me! Zaps you. *Journal of Adolescent and Adult Literacy, 43,* 720–725.

Fehring, H., & Green, P. (2001). *Critical literacies: A collection of articles from the Australian Literacy Educators' Association.* Newark, DE: International Reading Association.

Finders, M. (1996). *Just girls: Hidden literacies and life in junior high.* New York: Teachers College Press.

Fountas, I., & Pinnell, G. (2000). *Guiding readers and writers: Teaching comprehension, genre, and content literacy.* Portsmouth, NH: Heinemann.

Freebody, P., & Luke, A. (1990). Literacy programs: Debates and demands in cultural context. *Prospect, 5,* 7–15.

Gallagher, M., & Pearson, P. D. (1983). The instruction of reading comprehension. *Contemporary Educational Psychology, 8,* 317–344.

Gaskins, R. W., Gaskins, J. C., & Gaskins, I. W. (1991). A decoding program for poor readers—and the rest of the class too! *Language Arts, 68,* 213–225.

Gee, J. P. (1996). *Social linguistics and literacies: Ideology in the discourses* (2nd ed.). Bristol, PA: Taylor & Francis.

Gee, J. P. (2000). New people in new worlds: Networks, the new capitalism, and schools. In B. Cope & M. Kalnatzis (Eds.), *Multiliteracies: Literacy learning and the design of social futures* (pp. 43–68). New York: Routledge.

Gee, J. P. (2000, November). *What goes without saying: From the National Reading Panel to ownership in literacy.* Paper presented at the annual meeting of the National Council of Teachers of English, Milwaukee, WI.

Gutierrez, K. D., & Baquedano-Lopez, P., & Turner, M. G. (1997). Putting language back into language arts: When the radical middle meets the third space. *Language Arts, 74,* 368–378.

Hagood, M. (2000). New times, new millennium, new literacies. *Reading Research and Instruction, 39,* 311–328.

Hinchman, K. A. (1999). Querying reflective pedagogy in reading specialists' tutorial practica. In D. H. Evensen & P. B. Mosenthal (Eds.), *Reconsidering the role of the reading clinic in a new age of literacy* (pp. 133–148). Stamford, CT: JAI Press.

Hinchman, K. A., & Zalewski, P. (1996). Reading for success in a tenth-grade global studies class: A qualitative study. *Journal of Literacy Research, 26*(1), 91–106.

Jackson, A. W., & Davis, G. A. (2000). *Turning points 2000: Educating adolescents in the 21st century* (Report of the Carnegie Foundation of New York). New York: Teachers College Press.

Keene, E. O., & Zimmerman, S. (1997). *Mosiac of thought: Teaching comprehension in a reader's workshop.* Portsmouth, NH: Heinemann.

Kist, W. (2000). Beginning to create the new literacy classroom: What does the new literacy look like? *Journal of Adolescent and Adult Literacy, 43,* 710–718.

Klenk, L., & Kibby, M. (2000). Re-mediating reading difficulties: Appraising the past, reconciling the present, constructing the future. In M. Kamil, P. B. Mosenthal, P. D. Pearson, & R. Barr (Eds.), *Handbook of reading research* (vol. III, pp. 667–690). Mahwah, NJ: Erlbaum.

Ladson-Billings, G. (1997). *The dreamkeepers: Successful teachers of African American children.* San Francisco: Jossey-Bass.

Leu, D. J., & Leu, D. (1998). *Teaching with the Internet: Lessons from the classroom.* Columbus, OH: Christopher Gordon.

Luke, A., & Freebody, P. (1997). The social practices of reading. In S. Musratt, A. Luke, & P. Freebody (Eds.), *Constructing critical literacies* (pp. 185–226). Cresskill, NJ: Hampton Press.

Luke, A., & Freebody, P. (1999). A map of possible practices: Further notes on the four resources model. *Practically Primary, 4.* Retrieved January 15, 2001, from http://www.alea.edu.au/freebody.htm.

Luke, A., & Freebody, P. (2000) *Literate futures: Report of the literacy review for the Queensland State Schools.* Queensland: State of Queensland Department of Education. Retrieved January 15, 2001, from www.education.gld.gov.ua

Manzo, A., Estes, T., & Manzo, U. (2000). *Content area literacy: Interactive teaching for active learning.* New York: John Wiley.

Meek, M. (1983). *Achieving literacy: Longitudinal studies of adolescents learning to read.* London: Routledge & Kegan Paul.

Moats, L. C. (2000). *Speech to print: Language essentials for teachers.* Baltimore: Paul H. Brookes.

Moje, E. (2000a). *Adolescents' insights about literacy and learning in secondary schools.* Newark, DE: International Reading Association.

Moje, E. (2000b). "To be part of the story": The literacy practices for gangsta adolescents. *Teachers College Record, 102,* 651–690.

Moore, D. W., Bean, T. W., Birdyshaw, D., & Rycik, J. A. (1999). *Adolescent literacy: A position statement.* Newark, DE: International Reading Association.

Muspratt, S., Luke, A., Freebody, P. (Eds.). (1997). *Constructing critical literacies: Teaching and learning textual practice.* Cresskill, NJ: Hampton Press.

New London Group. (1996). A pedagogy of multiliteracies: Designing social futures. *Harvard Educational Review, 66*(1), 60.

Noddings, N. (1992). *The challenge to care in schools: An alternative approach to education.* New York: Teachers College Press.

Samuels, S. J. (1972). The effect of letter-name knowledge on learning to read. *American Educational Research Journal, 9,* 65–74.

Snow, C. E., Burns, M. S., & Griffin, P. (Eds.). (1998). *Preventing reading difficulties in young children.* Washington, DC: National Academy Press.

Vacca, R. (1998). Let's not marginalize adolescent literacy. *Journal of Adolescent and Adult Literacy, 41,* 604–609.

Williams, M. (2001). Making connections: A workshop for adolescents who struggle with reading. *Journal of Adolescent and Adult Literacy, 44*(7), 588–602.

Wilson, R. M., Hall, M. A., Leu, D. J., & Kinzer, C. (2000). *Phonics, phonemic awareness, and word analysis for teachers: An interactive tutorial.* Upper Saddle River, NJ: Prentice-Hall.

7 Connections beyond the Classroom

CENTRAL QUESTION: THINK AHEAD

How can I reach beyond my classroom to engage students with reading and writing?

Like other students, adolescents who struggle as readers in school some-times adopt a mentality of let's-just-give-teachers-what-they-want. Youth quite disaffected by school often spiral into an attitude of let's-not-give-teachers-what-they-want (Kos, 1991; Phelan, Yu, & Davidson, 1994). Individually and collectively, students at times express an attitude of let's-get-it-over-with, executing reading and writing assignments primarily to get a grade (Bintz, 1993; Brozo, 1990). Connecting students with people outside of classrooms can help counter this mind set.

Many teachers have found that reaching beyond classroom walls helps link adolescents with literacy. Learners who relate with individuals outside the classroom often find new meanings and motivations, new attitudes and interests (Epstein, 2001; Girard & Willing, 1996). Connecting with people outside classrooms is quite a visible aspect of current school efforts. We know one district that attributes much of its students' high achievement to formal partnerships with 130 different groups. These connections generate levels of thought and enthusiasm that surpass what is available during normal academics. Adolescents who read and write with children, peers, and adults outside classrooms develop literate identities.

A productive literate identity means that individuals consider themselves insiders to print—part of a fellowship of readers and writers (Alvermann, 2001). Individuals see themselves as partners within a literate public, entering a space where individuals share reading interests and techniques and where they identify with role models (Smith, 1988). They come to see themselves as responsible for and in control of their learning (Davidson, 1996; Welch & Hodges, 1997). Partnerships that reach beyond classrooms offer rich opportunities for adolescents to develop literate identities.

So far we have described numerous ways to promote literate identities and competencies through classroom partnerships. For instance, preceding chapters have described ways to create communities of learners who display respect and responsibility. They have explained collaborative practices such as quick book shares among peers and teacher–student conferences.

This chapter surveys six types of partnerships involving people outside middle and high school classrooms: home–school, cross age, community–school, cultural ties, professional development, and school structures.

Home–School Partnerships

Practically every school works to involve parents with their children's education (Christenson & Sheridan, 2001), and numerous formal and informal partnerships exist. Working as a team supports adolescents' literacy learning and identity. The following list describes common practices worth developing in home–school partnerships:

- Assisting with special projects at home, such as science fair or inquiry presentations
- Assisting with projects at school, such as dramatic presentations or student book publishing
- Attending open house
- Conferring with teachers and administrators (at school or home; by telephone or face to face) during regular opportunities and upon request

- Describing one's career—as well as on-the-job literacy activities—to a class
- Examining and acting on school handbooks, course information packets, and newsletters
- Monitoring course work completion such as homework and independent reading; signing and returning test papers and report cards
- Participating in booster clubs that support extracurricular activities such as athletics, band, and speech
- Serving as an external audience or an evaluator when students exhibit their academic accomplishments through portfolios or other presentations
- Serving in governance, budget, and decision-making roles
- Translating during meetings and conferences

These practices go beyond the normal practice of communicating what the school is doing. Efforts to connect family members and adolescents with reading and writing should focus not only on sending information home, but on bolstering home, school, and learner collaboration (Rycik, 1998). Along with the practices listed above, four that directly foster parental interaction

Cross-age tutoring within a family promotes literacy.

and involvement relative to literacy deserve emphasis: family book talks, interviews, compacts, and family resource centers.

Family Book Talks

Family book talks are book response practices similar to the classroom-based quick book shares and literature discussion groups described in Chapter 4. The following are standard family book talk procedures:

1. *Initiate the practice.* Teacher informs adolescents and family members of reasons for book talks (e.g., sharing personal reactions; learning from others' interpretations; relating with each other in new ways) and explains how they function. Information might be presented through beginning-of-the-year open houses, notices sent home, and classroom explanations. Book talk schedules and deadlines are specified. Some teachers have participants sign an informal contract agreeing to fulfill the book talk procedures.

2. *Form partnerships.* Adolescent and family member(s) form a book talk partnership. The family members consist of whoever is at home and is willing and able to participate—mother or father, grandfather or grand-mother, aunt or uncle, older brother or sister. Father–son, father–daughter, mother–son, mother–daughter, and combined family member partnerships all have something to offer. The book talk occurs in the primary language of the home, if desired.

3. *Decide what to read.* Teachers prepare a list of no more than 15 books and spend a class period introducing them. The books often come from depart-mental and library resources; many teachers align them with current unit topics. *The Fables of Aesop, The Girl Who Married the Moon,* and *Mysterious Tales of Japan* fit a unit on folklore; *Tell Them We Remember* and *The Man from the Other Side* reveal the Holocaust. Partners rank their top five selections, then teachers distribute books according to partners' orders of preference.

4. *Record responses.* Partners might write up their responses to what they read; this step is optional. Adolescents might record what they think of cer-tain chapters they just finished, then their partners might react to what was written. This back-and-forth correspondence can be done in letter format. Another plan is for partners to write simultaneously, then talk about what each wrote. Teachers frequently offer questions such as the ones presented in Table 4.2 to stimulate partners' responses to the books, although many part-ners produce their own questions or conversation starters.

5. *Talk about the readings.* Partners either talk about their responses when they finish reading sections of the book or when they finish reading the entire book. These book talk conversations might flow from prepared questions, from what the partners recorded, or from open, unstructured circumstances.

6. *Report on the experience.* Students might write their partners a letter commenting on the experience, sharing what became clear, and expressing appreciation for participating. Students also might write up a report for their teacher's analysis. Some youth attach audio- or videotaped records of their book talks. Family members' reports and comments certainly are appropriate, too. This final step 6 also is optional.

Family book talks offer several advantages. They enable adolescents and those at home to talk about how to relate to literary works (Morris & Kaplan, 1994). Sharing feelings, opinions, and strategies the books call forth can enhance future readings (Ciotti, 2001). Book talks also might strengthen family connections. Youth and adults who talk about book ideas and situations open doors to conversations not readily available during everyday life. Adolescents also might gain new insights into their heritages when they and an older family member read culturally relevant literature (Hansen–Krening & Mizokawa, 1997). For instance, an Asian American daughter learned more about her immigrant mother's family history and culture while participating in book talks about Amy Tan and Maxine Hong Kingston novels (Packard, 2001). The experience also supported the mother's English literacy development.

Interviews

Interviews consist of questioners conferring with others about their experiences and understandings. The family book talks just described can be considered joint interviews about novels. Adolescents might interview family members about countless topics. Interviewers typically obtain background on a topic and their interviewees before conferring; some kind of report typically wraps up the practice.

Family stories are a particularly fruitful area of inquiry appropriate for interviewing. Adolescents might construct a scrapbook reporting family members' experiences with the following:

Athletics/sports	Illnesses	Pets
Favorites	Jobs/occupations	Pranks
First encounters	Leaving home	Purchases
Holidays	Military	Schooling
House moves	Music	Vacations/car trips
Homecomings	Outdoor experiences	Winning

Subject matter teachers often have students interview family members about the unit topics being explored. For example, students might be instructed to ask the following questions:

What is the most important invention?

Who has affected history the most?
What are our biggest social problems?
In which decade were people better off?
What toxic agents are in our house?
What do we do—and what might we do—to reduce, reuse, and recycle?
How do you use mathematics on your job and in your personal life?
Who are your favorite authors? What are your favorite things to read?
How might the media be improved?

Interviewers report their findings orally during group and class discussions and in written form. Interviews often constitute only one source of information to be combined with others.

Compacts

Compacts, sometimes named contracts or covenants, define partners' expectations and responsibilities. Compacts crystallize student–family–teacher roles, although they exert practically no formal authority. They are most effective when they are one part of the multiple parts of a home–school partnership. Students, family members, and teachers sign educational compacts, if they choose, indicating that they agree to stated stipulations. Some possible home-based stipulations to include in a literacy compact are as follows:

- Student will read a self-selected book for at least 1 hour each week outside school.
- Student will talk at least once a week about what he or she is reading or writing in school.
- Student will complete homework prior to the day it is due.
- Student will submit one piece of writing to the class literary journal.
- Student will accomplish state standards.
- Student will attend or participate in at least one school artistic production such as a play, music, or dance performance.
- Student will read aloud to young family members at least once a week.

School-based literacy stipulations to include in a compact might come from the International Reading Association's adolescent literacy position statement (Moore, Bean, Birdyshaw, & Rycik, 1999). Items such as the following might be included:

- School will provide access to a wide variety of reading material.
- School will provide instruction that focuses on both the skill and desire to read increasingly complex material.
- School will provide assessment that shows adolescents their strengths as well as their needs.

- School will provide explicit instruction in comprehension and study strategies across the curriculum.
- School will respond to the characteristics of individual readers.

Family Resource Centers

Resource centers offer family members a place where they can join school personnel and others to promote education among their children and themselves. Many family centers serve as community night schools, enabling members to develop skills in technology and trades such as health or transportation. Others are connected with school guidance and counseling operations to address social service needs and higher education opportunities. Many centers address literacy, providing access to educational resources and training.

Literacy training programs teach family members how to support adolescents' reading, writing, and academic achievement (Cairney, 2000). Such a program might consist of about 10 sessions. Center coordinators or guest speakers could present ways family members might promote their adolescents' learning strategies, self-selected reading, and academic success skills. Ample opportunities for interaction could be offered to bolster family members' comfort and confidence with the ideas. Programs addressing adolescent literacy have implications for adult literacy, with older family members often learning the new reading and writing competencies intended for younger members.

Family resource centers also might offer programs for adolescents as parents. Parents take up many reading and writing issues when doing what is best for their children. For instance, teenage parents' literacy can be emphasized when inquiring into effective parenting in general and the literacy development of young children in particular (Johnson, Pflaum, & Poole, 1995/1996). Literacy lessons can be offered when dealing with parenting topics such as feeding schedules, childproofing the home, and toilet training. Literacy lessons are natural when examining book selection, oral reading, storytelling, and discussion with young children. Showing adolescent parents how to present *Pat the Bunny, Are You My Mother?* and *Corduroy* to their own children calls up the need to respond to literature at a proficient level. It provides a bridge to contemporary adolescent issues presented through more sophisticated literature such as *The House on Mango Street* and *I Know Why the Caged Bird Sings.*

Cross-Age Partnerships

Cross-age teams—older students working with younger ones—are flexible and powerful partnerships (Samway, Whang, & Pippitt, 1995). Various age groups can be combined: twelfth-grade students might meet kindergarteners; ninth-grade students might join third graders. Partners can be matched for a one-time-only meeting, or they might come together daily, weekly, biweekly, or monthly.

Both older and younger partners tend to benefit intellectually and emotionally in cross-age teams (Rekrut, 1994). They develop literacy competencies with word analysis and comprehension along with personal skills such as cooperation and responsibility. Buddy reading and tutoring are two especially promising cross-age structures that involve adolescents who struggle as readers in school.

Buddy Reading

Partners share books during buddy reading sessions, with one reading to another (Girard & Willing, 1996). This practice is patterned after the home practice of an adult reading to a child who is going to bed. Those presenting the book promote interest in it, read it aloud, and talk about it with their partner. Positive personal relations and insights into reading are common.

One variation on buddy reading projects involves young adults creating books to share with their partners (Avery & Avery, 2001). Such a project has four phases:

1. *Examine book craft.* Older students read and analyze currently published children's literature. They discern how features such as topic, illustrations, layout, plot, character development, and word choice contribute to book quality.
2. *Plan a book.* Older students form teams to design and write a book. They delegate tasks such as illustrating, writing, and editing each others' work en route to a finished product.
3. *Produce a book.* Using computer stations, art supplies, and book binding materials, students physically produce a book.
4. *Share.* Teams of older students take their original productions along with published favorites to a lower grade. Each team of older students might share their work with a group of younger ones for about 10 minutes, then each group of young students rotates to a new team of adolescents. Conversely, young students might present what they have to their older partners. Children might read aloud and talk about the children's literature they produced or that was published professionally. Follow-up notes and reports are appropriate.

A variation on this project is for older and younger students to produce books collaboratively. They might take up subject-related concepts such as neighborhoods or animal life cycles as well as literary ones such as fantasy or fables. Teams might share ideas and information on a topic, brainstorming future directions. They would interact during all the procedures just presented, not only when the books were completed.

Another variation is for younger and older students to communicate with each other prior to meeting face to face (Wilhelm, Baker, & Dube, 2001). Both groups might compose personal profiles, listing their interests, hobbies, preferences, and so on. (Parents might help complete young children's profiles.) Teachers then match buddies according to compatible profiles. Next, pairs exchange written notes and letters as well as video- or audiotaped passage tellings or retellings. After several exchanges, the pairs meet during a Reading Buddies Day celebration, share new—possibly desktop-published—stories, and enjoy the wrap-up experience.

Tutoring

Tutoring involves older students instructing younger ones (Berger & Shafran, 2000). In this partnership, tutors, like buddy readers, might share books, but they take the activity to another level by actually teaching lessons. After sharing a piece of literature, tutors might demonstrate how to determine the meanings of unfamiliar words in the passage, how to retell what they just read, or how to relate the passage ideas to their own lives.

One-to-one tutoring sessions enable teaching practices that are difficult to manage in whole-class settings. Tutors can record stories their young partners dictate, then practice identifying new words. They can respond immediately when individuals read orally. They might help arrange letter cards into words, and they might categorize word cards according to initial letters, rhyming words, or numbers of syllables. They might help sequence word cards into sentences.

Effective cross-age tutoring programs regularly support older students' efforts (Jacobson, et al., 2001). They prepare adolescents for practices such as sharing books, retelling stories through puppetry, structuring lessons, understanding the reading competencies being taught, managing behavior, and maintaining records. Such programs might follow a weekly schedule of Monday and Tuesday at the middle or high school planning lessons, Wednesday and Thursday at elementary schools presenting the lessons, and Friday back at the secondary school debriefing. Fridays can be spent identifying successes and challenges, reflecting on their tutee's status, and recording pertinent information.

Community–School Partnerships

Community–school partnerships unite adolescents with senior citizens, local business personnel, church officials, governmental leaders, police officers, fire fighters, and service group members, such as Rotarians and Optimists.

These arrangements set the stage for unique and significant understandings (Schnack, 2001). Adolescents and adults both might overcome stereotypes of each other, getting beyond punk or geezer preconceptions. They might generate new insights into others' perspectives, aspirations, and ways of being. Completing reading and writing activities jointly might promote both adolescents' and adults' confidence, pleasure, and competence with literacy. Community–school partnerships are next distinguished as volunteer or after-school programs.

Volunteer

Community volunteers acting on their own and as representatives of local groups can promote literacy much the same way as family members and cross-age teams just described. Community members might perform the following tasks:

- Assisting with special projects
- Describing career-related or personal experiences—including literacy-related activities
- Participating in book talks
- Responding to interviews
- Serving as an artist/author in residence
- Serving as an external audience or evaluator for student exhibitions
- Tutoring adolescents

Adolescents who produce oral histories, or biographies, of community members have especially rich opportunities to strengthen their reading and writing (Gilbert, 2001; Weinberg, 1996). They first examine professional biographies and memoirs such as *Tuesdays with Morrie, Black Like Me, October Sky, Incidents in the Life of a Slave Girl,* and *Black Elk Speaks,* then design a rubric for their finished projects stimulated by what the professionals have accomplished. Next, they design an interview for the particular respondent. They research areas related to the interviewee's past to ask appropriate questions. Finally, they conduct the interview, then write up and exhibit what was learned.

Community members frequently host adolescents at off-school sites through service learning initiatives. Some community groups sponsor book give-aways and read-alouds in child care centers, hospitals, and senior homes. Literacy events such as book fairs and shopping mall book celebrations also occur. Students participating in community food banks, health care centers, and recreational programs can read and write about issues related to their experiences.

Students also might visit people at work sites to familiarize themselves with out-of-school literacy expectations and norms of behavior. Job shadow-

School-to-work partnerships often involve literacy.

ing, internship, and mentoring arrangements are common among career-oriented, school-to-work transition programs.

Finally, many business and community groups at the local level and beyond grant money for educational purposes. School districts usually employ someone to locate and acquire this external funding. Teachers can check on proposals for funding literacy-related materials. Teachers often fund sets of books for classroom use, technology, and software through external sources.

After-School Programs

Classroom teachers can publicize after-school programs and encourage students to avail themselves of the services. Programs offered after school through agencies such as Boys and Girls Clubs, YMCA and YWCA, Urban League, public libraries, and church groups can help promote reading (McLaughlin, 2000). Along with offering a secure setting and controlled opportunities for social interaction, after-school programs often provide literacy opportunities such as homework help and free reading materials.

Some adolescents who struggle as readers face daily exigencies with chemical dependence and staying within the law; some are expelled from school. After-school programs that continue working with these individuals eventually might enable schools to welcome them back.

After-school book clubs held in public libraries can engage adolescents with print differently than school-sanctioned practices (Alvermann, Young, Green, & Wisenbaker, 1999). Such clubs might position reading and writing through technology and free discussions in ways that disaffected youth appreciate. Summer adolescent reading programs held in public libraries are promising community–school partnerships, too.

Cultural Ties

Literacy practices sanctioned by adolescents' cultural heritages might differ from the ones sanctioned by their schools. A cultural practice for retelling printed accounts might be for several members to join together and playfully recount excerpts; however, the dominant academic practice for retelling passages might be for individuals dutifully and on their own to recite passage events chronologically. Another culturally sanctioned practice might be to accept authoritative interpretations of a passage, whereas classroom expectations might entail critiquing ideas and exploring multiple perspectives.

Reading about people and situations identifiable as those from one's heritage differs from reading about people and situations from only one dominant group. Competing with each other differs from collaborating with each other. Validating contributions only from males at the expense of females differs from validating all contributions. And aspiring to the literacy demands of occupations that cultural groups traditionally enter differs from aspiring to the demands of school-sanctioned occupations. In brief, adolescents deserve instruction that acknowledges cultural ties while promoting literacy (Franquiz, 2001; Jimenez & Gamez, 1999; Kelly, 2001).

Advancement Via Individual Determination (AVID) is a suitable example of a successful high school literacy program that acknowledges cultural ties. AVID increases Hispanic and African American students' entry to college without loss of ethnic identity (www.avidonline.org; Mehan, Hubbard, & Villanueva, 1996). Students in this program meet daily in special classes. The goals and resources made available in this program emphasize literacy skills such as note taking, test-taking strategies, and general study tips. Teachers stress the value and possibility of attending college. Positive inclusive images adorn the walls. Role models from various sectors of the community regularly speak about their successes, emphasizing their uses of literacy. Students read biographies of famous people of color such as those of Malcolm X, Cesar Chavez, Wilma Mankiller, the Little Rock Nine, Desmond Tutu, Henry Cisneros, and Colin Powell. Students relate experiences connecting their personal and home lives with school and business spheres.

While assuming a literate identity in AVID, students maintain their cultural ones. Students create dual identities, developing school-sanctioned literate practices while maintaining ties with their community, family, and peers. They work toward bicultural and biliterate proficiencies. Border-crossing strategies to manage these dual identities consist of some students bringing nonacademic friends into academic settings, taking pride in speaking Spanish with friends and family, and planning to attend college in Mexico. Students also develop a consciousness about their educational and occupational futures. They display an awareness of their developing abilities to participate in mainstream practices, but they realize they still could expect to encounter discriminatory barriers.

Professional Development

Because teaching adolescents who struggle as readers is complex, instructional expertise does not occur automatically or immediately. Becoming an excellent teacher requires much time, effort, and support. It means continually seeking improvement—participating in ongoing professional development. Such efforts characterize noteworthy adolescent literacy school programs (Langer, 2000). Study groups and professional associations are two means of effectively supporting professional development.

Study Groups

Study groups consist of teachers affiliating with each other while attending to particular instructional concerns (Birchak, et al., 1998). School program goals frequently are highlighted, and teachers individually and collectively solve problems relative to meeting goals. Biweekly sessions typically begin with 20 minutes of open-ended sharing, move to focused consideration of a selected issue, and end with an action plan.

During study groups knowledge is shared in an open, collegial manner so individuals can use it as they desire. Teachers critically examine their beliefs and actions relative to a classroom concern, frequently recording ideas in a journal. They review standards and the professional literature, consult with knowledgeable others, and converse among themselves. They explore multiple indicators of student achievement such as standardized test scores, performance with class assignments and projects, and students' anecdotal comments.

Study group partners plan instructional initiatives for themselves, then later report what happened. Literacy initiatives range from deepening students' responses to literature, to strengthening word analysis competencies, to refining reciprocal teaching procedures. Partners might support each other's initiatives by sharing resources, coaching each other, visiting one another's classes, videotaping class actions, evaluating what students produce, and providing feedback. They might react to one another's teaching portfolio presentations.

Study groups are peer-level partnerships that can evolve from mere gatherings to actual communities. Having teachers voluntarily join particular groups rather than assigning them is one way to encourage communal action. Another way to promote collaboration is to have a vision of what distinguishes beginning professional development communities from mature ones. Table 7.1 delineates a comparison of these two types of communities that

TABLE 7.1   Comparison of Beginning and Mature Professional Development Communities

	Beginning Community	Mature Community
Formation of Group Identity and Norms of Interaction	Identification is with subgroup	Identification is with whole group
	Belief that individuals are interchangeable and expendable	Belief that group is enriched by multiple perspectives (sense of loss when member leaves)
	Undercurrent of incivility	Civil interactions
	Sense of individualism overrides responsibility to group's functioning	Sense of community shapes responsibility for and regulation of group's functioning behavior
Understanding Differences/ Navigating Fault Lines	Denial of differences	Understanding and productive use of differences
	Conflict goes backstage, hidden from view	Conflict is an expected feature of group life and is dealt with openly and honestly
Negotiating the Essential Tension	Lack of agreement over purposes of professional community	Recognition that teacher learning and student learning are fundamentally intertwined
Taking Communal Responsibility for Individuals' Growth	Belief that teachers' responsibility is to students, not colleagues; intellectual growth is the responsibility of the individual	Commitment to colleagues' professional growth
	Belief that contributions to group are acts of individual volition	Acceptance of rights and responsibilities of community membership

might help participants acknowledge beliefs and interactions that distinguish mere gatherings from responsive study groups (Grossman, Wineburg, & Woolworth, 2000).

Professional Associations

Professional associations unite members with colleagues. One type of professional educational association involves postsecondary schools. People from community colleges, technical schools, and universities might form partnerships with public schools through professors in residence, joint committee participation, recertification credit programs, professional development schools, and graduate programs. Postsecondary educators usually are quite adept at orienting adolescents to future possibilities.

Educational organizations such as the International Reading Association and the National Council of Teachers of English (see their websites in
Table 7.2) hold local, regional, and national professional development meetings on literacy. Their professional journals, the *Journal of Adolescent and Adult
Literacy* and *English Journal,* contain much about the reading and writing of
adolescents. Program descriptions, unit and lesson plans, book lists, instructional models, theoretical essays, research reports, and other professional
development resources are available through outlets listed in Table 7.2.

TABLE 7.2   Professional Development Resources

Literacy Associations and Centers

American Library Association	www.ala.org
Center on English Learning and Achievement	http://cela.albany.edu/
International Reading Association	www.ira.org
National Council of Teachers of English	www.ncte.org
National Reading Conference	http://nrc.oakland.edu/
Reading Online: A journal of K–12 practice and research of the International Reading Association	www.readingonline.org/
Young Adult Library Services Association	www.ala.org/yalsa

General Education Associations

Association for Supervision and Curriculum Development	www.ascd.org
National Association of Secondary School Principals	www.nassp.org
National Education Association	www.nea.org
National Middle School Association	www.nmsa.org
National Staff Development Council	www.nsdc.org

Research, Development, Service, and Information Sources

Center for Research on Education, Diversity, and Excellence	www.cal.org/crede/pubs
Center for Research on the Education of Students Placed At Risk	www.csos.jhu.edu/crespar/CReSPaR.html
Education Commission of the States	www.ecs.org
Regional Educational Laboratory Network	www.relnetwork.org
National Institute of Child Health and Human Development: Reading Research Resources	www.nichd.nih.gov/crmc_cdb/reading.htm
National Board of Professional Teaching Standards	www.nbpts.org
National Network of Partnership Schools	www.csos.jhu.edu/p2000
Northwest Regional Educational Lab (6+1 Trait Writing)	www.nwrel.org/assessment/
Office of Educational Research and Improvement	www.ed.gov/offices/OERI/
Wisconsin Literacy Education and Reading Network Services	http://wilearns.state.wi.us/
Writing Opportunities and Reading Development for Student Success (WORDSS)	www.unf.edu/dept/fie/WORDSS/ index.htm

School Structures

School structures encompass work schedules, resources, and duties that policymakers arrange so schools function. Although administrators generally are responsible for organizing the work of schools, teachers' voices can be heard through school leadership roles, committee memberships, and speaking out individually. Reaching to school structures as a way to promote adolescents' literacies is a somewhat indirect, systemic approach, usually initiated by administrators. But it is one that deserves serious consideration by all educators. This section presents five types of school structures to consider as ways to promote literacy: literacy across the curriculum, library–media centers, school success courses, personalized schools, and full-service schools.

Literacy across the Curriculum

In schools that promote literacy across the curriculum, subject matter teachers guide students to read as scientists, historians, journalists, and so on. Previous chapters in this book have already highlighted ways for teachers to accomplish this. Weaving reading and writing through all subject matter units of instruction, as presented in Chapter 4, is essential.

A primary reason for promoting literacy across the curriculum is that content-area teachers can best teach the reading and writing competencies associated with their disciplines (Moore, Moore, Cunningham, & Cunningham, 1998). Reading to solve geometric problems in mathematics classes differs from interpreting poetry in language arts classes; and both differ from inquiring into life cycles in biology. Literacy functions differently in the various disciplines, so teachers who are qualified in each should be the ones to teach students how to read and write in each.

Terminology also differs from class to class, with technical words such as *hypotenuse, onomatopoeia,* and *photosynthesis* appearing mainly in specific disciplines. Simpler terms such as *cell, ground, angle,* and *ray* appear across all disciplines, but they have different meanings in each one. Again, subject matter specialists are in the best position to teach the new words. Finally, adolescents seem most receptive to reading and writing instruction when they need it to perform specific assignments. Teaching students how to take laboratory notes occurs best in science class when lab notes are needed—not in a reading class as a stand-alone exercise.

Library–Media Centers

Librarians and media specialists are valuable partners for teachers working with adolescents who struggle as readers (Humphries, Lipsitz, McGovern, &

Wasser, 1997). They are especially useful when providing readers access to appropriate materials during self-selected reading and inquiry projects. When teachers launch new units, library–media specialists often visit classrooms and publicize pertinent materials. They display books, read aloud brief portions, and comment on how they fit course contents.

These specialists also directly promote individuals' efforts with reading. They set up adolescents with reading improvement CDs, videos, and computer software designed for individuals' work pace and protection from peers' hurtful comments (Hasselbring, Goin, Taylor, Bottger, & Daley, 1997). When students are conducting inquiry, specialists help them use electronic networks and search engines to access and compile information. Librarians and media specialists also frequently take the lead during school district, state, and national literacy incentive programs.

School Success Courses

Because getting off on the right foot is essential for succeeding later in secondary school (Roderick & Camburn, 1999), many educators are instructing students early on about what it takes to succeed (Gaskins, 1998). Reading specialists frequently affiliate with others in preparing and presenting courses that have titles like Success Seminar, Dynamics of Effective Learning, and Freshman Experience. Course offerings range beyond print-related proficiencies to general academic ones, knowing that students who do not focus on school also do not focus on school-based reading and writing. Topics such as the following frequently are examined:

> *Class orientation:* mission of the course, connecting with academics, rules and procedures
>
> *School orientation:* mission of the school, history and traditions, administrators and faculty, support services, extracurricular opportunities, FAQs
>
> *Role models:* school alumni, community leaders, national and international heroes, visualizing success
>
> *Personality types:* Myers–Briggs indicators, learning styles and preferences, creating compatible productive learning environments
>
> *Goal setting:* charting a course to the future, career pathways, personal fulfillment, decision making
>
> *Managing time:* determining and scheduling priorities, knowing when and how to say no, controlling procrastination
>
> *Learning how to learn:* taking charge of learning, habits of effective learners, note taking, reciprocal teaching, test taking

Literacy: reading interests and habits, strengths and limitations, personal and academic uses, word study

Inclusion: celebrating diversity, honoring others' customs and strengths

Protocol: teamwork, getting along with others, societal and workplace etiquette, assertive communication

Conflict resolution: anger management, stress management, channeling emotions

Self-actualization: becoming all you can become

Instructional activities and assessments such as the following are included with school success courses:

Guest speakers	Teacher and peer modeling
Tours	Self-assessments
Print and online resources	Notebooks and reflective journals
Role plays and simulations	Inquiry projects with rubrics

Personalized Schools

Personalized schools emphasize social arrangements that foster close student–teacher relationships (Murphy, 2001; National Association of Secondary School Principals, 1996). One goal of personalized schools is to cultivate relationships that nurture reading and writing.

Personalized instruction is a special hallmark of middle schools, which feature groups of students enrolled with interdisciplinary teams of four or five teachers (Jackson & Davis, 2000). This structure promotes coherence among subject matter and literacy instruction as well as attention to individual students. Interdisciplinary teams respond to learners' needs for a personal human touch. They encourage—indeed, they often require—academic development of all students, acting on the belief that all can learn.

Block scheduling is another school structure implemented in the name of personalization. Students remain with one teacher and course for spans of time exceeding the traditional 50 minutes per day. Spending long amounts of time together encourages teachers and students to develop ideas and form personal relationships. During these classes teachers can schedule long-term reading and writing practices that enable concepts and strategies to be developed fully.

Advisory programs match students with teachers specifically to address personal concerns. Teachers serve as guides, mentors, and counselors—as student advocates—relative to peer interactions, approaching difficult teachers, minor health problems, and so on. Teachers guide students to become self-advocates—individuals who specify their own problems and determine their own possible solutions.

Full-Service Schools

Many adolescents who struggle as readers face social, emotional, and physical concerns that potentially disrupt learning. Chemical dependence, staying within the law, and parenthood—to name a few—readily distract from literacy learning. Teens who immigrate to the United States and find themselves amid a strange language and set of customs often feel uprooted. In extreme cases, youth might be in crisis due to bullying, sexual harassment, emotional or physical abuse, and homelessness. Full-service schools acknowledge these exigencies when structuring academic assistance (Calfee, Wittwer, & Meredith, 1998; Dryfoos, 1994).

Full-service schools provide personal and social supports intended to connect students with academics. Class times are adjusted to students' work and parenting schedules, with meetings occurring throughout the day and in the evening. Some classes are delivered via technology so individuals can access lessons whenever time is available.

Full service means providing attendance initiatives, after-school programs, and career counseling. Nutrition, weight management, health, and dental screenings are available. Substance abuse counseling and mental health support groups exist. Adolescent parents have access to child care when they attend school. Case management, crisis intervention, and court-mandated services are available.

Additional services include placing struggling readers in academically rigorous courses and supporting them. Schools provide guest speakers, readings, and presentations that call attention to the idea that social groups possibly interfering with academic success can be accommodated. Emphases are on individual decision making, personal responsibility, and ways to manage multiple identities in today's society. Teachers mediate difficulties between students and college-bound course instructors, involve parents, and supervise entry to academic situations beyond high school. They connect adolescents with institutions of higher learning through recruiters, school alumni currently enrolled in higher education, and field trips. Full-service schools arrange conditions that support adolescents' involvement with academics, including reading and writing.

Conclusion

Connecting with others outside classrooms is a big job. Assistant superintendents, district personnel, and assistant principals often join with teachers in establishing partnerships. One high school assistant principal for student services that we know refers to herself as the *special assistant for partnerships*. Recognizing the value of partnerships, she independently and informally devotes substantial time to connecting her school's efforts with others. Teachers go to her as the informal coordinator for partnerships; she will soon become the formal coordinator.

Connecting reading and writing with people beyond classroom walls enriches normal academics. Adolescents who read and write in concert with young children, family members, library–media specialists, community volunteers, and cultural icons take their literacy to new levels. They refine their identities as literate individuals. Teachers who connect with others through study groups, professional associations, literacy across the curriculum initiatives, and personalized work structures access a broad range of services for themselves and their students.

CENTRAL QUESTION: THINK BACK

How can I reach beyond my classroom to engage students with reading and writing?

To answer fully this chapter's central question, build on the following key concepts:

- Promote home–school partnerships through (1) family book talks, (2) interviews, (3) compacts, and (4) family resource centers.
- Develop cross-age teams through (1) buddy reading and (2) tutoring.
- Build community–school partnerships through (1) volunteer agencies and (2) after-school programs.
- Acknowledge cultural ties.
- Participate in professional development through (1) study groups and (2) professional associations.
- Commit to five school structures that promote literacy: (1) literacy across the curriculum, (2) library–media centers, (3) school success courses, (4) personalized schools, and (5) full-service schools.

REFERENCES

Alvermann, D. E. (2001). Reading adolescent's reading identities: Looking back to see ahead. *Journal of Adolescent and Adult Literacy, 44,* 676–690.

Alvermann, D. E., Young, J. P., Green, C., & Wisenbaker, J. M. (1999). Adolescents' perceptions and negotiations of literacy practices in after-school book clubs. *American Educational Research Journal, 36,* 221–264.

Avery, C. W., & Avery, K. B. (2001). Kids teaching kids. *Journal of Adolescent and Adult Literacy, 44,* 434–435.

Berger, A., & Shafran, E. A. (2000). *Teens for literacy: Promoting reading and writing in schools and communities.* Newark, DE: International Reading Association.

Bintz, W. P. (1993). Resistant readers in secondary education: Some insights and implications. *Journal of Reading, 36,* 604–615.

Birchak, B., Connor, C., Crawford, K., Kahn, L., Kaser, S., Turner, S., & Short, K. (1998). *Teacher study groups: Building community through dialogue and action.* Urbana, IL: National Council of Teachers of English.

Brozo, W. G. (1990). Hiding out in secondary classrooms: Coping strategies of unsuccessful readers. *Journal of Reading, 33*(5), 324–328.

Cairney, T. H. (2000). Developing parent partnerships in secondary literacy learning. In D. W. Moore, D. E. Alvermann, & K. E. Hinchman (Eds.), *Struggling adolescent readers: A collection of teaching strategies* (pp. 58–65. Newark, DE: International Reading Association.

Calfee, C., Wittwer, F., & Meredith, M. (1998). *Building a full-service school: A step-by-step guide.* San Francisco: Jossey–Bass.

Christenson, S. L., & Sheridan, S. M. (2001). *Schools and families: Creating essential connections for learning.* New York: Guilford.

Ciotti, H. (2001). Including parents in the fun: Sharing literary experiences. *English Journal, 90,* 52–59.

Davidson, A. L. (1996). *Making and molding identity in schools: Student narratives on race, gender, and academic identity.* Albany: State University of New York Press.

Dryfoos, J. G. (1994). *Full-service schools.* San Francisco: Jossey–Bass.

Epstein, J. L. (2001). *School, family and community partnerships: Preparing educators and improving schools.* Boulder, CO: Westview Press.

Franquiz, M. E. (2001). It's about YOUth! Chicano high school students revisioning their academic identity. In M. de la Luz Reyes & J. J. Halcon (Eds.), *The best for our children: Critical perspectives on literacy for Latino children* (pp. 213–228). New York: Teachers College Press.

Gaskins, I. W. (1998). There's more to teaching at-risk and delayed readers than good reading instruction. *The Reading Teacher, 51,* 534–547.

Gilbert, B. (2001). Designing a town-based writing project. *English Journal, 90*(5), 88–94.

Girard, S., & Willing, K. R. (1996). *Partnerships for classroom learning: From reading buddies to pen pals to the community and the world beyond.* Portsmouth, NH: Heinemann.

Grossman, P., Wineburg, S., & Woolworth, S. (2000). *What makes teacher community different from a gathering of teachers?* Retrieved September 12, 2001, from http://depts.washington.edu/ctpmail/pubslist.html.

Hansen–Krening, N., & Mizokawa, D. T. (1997). Exploring ethnic-specific literature: A unity of parents, families, and educators. *Journal of Adolescent and Adult Literacy, 41,* 180–189.

Hasselbring, T. S., Goin, L., Taylor, R., Bottge, B., & Daley, P. (1997). The computer doesn't embarrass me. *Educational Leadership, 55*(3), 30–33.

Humphries, J. W., Lipsitz, J., McGovern, J. T., & Wasser, J. D. (1997). Supporting the development of young adolescent readers. *Phi Delta Kappan, 79,* 305–311.

Jackson, A. W., & Davis, G. A. (2000). *Turning points 2000: Educating adolescents in the 21st century.* New York: Teachers College Press.

Jacobson, J., Thrope, L., Fisher, D., Lapp, D., Frey, N., & Flood, J. (2001). Cross-age tutoring: A literacy improvement approach for struggling adolescent readers. *Journal of Adolescent and Adult Literacy, 44,* 528–536.

Jimenez, R. T., & Gamez, A. (1999). Lessons and dilemmas derived from the literacy instruction of two Latina/o teachers. *American Educational Research Journal, 36,* 265–301.

Johnson, H. L., Pflaum, S., & Poole, P. (1995/1996). Focus on teenage parents: Using children's literature to strengthen teenage literacy. *Journal of Adolescent and Adult Literacy, 39,* 290–296.

Kelly, M. M. (2001). The education of African-American youth: Literacy practices and identity representation in church and school. In E. B. Moje & D. G. O'Brien (Eds.), *Constructions of literacy: Studies of teaching and learning in and out of secondary schools* (pp. 239–259). Mahwah, NJ: Lawrence Erlbaum.

Kos, R. (1991). Persistence of reading difficulties: The voices of four middle school students. *American Educational Research Journal, 28,* 875–895.

Langer, J. (2000). Excellence in English in middle and high school: How teachers' professional lives support student achievement. *American Educational Research Journal, 37*(2), 397–439.

McLaughlin, M. (2000). *Community counts: How youth organizations matter for youth development.* Washington, DC: Public Education Network. Retrieved September 16, 2001, from www.publiceducation.org.

Mehan, H., Hubbard, L., & Villanueva, I. (1996). *Constructing school success: The consequences of untracking low achieving students.* New York: Cambridge University Press.

Moore, D. W., Bean, T. W., Birdyshaw, D., & Rycik, J. A. (1999). *Adolescent literacy: A position statement.* Newark, DE: International Reading Association, Commission on Adolescent Literacy.

Moore, D. W., Moore, S. A., Cunningham, P. M., & Cunningham, J. W. (1998). *Developing readers and writers in the content areas, K–12* (3rd ed.). New York: Longman.

Morris, N. C., & Kaplan, I. (1994). Middle school parents are good partners for reading. *Journal of Reading, 21,* 130–131.

Murphy, J. (2001). *The productive high school: Creating personalized academic communities.* Thousand Oaks, CA: Corwin Press.

National Association of Secondary School Principals. (1996). *Breaking ranks: Changing an American institution.* Reston, VA: Author.

Packard, B. W-L. (2001). When your mother asks for a book: Fostering intergenerational exchange of culturally relevant books. *Journal of Adolescent and Adult Literacy, 44,* 626–633.

Phelan, P., Yu, H. C., & Davidson, A. L. (1994). Navigating the psychological pressures of adolescence: The voices and experiences of high school youth. *American Educational Research Journal, 31,* 415–447.

Rekrut, M. D. (1994). Peer and cross-age tutoring: The lessons of research. *Journal of Reading, 37,* 356–362.

Roderick, M., & Camburn, E. (1999). Risk and recovery from course failure in the early years of high school. *American Educational Research Journal, 36,* 303–343.

Rycik, J. (1998). From information to interaction: Involving parents in the literacy development of their adolescent. *NASSP Bulletin, 82*(600), 67–72.

Samway, K. D., Whang, G., & Pippitt, M. (1995). *Buddy reading: Cross-age tutoring in a multicultural school.* Portsmouth, NH: Heinemann.

Schnack, P. (2001). Partners in reading: A community reading/writing project. *English Journal, 90,* 95–101.

Smith, F. (1988). *Joining the literacy club: Further essays into education.* Portsmouth, NH: Heinemann

Weinberg, S. K. (1996). Unforgettable memories: Oral history in the middle school classroom. *Voices from the Middle, 3*(3), 18–25.

Welch, O. M., & Hodges, C. R. (1997). *Standing outside on the inside: Black adolescents and the construction of academic identity.* Albany: State University of New York.

Wilhem, J. D., Baker, T. N., & Dube, J. (2001). *Strategic reading: Guiding students to lifelong literacy, 6–12.* Portsmouth, NH: Boynton/Cook.

CHAPTER

8 Classroom Assessments

CENTRAL QUESTION: THINK AHEAD

How are adolescents' reading and writing competencies best evaluated?

Literacy has assumed great visibility since the middle 1990s when educational reformers enacted sweeping accountability measures. A public spotlight now shines on reading, and countless assessments are in place. This situation greatly influences adolescent literacy instruction.

Assessing literacy for evaluation purposes is multidimensional. State-mandated standards establish expectations for what students are to be able to do; they determine what is to be accomplished (Kendall & Marzano, 2000).

Standards present a common focus for directing academic growth. For instance, the Arizona Department of Education mandates numerous reading and writing standards (see www.ade.state.az.us/standards). Arizona educators—like many others—are shaping their instruction to enable students to accomplish the following literate actions:

1. Using structural analysis skills such as identifying root words, prefixes, suffixes, and word origins to decode words unfamiliar in print
2. Drawing defensible conclusions based on events and settings
3. Identifying the sequence of activities needed to carry out a procedure
4. Evaluating technical journals or workplace documents for purpose, organizational pattern, clarity, reliability and accuracy, and relevancy of information

Assessments, which measure what students have attained, are often today used for evaluating schools' achievement of standards. For instance, state-mandated assessments determine students' proficiencies with using structural analysis, drawing defensible conclusions, identifying sequences of activities, evaluating journals or documents, and so on.

State-mandated standards and assessments have complicated educators' efforts (Valencia & Wixson, 2000). On the one hand, these standards and assessments have promoted literacy improvement initiatives. More and more educators and members of the public are concerning themselves with adolescents' literacy development. On the other hand, state standards and assessments are at risk of obstructing improvement efforts. Understanding uses of assessment sheds light on this situation.

Uses of Assessment

Assessment is gathering information to monitor actions and inform decisions (Linn, 1989). It is a regular part of decision making. People regularly gather information to help determine how they are doing in the present and help decide what to do in the future.

Specific uses of assessment differ, a condition that became exceptionally clear to David when John, his then 15-year-old son, returned home from a first-ever golf game. David doesn't golf, but his father—John's grandfather—was an avid golfer, and David was eager to know whether granddad's aptitude, ability, and passion for the game simply skipped him and ended up in the grandson. David also was very willing to foster his son's efforts with the game, but he wanted to know what needed fostering. So when John returned from the game, David was curious and asked how it went. In a rather cryptic manner John reported, "I shot 118."

This assessment, reported as shooting 118, was somewhat informative. David realized that John was far from a par of 72 (the performance standard set by the course designers) and that he was roughly equivalent to what absolute beginners with some aptitude for the game typically accomplish. But the report of 118 didn't come even close to telling David all that he wanted to know for assessment purposes:

> Did this score accurately reflect John's skill—would he score about the same with several rounds of golf?
>
> How did John like the game?
>
> How did John do driving the ball off the tee, using his long irons, his short irons, his putter?
>
> How did John do with his grip, his stance, his club selection, and his ability to shift weight during his swing?
>
> How did John handle the course layout and conditions?
>
> Did John and his friends perform golf etiquette well, moving along with the other players and not hindering anyone's play?

The 118 score provided a rough, general indication of golf proficiencies and preferences, but it went only so far. The single score was telling, but it did not tell the whole story. To evaluate John's golfing future and contribute meaningfully to his development, David would need to play many rounds with his son.

Just as with golf, reading scores go only so far. Reading assessments serve different purposes for different audiences. An informative way to view these assessments is to distinguish them between high-stakes and classroom-support purposes.

High-Stakes Assessments

High-stakes assessment means that one test is used as the basis for important decisions. Individuals' futures are at stake with such an assessment; much depends on performance with a particular test. For instance, high-stakes assessments exist for determining which students graduate from high school, which are promoted from one grade to another, and which are eligible for special programs and institutions. High-stakes assessments also exist for deciding which teachers receive pay raises, which receive remedial attention, and which are terminated from their teaching positions. This form of assessment became popular during the mid-1990s amid educational emphases on accountability.

High-stakes assessments typically are reported as single, concise scores, like 118. Such a number allows easy access, allowing decision makers to determine efficiently what to do. On the basis of a single score, authorities efficiently sort people into categories, determining who goes where and who gets what.

However, as in the case with John's golf score, much more than a single overall number is needed to inform appropriate decisions about particular individuals in particular situations. Because of this, many educators oppose reliance on a single score for deciding individuals' educational futures. For instance, the International Reading Association (IRA) Board of Directors issued a May 1999 position statement disapproving high-stakes assessment that opened with these words:

> The Board of Directors of the International Reading Association is opposed to high-stakes testing. . . . Our central concern is that testing has become a way of controlling instruction as opposed to a way of gathering information to help students become better readers. (International Reading Association, 1999)

Perhaps the best support for the IRA concerns is available in publications by the National Center for Fair and Open Testing (www.fairtest.org) and in scholarly reports published in the professional educational literature (e.g., Amrein & Berliner, 2002; Hoffman, Assaf, & Paris, 2001; McNeil, 2000). These references convincingly support the claims by the IRA that high-stakes tests have negative effects. Additionally, professional associations not linked directly to literacy learning, such as the American Educational Research Association (www.aera.net), the American Psychological Association (www.apa.org), and the National Council on Measurement in Education (www.ncme.org), provide guidelines that require multiple—not single—measures as the basis for any substantive decision affecting any individual. Practically all test publishers' technical manuals recommend multiple measures, too.

Teachers who work effectively with adolescents who struggle as readers acknowledge the demands as well as the pitfalls of high-stakes assessments. Many teachers contest these tests by speaking out against them at school board and school meetings, writing to local newspapers, and lobbying politicians (Kohn, 2000). But even when opposing high-stakes assessments, educators are required to prepare students for them. Educators face the task of providing a high-quality overall education that prepares students for life— as well as for a particular state-mandated exam.

Research by Langer (2000) shows how those in high-performing schools regularly review the expectations and results of statewide assessments, then instruct students in ways directly leading to their eventual success. These teachers employ a wide range of goal-directed practices, consistently focusing on student achievement. They coordinate teaching practices such as writing workshops and reciprocal teaching according to a plan that keeps test goals in mind. They orchestrate practices so students acquire meaningful competencies and positive attitudes, including what it takes to pass state tests. Assessments that support classroom instruction are commonly used in such schools.

Classroom-Support Assessments

Classroom supports occur during everyday events involving teachers and students. They involve students' performances with activities such as journal entries, book responses, inquiry projects, and teacher-made tests. The International Reading Association's Adolescent Literacy Commission position statement endorses classroom-support assessments this way: "Adolescents deserve assessment that shows them their strengths as well as their needs and guides their teachers to design instruction that will best help them grow as readers" (Moore, Bean, Birdyshaw, & Rycik, 1999, p. 6).

Classroom-support assessments are an ongoing, cyclical process. It entails teachers and students determining what needs to be learned (e.g., taking notes, solving word problems, interpreting poetry), engaging in instruction, monitoring performance, then determining what next needs to be learned. Events flow through one another as teachers and students constantly observe their performance, gather data, and decide next steps.

Classroom-support assessments promote learning in large part by maintaining focus (Shepard, 2000). Setting aside time during initial teaching to show how reading and writing will be assessed clarifies literacy expectations and signals what is important. This practice focuses teachers on what needs to be taught, and it focuses students on what needs to be learned. It directs everyone's efforts, fostering goal-oriented classrooms.

Classroom-support assessments also promote learning through self-assessment. Teachers and students determine how they are doing. Teachers find out for themselves what they need to reteach, and learners determine for themselves what they still need to learn. Teachers who promote self-assessment involve students as well as themselves in estimating classroom learning. Students learn to apply the same criteria as teachers do to their literacy performance. Bringing students into the assessment process this way promotes self-awareness and independence, eliminating students' reliance on others. Self-assessments can be promoted in numerous ways:

1. Students and teachers establish instructional goals (e.g., becoming an independent lifelong learner), display them, refer to them throughout the course, and reflect on progress toward them.
2. Learners gauge their reading and writing by rating their specific performances and supporting their ratings. Students might answer open-ended inquiries such as, "I rate my summaries . . . because . . . " This might occur during small-group conversations, individual conferences, or as journal entries.

3. Portfolio self-assessments might ask students: "What do you think is the best piece of work in this collection? Explain why" and, "With which piece of work are you least satisfied? Explain why."

4. During teacher–student conferences learners think through how well they accomplished reading and writing strategies such as learning key vocabulary and following the author's organization.

5. After teachers direct instruction with strategies such as graphically organizing information or noting meaningful parts of words, learners estimate how well they performed the strategies in their assignments.

6. During units' culminating activities learners reflect orally or in writing on their work and growth as learners. For instance, they might answer questions such as, What advice would you give someone who is doing this project next year? and, What did you find out about your reading and writing while completing this project?

Classroom-Support Assessments

This section describes classroom-support assessments that are appropriate for adolescents who struggle as readers. Each goes far in maintaining focus and promoting self-awareness. Each can be used in multiple situations. These assessments consist of guidelines found in the professional literature, which need to be adapted locally. They comprise informal procedures that play out differently in different classrooms. (For a description of more formal, externally designed assessments that you might import into your classroom, consult the ERIC/AE Test Locator [http://ericae.net/testcol.htm#ETSTF], which is a joint project of the ERIC Clearinghouse on Assessment and Evaluation, the Educational Testing Service, the Buros Institute of Mental Measurements, and others.) The classroom-support assessments described in this section include rubrics, portfolios, conferences, and diagnostic inventories.

Rubrics

Rubrics, or scoring guides, are useful for directing and monitoring complex learning activities (Arter & McTighe, 2001). A regular part of framing instructional units, as presented in Chapter 3, involves designing rubrics. Teachers and students with clear rubrics—along with clear topics, standards-based outcomes, essential questions, and culminating activities—have a powerful means of maintaining focus and self-assessing progress.

The term *rubric* is connected with *ruby*, derived from the Latin *ruber*, which denotes the color red. Traditional assessments of students' papers were marked with red ink. Contemporary assessments include features unrelated to color, as the rubric in Figure 8.1 for a personal story indicates. This personal story rubric, like a traditional task analysis, simplifies what is com-

Beginning Action						
Story problem is clear.	4	3	2	1		Story problem is unclear.
Ending Action						
Solution to the problem could really happen.	4	3	2	1		Solution to the problem probably would not happen.
Creativity						
Story events go beyond the examples presented during class.	8	6	4	2		Story events are practically identical to the examples presented during class.
Mechanics						
Spelling, grammar, and legibility promote understanding of the story.	4	3	2	1		Spelling, grammar and legibility interfere with understanding of the story.
On Time						
Yes	2	0		No		

FIGURE 8.1   Sample Personal Story Rubric

plicated, providing entry points into the overall task. It specifies the essential components of the performance, breaking down complexities into manageable proportions. To produce such a rubric, follow these five steps:

1. *Envision students' best performance.* Examine the reading or writing assignment, asking, "What should students produce to be successful?" Consult published resources and colleagues for ideas. Whenever possible, involve your students in deciding what the products should exemplify. Additionally, examine the work products that students completed in the past. These products provide good models for current students; they can see what you are talking about. A good rule of thumb is to provide at least two models so students do not lock in on one as the only possibility.
2. *Generate criteria.* Criteria are the specifics that make up a successful product. The personal story rubric in Figure 8.1 contains five criteria: beginning action, ending action, creativity, mechanics, and on time.
3. *Generate indicators.* Indicators describe the points on a continuum of performance; they often describe only high- and low-quality performance. For instance, the rubric in Figure 8.1 contains the item "Story problem is clear" as a high-quality indicator for the beginning action criterion.
4. *Generate scales.* Scales indicate the scores student can earn relative to the criteria. The rubric in Figure 8.1 contains 4 as the highest possible score

for the beginning action criterion and 8 as the highest possible score for creativity.

- Many authorities recommend a 4-point scale so scores fall on one end or the other of the continuum; a 3-, 5-, or 7-point scale allows scorers to regress to the middle.

- Note that the last scale in Figure 8.1, for the on-time criterion, contains only 2 points. Such a dichotomous checklist is appropriate for yes–no decisions that do not address quality (e.g., cover sheet attached, five references cited, typed double-spaced).

5. *Revise the rubric.* Conduct a pilot test of the rubric to see what revisions are needed. Elicit student input. (In fact, involving students in initially creating rubrics helps them see themselves as readers and writers as the year progresses.) Modify the rubric after trying it out. Clarify and develop it.

Rubrics support instruction well. When working with personal stories, for instance, teachers and students can use a personal story rubric as a guide during whole-class presentations, peer planning, individual writing, peer revising, and teacher–student conferences. This rubric also could be used by combinations of students, teachers, mentors, peers, parents, and external evaluators. The criteria help maintain focus and promote self-assessment in all these circumstances.

Another way rubrics support classroom instruction is by contributing to a sense of fairness. Adolescents who struggle as readers often vehemently disdain hidden agendas and arbitrary scoring, so they tend to appreciate the openness and consistency of rubrics. By making public what is being taught and tested, rubrics display expectations visibly and explicitly. Such a fair and impartial practice goes far in engaging adolescents.

Rubrics also support complex teaching and learning outcomes that traditional tests miss (Bauer, 1999; Stiggins, 1997). They fit authentic relevant reading and writing requirements encountered practically anywhere. They can be used to help students attend to such aspects of reading comprehension as determining importance, discerning organization, being strategic, summarizing, forming images, grasping literal information, connecting authors' ideas, relating authors' ideas to what is known, applying, and synthesizing information from various sources. For instance, the rubric presented in Figure 8.2 addresses the complexities of students interacting in small groups. This rubric is good for assessing student performance during literature discussions or book clubs.

Finally, rubrics are especially appropriate with long-term tasks because they list what counts (e.g., http://rubistar.4 teachers.org). They serve to maintain focus and provide feedback with projects completed over time such as book responses, laboratory investigations, library or community inquiries, and portfolio construction. To illustrate, rubrics might be constructed for a

Productivity					
We remained focused, efficiently accomplishing much.	4	3	2	1	We often lost focus, working inefficiently and accomplishing little.
Participation					
Everyone was an insider, contributing ideas.	4	3	2	1	Some people were outsiders, contributing little.
Communication					
We listened attentively and responded to ideas; interactions were give-and-take.	4	3	2	1	We often disregarded ideas; interactions frequently were one-sided.
Climate					
We disagreed agreeably; the atmosphere was friendly and relaxed.	4	3	2	1	We often disagreed disagreeably; the atmosphere was tense and quarrelsome.
Roles					
Each member played preferred (or assigned) roles to help the group move along.	4	3	2	1	Only a few played preferred (or assigned) roles to help the group move along.

FIGURE 8.2   Sample Student Group Interaction Rubric

senior project containing the following extended sequence of activities: (1) topic selection, (2) project agreement, (3) progress journal update, (4) presentation plan, (5) preliminary draft, (6) final draft, and (7) presentation.

Portfolios

Portfolios are collections of student work saved over time. They contain material selected by the student, the teacher, and the student and teacher working collaboratively. By participating in showcasing their work in portfolios, students actively engage in self-assessment, reflecting on their development as readers and writers. Teachers obtain insight into student progress by viewing samples of students' performance with actual classroom tasks assembled over time. They have access to a wide range of information.

Although educators typically focus on portfolios when assessment is the topic, many educators have begun suggesting that portfolios belong in presentations of instruction because they affect learning so powerfully (Clark, Chow-Hoy, Herter & Moss, 2001). This ambivalence about when to discuss portfolios attests to the interconnectedness of teaching and assessing. Mitchell, Abernathy, and Gowans (1998) present an especially sensible four-step approach

1. *Planning the focus*
   What am I attempting to assess?
   What can I expect to know about a student from his/her portfolio?
   What is my definition of a portfolio for this assignment?

2. *Selecting the content*
   How will content for portfolios be selected?
   Who will select materials?
   What resources can be used?

3. *Adding materials and building a portfolio*
   Will materials be added on an ongoing basis?
   What decision criteria will be used for including materials?
   How will materials be displayed?

4. *Providing feedback*
   How will feedback be provided?
   How will the portfolio be evaluated?

FIGURE 8.3   Portfolio Plan

Source: From Mitchell, Abernathy, and Gowans, 1998.

with accompanying sets of questions for literacy portfolios. This approach is reproduced in Figure 8.3.

Teacher–Student Conferences

Conferences are opportunities for students to meet with a teacher and talk about what they are learning. These classroom-support assessments can be time consuming, yet a powerful means of mediating the insights of adolescents who struggle as readers and writers. For reasons ranging from protecting students' privacy and self-esteem to mediating complex understandings particular to individuals, teachers find them one of the most effective contexts for working with adolescents who struggle with reading or writing.

When emphasizing reading, you may ask students to read aloud and discuss the meaning of a short segment of self-selected or assigned material, allowing you to determine their oral reading proficiencies with and attitude toward the material. You may want to note oral reading miscues on a photocopy, using coding systems described for informal reading inventories (Johnson, Pikulski, & Kress, 1987). These markings include such notations as circling omitted words, inserting substituted words or mispronunciations, and underlining repetitions. Remember that the most easily read texts are at least 90 percent decodable, but that this acceptability rate can vary, depending on an individual's interest in or prior knowledge of the material. Conferences then promote reflection on the part of students and teachers about patterns in and numbers of oral reading miscues (Goodman & Marek, 1996). Conferences can also attend to strengths and weaknesses in comprehension of this same passage.

You can confer with individual students as well as with groups, although you must be careful not to embarrass students who struggle as readers and writers in front of peers. Many teachers designate certain students for every other Monday, for every other Tuesday, and so on to ensure that they meet all students regularly. Conferences typically last about 5 minutes per individual and occur while remaining class members are involved with individual tasks such as silent reading, projects, or study guides.

During a reading conference, students might select a few paragraphs to read orally to the teacher, explain why they selected the particular text, and describe how it fits with what was read so far. Some teachers prefer selecting a passage themselves from the portion of text read so far. In some cases, teachers might want to ask a student to read aloud graded lists of words (Fry, Kress, & Fountoukidis, 2000) or a series of leveled passages because a more extensive collection of oral reading miscues makes it easier to discern patterns for teaching. Bear and his colleagues (Bear, Invernizzi, Templeton, & Johnston, 1999) provide a dictated spelling assessment that allows teachers and students to consider in even more detail students' knowledge of such patterns in words. Teachers can also invite students to read aloud and reflect on written work already submitted and scored for high-stakes assessments so that efficient and effective interventions related to these assessments can be developed.

Establishing a consistent focus for the conference across all students promotes trustworthiness in what you learn. During a writing or portfolio conference, students can be prompted systematically with the following inquires: What do you like about this piece? Explain the beginning, middle, and end of this piece. What do you hope to learn more about?

Conferences add a personal, human touch, augmenting the relationship between a teacher and student that is difficult to achieve in pencil-and-paper communications. Conferences can be informal conversations about the general status of what students are reading and writing, or they can be somewhat structured and systematic, centered on what it takes to accomplish something specific: a book being read, a paper being written, a project being completed. Note that collecting consistent data over time in an interactive literacy portfolio provides a basis for discussing growth and needed attention. Be sure to document pertinent comments and information from other contexts that also help individuals consider current status. Follow up this information at later conferences.

Diagnostic Inventories

Diagnostic inventories are informal classroom-based instruments that provide information concerning specific reading and writing competencies. They are diagnostic because they analyze selected aspects of a situation; they are inventories because they itemize situations—they are not used for grading.

As shown in Chapter 5, teachers often have students complete getting-to-know-you exercises during the first few days of school. Our hypothetical teacher had students respond to five questions on the back of a card:

1. How do you feel about reading?
2. What have you enjoyed reading in the past?
3. What does someone have to do to be a good reader?
4. What are you involved in before or after school that might affect your class performance?
5. What can I do to help you improve your reading the most?

Many secondary school teachers have individuals complete more detailed diagnostic reading and writing inventories during class time. Doing so serves several functions:

1. Highlighting literacy as an important feature of the class.
2. Providing a springboard to initiate instruction in needed reading and writing competencies.
3. Bringing students into the assessment process.
4. Screening individuals (identifying those at different ranges of performance, especially those in need of substantial accommodations and adaptations)
5. Starting off the academic semester or year with a businesslike introduction; establishing classroom climate and procedures

A sample beginning-of-the-year diagnostic inventory is presented in Figure 8.4. It addresses four categories of literacy. You might use it as an entry into selected parts of reading instruction in your course. You might invite students to add it to their literacy portfolios and to revisit parts of it during the course.

Grading

Reporting grades for individual students every few weeks is a prominent school practice involving assessment (Marzano, 2000). Grades formally report evaluations of student performance. They carry much official weight, serving as bases for motivation, recognition, graduation, and postsecondary options. Administrators use grades when counseling and placing students into classes, programs, and institutions. When teaching adolescents who struggle as readers, grades count. When designing your grading plan, consider its components, weights, performance norms, and fairness.

1. *Parts of the class text*
   On what page does Chapter 3 begin?
   Where would you look in the text to find the meaning of *paleozoic*?
   What purpose do the annotations on page 68 serve?

2. *Study strategies*
   What do you do when you come to a difficult word in the text?
   What do you do when you come to a difficult section in the text?
   What do you do to help you remember information and ideas?
   How do you prepare for a test?

3. *Writing*
   Pretend you are a park naturalist and describe to a group of tourists the rock strata presented in the figure on page 33.

4. *Attitude and Interest*
   List the last three books you have read.
   Name your favorite authors.
   Have you ever reread a book? If so, name it/them here.
   List what you read other than books.

FIGURE 8.4   Sample Diagnostic Inventory

Components

As with rubrics, design a grading plan that breaks down expectations into meaningful yet manageable components. Simplify the course expectations so students understand what is needed to succeed. Your course expectations might consist of some of the following components:

- Bell work, seat work, daily work, homework
- Classroom activities, special assignments
- Journals, learning logs, lab reports, notebooks, portfolios
- Book response activities
- Inquiry projects, research reports
- Demonstrations, exhibitions, oral reports
- Quizzes, tests, unit exams, final course exams
- Performance on department, school, school district, or statewide assessments

Educators often wrestle over whether to grade students' general academic conduct, which consists of factors such as decorum, work habits, attendance, neatness, and effort. Haladyna (1999) asserts that including general conduct or any of its subdivisions in an overall course grade is "arguable" (p. 46); pros and cons exist. Teachers generally want to promote general academic conduct and reward students who display good conduct. Likewise, employers often report valuing general conduct highly when recruiting and retaining employees, so including it when determining a grade is sensible. Indeed, many secondary teachers regularly grade low-achieving students higher than their performance alone might justify when those students clearly demonstrate positive general academic conduct (McMillan, 2001).

However, high grades might convey a false impression of high academic achievement, producing concerns about grade inflation and social promotion. Assessing general academic conduct also can be quite subjective. The best advice seems to be to include general academic conduct in grading when you are convinced it is justified in your class. But be sure to explain why you are including it, and specify how you will evaluate it. Concrete indicators of work habits and effort, such as bell work and journal entries, are available. Additionally, consider reporting conduct as an entity separate from achievement as countless elementary schools do.

An issue related to grading general academic conduct, that of grading students' class participation, also is arguable. Assessing participation might penalize individuals who prefer remaining quiet during class, and it might stimulate senseless activity. But evaluating the degree to which students are involved with and contributing to ongoing class processes has merit, too. The best advice here seems to be to quantify participation according to concrete indicators that frequently are assessed as pass/fail, such as completed bell work, journal entries, homework, minutes read, and so on. Reasonably completing each task earns points and points translate into certain grades. If oral participation counts, then notify the class that Participation Time is occurring, invite comments equitably, and record instances of appropriate responses.

Components of a grading plan that are not supportable involve students' personal attributes. Avoid grading on the basis of reputation, personality, enthusiasm, communication style, or interpersonal skills. Guard against being influenced by individuals' appearance, height, grooming, and hygiene. Do not determine grades according to how students fit with any overt or covert predispositions toward race, class, gender, ethnicity, or religion.

Finally, students' emotional and motivational needs come into play relative to low grades, especially ones earned early in the semester. Students might despair of achieving success if they receive failing grades before they catch on to course expectations the first few weeks of school. Many teachers acknowledge this by dropping two or three of the lowest grades when computing overall scores. They also guard against assigning zeroes, knowing that such a score statistically skews grades so low that recovery is difficult. If a failing grade is 50 or 60 percent of the total, then recording that percentage might be more appropriate than recording a zero.

Weights

Along with deciding components to be included in a grade, decide the weights for each. Decide relative emphases: what each component is worth and what proportion of the overall grade each represents. For instance, components and their weights in a history class might be as follows:

History Grading Plan

Component	Weight
Tests	30%
Quizzes	20%
Bell work	5%
Book Projects	45%
Total	100%

This history grading plan weights test and quiz performance as half the course grade. It includes bell work, yet assigns it only 5 percent of the grade. A noteworthy emphasis is on book projects. Nearly half the course grade depends on project-based performance involving print.

Now contrast the history grading plan with a plan for a mathematics class:

Mathematics Grading Plan

Component	Weight
Tests	40%
Quizzes	20%
Homework	15%
Class work	20%
Projects	5%
Total	100%

This mathematics plan is similar to the history one in regard to its emphases on tests and quizzes, but it differs substantially with regard to homework, class work, and book projects. Whereas the history plan neglects homework, this plan emphasizes homework, apparently so students regularly practice after school what is presented during class. It also emphasizes class work, apparently so students concentrate on daily assignments done at their seats. It deemphasizes reading projects, thus advertently or inadvertently devaluing literacy.

Performance Norms

Grading plans also depend on your view of appropriate norms of performance. How will you determine success? What constitutes acceptable achievement? Three possible norms for grading follow.

Curriculum-Referenced Norms.   Curriculum-referenced norms compare student performance with uniform-stated guidelines derived from the school curriculum. Rubrics are good illustrations of curriculum-referenced norms because they specify criteria and explain levels of performance relative to each criterion. Additionally, teachers often use students' products from previous classes as models, or anchors, to exemplify various levels of performance. If rubrics are not appropriate, such as when using multiple-choice tests or computing time spent reading, educators still predetermine acceptable performance.

Improvement.   Grades based on improvement involve comparing individuals' current performances to their previous performances. Such a norm evaluates today's performance on the basis of yesterday's performance and determine how much an individual has gained. Rewarding improvement tends to motivate students, and it emphasizes the idea of individuals bettering themselves. However, adolescents' initial performance might be low inadvertently—or purposefully to manipulate the system—so assessing improvement becomes quite complicated.

Class Rank.   Class rank means using relative standing among peers to assign grades. It involves comparisons among students, evaluating individuals according to their position amid the range of performances in class. High, middle, and low standings are determined by one's performance relative to others in class. Problems with using rank are that it varies according to whomever happens to be in class and it pits students against each other rather than an impersonal, particular level of achievement.

Most assessment authorities today advocate curriculum-referenced norms (Cross & Frary, 1999). We agree with this stance, while affirming the value of tweaking such norms when individuals demonstrate irrefutable, noteworthy improvement. Teachers' personal, professional judgments, used sparingly when assigning course grades, deserve recognition.

Fairness

Grading fairly is vital to a successful classroom plan. Educators need to maintain high expectations for all students; they also need to accommodate students' diverse learning styles, preferences, and needs (Thompson, Quenemoen, Thurlow, & Ysseldyke, 2001). Adolescents who struggle as readers and writers in school—like all students—deserve equitable opportunities to obtain high grades. Moreover, students are apt to engage school more fully knowing they have a fair chance to score well despite their reading and writing difficulties. Consider four ways to ensure fairness in your grading practices: using broad samples of achievement, modifying test accommodations, offering opportunities to go the extra mile, and making continued updates.

Broad Samples of Achievement.   Grades based only on tests privilege those who do well with tests. Grades based solely on essays favor good essay writers. Be sure to include multiple measures of student performance when determining grades.

Fair classrooms offer students multiple, alternative ways to demonstrate their learning during the grading period. Grades are based on tests as well as on everyday work products. Daily practice assignments are balanced with independent inquiries. Book responses include oral, written, and artistic options. Teachers direct students to some readings, and students self-select others. Well-rounded sets of opportunities such as these treat diverse students fairly.

Having students collaborate in cooperative groups produces much literacy learning, but assigning group grades to individuals is problematic. Questions of fairness regularly result, with individuals claiming (rightly or wrongly!) that certain industrious members did all the work while slackers avoided it yet reaped unearned grades. The common solution to this situation is to reward collective performance through special recognition and praise, and grade only individual performance. Promote the idea of group members helping each other; assess individuals through test results and what they contributed to specific components of group projects.

Test Accommodations.   A fair way to assess students with special reading and writing needs is to modify test procedures and contents in ways that allow them to demonstrate what they know without punishing them for their disability. Those who are charged with supporting the literacy development of struggling readers and writers may especially want to help classroom teachers consider such accommodations. For instance, students might be offered the following accommodations:

- Test directions given orally and in writing
- As much time as needed
- The test broken down into parts to be taken at different times
- A different test site, away from distractions
- Questions read orally
- Clarifications of the questions
- Alternative readings to react to
- Responses to be recorded on tape or by another person
- Interpreters for clarifying the test and recording responses

Along with these accommodations, fairness is promoted when students conceal their names on tests, using a number or some other way to maintain anonymity. This avoids the possibility of scorers' unintentional biases affecting the evaluations.

Opportunities to Go the Extra Mile.   Grading fairly dictates offering students the chance to continue working until they achieve a measure of success. Extra-credit opportunities are one way to address this. A sensible approach to extra credit is to design a standard task that can connect with every instructional unit. For instance, history teachers accept biographies of individuals who acted during the era being studied. Mathematics teachers have students produce simplified descriptions of problem-solving operations relative to the current topic. Language arts teachers take forms of writing associated with the current unit.

Many teachers accept extra-credit work only when individuals have completed assigned work acceptably. They also limit extra-credit points so students might raise their course grade a predetermined amount, perhaps half a letter grade.

Offering students opportunities to resubmit assignments and retest themselves also enables them to go the extra mile. Resubmissions and retestings are consistent with cognitive learning theory (Bloom, 1976) and the belief that all students can learn but that some require more time than others. This practice fits well with teacher–student and student–student conferences, too. Although retests and resubmissions are excellent in principle, the paperwork they generate in reality is daunting. One reasonable approach entails four steps: (1) students submit final drafts; (2) the teacher grades the drafts according to a rubric, comments on the drafts, and returns them; (3) students revise the drafts according to the teacher's comments and submit new drafts; and (4) if revisions are appropriate, the teacher then enters the original grade in the grade book and gives the rubric to the student along with the final draft.

Continual Updates.   A final way to grade fairly is to ensure that students and those who care for them at home always know their course standing. Continual updates limit any unpleasant or unproductive surprises, and, as previously noted, they promote self-assessment.

School policies for reporting progress might call for grades to go out every 3 weeks, but consider updating students every day. Continual updates are possible when students record and maintain their own progress. They also are possible by posting daily computer-generated spreadsheets. Conferences during class and appointments before and after school promote ongoing dialogue about academic standing. Many teachers automatically contact students' homes when individuals perform below certain levels. More and more schools are putting up websites for teachers to post their grade books online.

Conclusion

Literacy assessments serve many purposes. Classroom-support assessments can represent students' best interests by showing students their strengths as well as what needs improvement. Assessments can help students focus on their learning and self-regulate their progress. Wrapping assessments into a fair grading plan goes far in promoting reading and writing development.

CENTRAL QUESTION: THINK BACK

How are adolescents' reading and writing competencies best evaluated?

To answer fully this chapter's central question, build on the following key concepts:

- Distinguish assessments according to high-stakes and classroom-support uses.
- Employ classroom-support assessments such as (1) rubrics, (2) portfolios, (3) teacher–student conferences, and (4) diagnostic inventories.
- Assign curriculum-referenced course grades.
- Ensure fair grading through (1) broad samples of achievement, (2) test accommodations, (3) opportunities to go the extra mile, and (4) continual updates.

REFERENCES

Amrein, A. L., & Berliner, D. C. (2000). High-stakes testing, uncertainty, and student learning. Education Policy Analysis Archives, 10 (18). Retrieved March 28, 2002 from http://epaa. asu.edu/epaa/v10n18/.

Arter, J., & McTighe, J. (2001). *Scoring rubrics in the classroom: Using performance criteria for assessing and improving student performance.* Thousand Oaks, CA: Corwin.

Bauer, E. B. (1999). The promise of alternative literacy assessments: A review of empirical studies. *Reading Research and Instruction, 38,* 153–168.

Bear, D., Invernizzi, M., Templeton, S., & Johnston, F. (1999). *Words their way: Word study for phonics, vocabulary, and spelling instruction.* Englewood Cliffs, NJ: Prentice-Hall.

Bloom, B. S. (1976). *Human characteristics and school learning.* New York: McGraw-Hill.

Clark, C., Chow-Hoy, T. K., Herter, R. J., & Moss, P. A. (2001). Portfolios as sites of learning: Reconceptualizing the connections to motivation and engagement. *Journal of Literacy Research, 33,* 211–241.

Cross, L. H., & Frary, R. B. (1999). Hodgepodge grading: Endorsed by students and teachers alike. *Applied Measurement in Education, 12*(1), 53–72.

Fry, E., Kress, J., & Fountoukidis, D. (2000). *The reading teachers' book of lists.* New York: Prentice-Hall.

Goodman, Y., & Marek, A. (1996). *Retrospective miscue analysis: Revaluing readers and reading.* Katonah, NY: Richard C. Owen.

Haladyna, T. (1999). *A complete guide to student grading.* Boston: Allyn and Bacon.

Hoffman, J. V., Assaf, L. C., & Paris, S. G. (2001). High stakes testing in reading: Today in Texas, tomorrow? *The Reading Teacher, 54,* 482–492.

International Reading Association (1999). *High-stakes assessments in reading: A position statement of the International Reading Association.* Newark, DE: Author. Retrieved October 10, 2001 from www.reading.org.

Johnson, M., Pikulski, J., & Kress, R. (1987). *Informal reading inventories* (2nd ed.). Newark, DE: International Reading Association.

Kendall, J. S., & Marzano, R. J. (2000). *Content knowledge: A compendium of standards and benchmarks for K–12 education* (3rd ed.). Aurora, CO: Mid-Continent Regional Educational Laboratory. Retrieved September 8, 2001, from www.mcre.org/standards-benchmarks/.

Kohn, A. (2000). *The case against standardized testing: Raising scores, ruining the schools.* Portsmouth, NH: Heinemann.

Langer, J. (2000). Excellence in English in middle and high school: How teachers' professional lives support student achievement. *American Educational Research Journal, 37,* 397–439.

Linn, R. L. (Ed.). (1989). *Educational measurement.* New York: Macmillan

Marzano, R. J. (2000). *Transforming classroom grading.* Alexandria, VA: Association for Supervision and Curriculum Development.

McMillan, J. H. (2001). Secondary teachers' classroom assessment and grading practices. *Educational Measurement: Issues and Practices, 20* (2), 20–32.

McNeil, L. M. (2000). *Contradictions of school reform: Educational costs of standardized testing.* New York: Routledge.

Mitchell, J. P., Abernathy, T. V., & Gowans, L. P. (1998). Making sense of literacy portfolios: A four-step plan. *Journal of Adolescent and Adult Literacy, 41,* 384–386.

Moore, D. W., Bean, T. W., Birdyshaw, D., & Rycik, J. A. (1999). *Adolescent literacy: A position statement.* Newark, DE: International Reading Association, Commission on Adolescent Literacy.

Shepard, L. A. (2000). The role of assessment in a learning culture. *Educational Researcher, 29,* 4–14.

Stiggins, R. J. (1997). *Student-centered classroom assessment.* Upper Saddle River, NJ: Merrill.

Thompson, S. J., Quenemoen, R. F., Thurlow, M. L., & Ysseldyke, J. E. (2001). *Alternate assessments for students with disabilities.* Thousand Oaks, CA: Corwin.

Valencia, S. W., & Wixson, K. K. (2000). Policy-oriented research on literacy standards and assessments. In M. J. Kamil, P. B. Mosenthal, P. D. Pearson, & R. Barr (Eds.), *Handbook of reading research* (Vol. 3, pp. 911–935). Mahwah, NJ: Lawrence Erlbaum.

9

Program Leadership

CENTRAL QUESTION: THINK AHEAD

How can I involve my school administrators and colleagues with literacy?

We frequently hear this question—or one very much like it—after our adolescent literacy staff development and conference presentations. We take it to mean that the workshop and conference attendees accept the idea of directly addressing adolescents' literacies, but they are looking for administrative and collegial support to extend their efforts. They realize the value of comprehensive reading programs.

Comprehensive secondary school reading programs have been recommended since the early 1900s (Moore, Readence, & Rickelman, 1983). Toward the end of the twentieth century, about half the secondary schools in a large survey claimed that they maintain such a program, but about one-fifth said they did so through their special education departments, and about one-tenth noted that no special programs existed (Barry, 2000). The tying of high-stakes literacy assessments to graduation and school funding as part of the accountability movement begun in the 1990s means that this situation is changing. More attention is being paid to comprehensive literacy programs for older students.

This attention is long overdue because, as noted earlier, the National Assessment of Educational Progress reports that reading scores among adolescents have remained virtually unchanged for about 3 decades (Campbell, Hombo, & Mazzeo, 2000). These scores suggest that most U.S. adolescents can read school materials at a basic level. However, far fewer read such materials at the more advanced levels required by the new high-stakes assessments.

At the same time, evolving technologies suggest new literacy competencies of a type that are more likely to be tested by life than by school assessments (New London Group, 1996). Such competencies are far more complex and multidimensional than what is covered on any current assessments. They require flexible communication and problem-solving abilities that can be shifted and shaped to apply to a variety of constantly changing media. Indeed, teenagers have been observed to develop skills, often outside school, that fit the requirements of the new literacies better than anything that is required by school (Gee, 2000).

This chapter explains how to begin and maintain schoolwide programs that promote literacy development among all secondary school students. However, like the rest of this book, this chapter devotes special attention to adolescents who struggle as readers and writers. It details actions for engaging school and school district administrators, as well as teachers and parents, in developing adolescents' literacies.

Beginning a Schoolwide Literacy Program

In 1999 the International Reading Association Board of Directors endorsed a document composed by members of its Adolescent Literacy Commission entitled *Adolescent Literacy: A Position Statement* (Moore, Bean, Birdyshaw, & Rycik, 1999). This position statement contains seven research-based principles that can serve as the basis for adolescent literacy program development. It contends that adolescents deserve the following assistance:

1. Access to a wide variety of reading materials that they can and want to read

2. Instruction that builds both the skill and desire to read increasingly complex materials
3. Assessment that shows them their strengths as well as their needs and that guides teachers to design instruction that will best help them grow as readers
4. Expert teachers who model and provide explicit instruction in reading comprehension and study strategies across the curriculum
5. Reading specialists who assist individual students having difficulty learning how to read
6. Teachers who understand the complexities of individual adolescent readers, respect their differences, and respond to their characteristics
7. Homes, communities, and a nation that support their efforts to achieve advanced levels of literacy and provide the support necessary for them to succeed

This list provides important premises for developing a schoolwide literacy program. These premises likely make great sense to those who agree with the idea that youth are not finished learning to read after having learned to decode letter–sound relationships. Indeed, although readers can develop a certain amount of competence that can be applied across contexts, they do not become literate in a finite way as long as unfamiliar worlds remain on the horizon. This suggests the need for ongoing literacy development for each new context, a need for which those who develop adult workplace literacy programs can attest. Literacy learning is a lifelong process, one in which increasingly flexible and specialized skills are needed for success in specific disciplines and contexts.

However, U.S. middle, junior, and senior high schools usually are orchestrated in ways that focus with increasing intensity on discipline-specific learning as grade levels progress. The structure and focus of secondary schools often precludes the widespread implementation of comprehensive literacy programs (O'Brien, Stewart, & Moje, 1995). In our experience, secondary school structures mitigate against developing strategies for learning content, including those related to reading and writing. When students struggle with assigned reading and writing, teachers often dumb-down their expectations. They use techniques such as factual study guides and tell students what to fill in as the basis for examinations in lieu of teaching students to engage in the in-depth reading and study suggested by literacy theorists, the new high-stakes assessments, and the workplace. Even less attention is paid to the new literacies suggested by our evolving technologies.

Within factually focused settings, some students who struggle as readers and writers receive help that enables them to complete homework that is modified in deference to their difficulties. Some are no longer offered the possibility of extended literacy instruction, and are invited, instead, to participate only in shortsighted vocational training to increase their employability.

Such students are not given the chance to participate in content study with classmates, to have their existing literacies recognized, to succeed with new high-stakes assessments, or, ultimately, to participate in a meaningful way in our increasingly literate society. In addition, better readers and writers are left to their own devices to figure out needed competencies.

Thus, providing adolescents the literacy support services they deserve connotes important schoolwide changes that involve everyone in a school (Buehl, 1998; Moore, in press; Wepner, Strickland, & Feeley, 2002). Such a move cannot be quickly implemented by administrative mandate. Rather, it results from deep study that moves secondary school personnel and the community from blaming the teachers and parents who preceded them. Such a move means assuming responsibility for helping preteens and teens who present themselves at the classroom door extend their literacy skills in new, more complex ways. The move is best led by literacy teams.

Literacy Teams

Secondary schools that have successfully implemented comprehensive literacy programs determine a way to affect change that works for the adolescents and teachers within a particular situation. Collaborative groups form to study the conditions in the school and review approaches that are recommended in the literature on promoting literacy in secondary schools (Anders, 1998). They decide the kind of culture and actions they want to develop in a school, and they set short- and long-term goals to begin to achieve these changes (Anders, Hoffman, & Duffy, 2000).

Who belongs on such a literacy team? Anders and her colleagues suggest that it is best to work with volunteers, that is, members of an instructional staff who are willing to become involved and to consider changing their repertoire in light of a school's literacy-related concerns.

How might one solicit such volunteers? In one model, building administrators and literacy specialists collaborate to discern a few of the most influential, enthusiastic, and effective staff in their building and invite these individuals to a discussion table to plan the program. In another model, a kick-off faculty meeting announcing a building-wide focus might begin with a presentation and discussion of student performance data, gleaned from high-stakes assessments, classroom performance data, and student and teacher anecdotal report. Volunteers are solicited as a result of this discussion.

In either case, Conley (1989) recommends that representatives of various school constituencies be involved on such a team. Reading specialists can contribute expertise and resources. They might take the lead, gathering literacy-related needs of staff and students in a particular building. (For more information about what a reading specialist might do, go to the International Reading Association's website [www.reading.org] and consult the *Roles of a Reading Specialist* position statement by using the home page shortcuts bar.)

Subject-area specialists can give advice regarding reading and writing needs specific to their disciplines. Special education resource teachers can provide advice about students identified as having special learning needs. A guidance counselor and social worker can advocate for emotional and health supports that shape literacy. Students can represent their points of view, especially at the high school level. It is critical that administrators approve of and be part of such a team because they are likely to have the broadest sense of available resources and needs that can be brought to bear on literacy-related concerns. Finally, business, community, and family members might be included.

Members of this team study assessment data and consider the available literature on adolescent literacy in a systematic, self-critical way, perhaps beginning with this text and the aforementioned position statement from IRA. They discuss short- and long-term goals for the entire school population and lay out a plan of action for the building that includes all the program components noted in this chapter. They meet consistently, on a long-term basis, so results can be gauged and used as a basis for refining plans and goals.

Setting Goals

Think back to the Four Ps presented in Chapter 1. One item, purpose, is as important for a comprehensive reading program as it is for a class or an instructional unit. When referring to a program's purpose, we use the more common term *goal.*

A good overall goal for a schoolwide comprehensive literacy program is to ensure that adolescents develop the communicative skills they need to succeed in and improve the changing world. This overall goal could encompass the metaphors for reading presented in Chapter 1 as well as the four resources model described in Chapter 6, ensuring that students learn to extend their competencies through multiple roles and in varieties of oral, written, and multimediated academic and nonacademic contexts.

Articulating attainable short-term goals and objectives suitable to a specific school context and particular grades is critical to a comprehensive program's success. Such goals should consider the needs of readers and writers of varying skills as well as which teachers are most likely to be willing to begin implementation. Worthwhile goals will address students' development of the strategic literacy practices needed across the disciplines. In addition, they will consider forging connections between in-school academic literacies and such out-of-school literacies as zines and lyrics reading, instant messaging, or even graffiti writing (Fabos, 2000; Finders, 1996; Moje, 2000b).

Such short-term goals should be concerned with students' performance on high-stakes state assessments and college entrance examinations in some kind of reasonable way. Thus, if most of the students in a particular school district usually score 1200 or above on their SATs, a goal for a high school literacy program might be to maintain this performance while paying more attention to development of computer-related or other out-of-school literacies. However, if students are struggling to pass the high-stakes language arts assessment required for high school graduation, then a high school will want to focus on developing strategic reading and writing in a variety of contexts.

As Conley (1989) points out, young adolescents differ from older adolescents. They need help making the transition from elementary school to the rigors of discipline-specific study. Middle school goals should address expectations that adolescents perform adequately on assessments as well as help them develop the discipline-specific literacy skills of academic and out-of-school contexts.

Most states have determined specific expectations for language arts development pursuant to grade levels. Clearly, a literacy team in any school will want to develop goals and objectives congruent with their state's requirements for particular grade levels. For instance, students in New York State are expected to achieve four standards, the first of which is that students will read, write, speak, and listen for information and understanding. Expected performances relative to this and other standards are then delineated (e.g., locating and using school and public library resources independently to acquire information; applying thinking skills such as defining, classifying, and inferring to interpret data, facts, and ideas from informational texts). Students are expected to meet these standards as they read a minimum of 25 books or the equivalent per year across all content areas and standards, write at least 1,000 words per month, and listen and speak on a daily basis (www.nysed.gov/ciai/pub.html#cat2).

To be practical, short-term goals will take into account what is actually tested on local and state assessments (Langer, 2000). Such assessments are designed for congruence with state standards. At the same time, they require particular types of tasks and scoring criteria that can be helpful for teachers and their students to review, practice, and even critique prior to sitting for examination.

As stated in Chapter 6, one teacher aptly described such work to Kathy as "assessment literacy." This teacher noted that she, like many other teachers, incorporated testlike tasks into her instructional routine to prepare students for what was to be included on tests. She observed that this task became much easier once she had participated on the scoring teams for these tests. She learned to consider in detail the ways in which students interpret typical tasks.

This teacher's cautions about this approach, however, agree with our own. One wouldn't want to set all one's goals around testing tasks, or one would be presenting a limited view of literacy, as is argued well by the national professional organizations cited in Chapter 7 (see Table 7.2). Students can be invited to understand and critique the assessment program so that they knowingly approach testing occasions, making good choices about how to represent themselves. They can be taught to take tests strategically and confidently as presented in Chapter 4. Without such opportunities to mediate students' perceptions toward testing, one risks being surprised and heartbroken by the eighth grader Kathy observed, who became frustrated and embarrassed during one test, walking out of the room, mumbling, "F— New York State," and never returning to school.

The literacy team should be clear to set reasonable short-term goals for the entire range of adolescent literacy learners in all school contexts. Some adolescent readers and writers struggle with reaching desired proficiency with academic literacy tasks and exit examinations. Programs must set reasonable goals for these teenagers, with programming based on achievable and success-oriented steps that make explicit progress toward defined and increased proficiency. They must discern and make the most of all students' existing academic and nonacademic competencies.

Goal setters should survey teachers, students, parents, and community members about the range of adolescents' reading skills and needs. A literacy team might consider a literacy model as a base, such as Luke and Freebody's (1999) four resources model, and survey constituents to ask whether and how students should be able to demonstrate particular competencies relative to each area of the model. The literacy team can then consider results as they use the model to determine appropriate courses of action for staff and students in a particular building.

The literacy team also will want to consider carefully how to express goals and objectives, perhaps following a well-tested curriculum development model, such as *Dimensions of Learning* (Marzano, et al., 1997) and *Understanding by Design* (Wiggins & McTighe, 2000). It can seem as though wording and structuring goals and objectives is a form of whistling in the wind when real action is needed in the face of struggling teenaged readers and writers. But our experience has been that such discussions are quite beneficial. They provide a structured way for collaborators to merge multiple perspectives and to proceed from study group to action. At the same time, any articulation of goals and objectives should be considered a work in progress, a draft awaiting revision pending results of evaluation or new ways of thinking about literacy that is required of students. Ongoing revisions should be scheduled accordingly.

Involving Staff

Like any profession, secondary school teachers and administrators have various strengths. Some conceptualize content knowledge excellently. Others have amazing rapport with adolescents. Some are good at supporting the instructional development of colleagues. Still others can do several of the preceding things with reasonable facility. All go to work each day intending to perform well in a very complex setting. This is the place to begin a literacy-related initiative.

Because of day-to-day struggles with adolescents' varying needs, all secondary school teachers and administrators have thought long and hard about literacy, despite the fact that some may look more successful than others. Secondary school reading programs work best when personnel participate in ways that respect their perspective (Vacca, 1989).

Administrators clearly should be involved in all aspects of a schoolwide literacy program, although leadership may come from an administrator or literacy specialist with the help of the literacy team. It may then be tempting to mandate all teachers' participation in a schoolwide literacy program. However, research suggests that beginning with volunteers is best (Anders, et al., 2000). The volunteer pool will build as teachers begin to see that pedagogical ideas make a difference in colleagues' classrooms.

Volunteers might come from one cross subject–area team to address literacy-related teaching strategies. Conversely, it might be helpful to have a team of teachers within a specific subject area such as science or social studies to initiate study and support together. The literacy team should decide on an approach that's right for their situation, and they should be certain that they have willing participants.

Many teachers also have experiences with previous literacy-related initiatives. For instance, at some point in their careers, many teachers took classes or participated in staff development in something called "content-area reading." Others have taken methods classes in which literacy strategies are promoted. Thus, any invitation for teachers to rework their teaching with more attention to literacy practices should be made with an awareness of teachers' previous experiences in this area. Any approach used has to appreciate and be willing to bend in the face of these individuals' insights.

A study group approach, presented in Chapter 7, is a productive partnering way to begin implementing a comprehensive literacy program. In this approach, teachers read texts or articles and create a plan for implementing the ideas in the readings after much study and discussion. They talk to colleagues about their particular students and required content, and they determine most appropriate applications for ideas that are provided. They also can elicit feedback from their colleagues or from an outside consultant so they can refine their use.

Some prepared staff development programs, such as Creating Independence through Student-Owned Strategies (www.project criss.org) and the Strategic Literacy Initiative (www.WestEd.org/stratlit), recommend coaches as partners for teachers trying to implement recommended strategies. Absent these coaches from a home-grown program, teachers from the literacy team and other study group teachers can be invited to observe or teach together. They can then use their enhanced understanding of a particular classroom context to offer suggestions for optimum implementation.

Of course, to be effective, coaches need to think about finding something to praise in each observed lesson. Effective coaches also begin by asking teachers with whom they work which concerns they most want to address prior to raising their own concerns for the teachers' implementation. If left to their own critiques because a teacher doesn't ask for advice, effective coaches focus on improving one area at a time so as not to overwhelm their colleagues. Coaches should talk as they would want others to talk with them—with humor, insight, and respect for their partners' expertise.

Creating a Culture

Respect and enthusiasm for adolescents' beliefs, concerns, and literacies permeate the culture of a school that is committed to improving adolescent literacy. Even if programming itself begins with a small pool of volunteer staff, the school must be convinced of the need to focus on literacy development. Some schools name and publicize their programs with posters and other public relations efforts. Others choose acronyms to represent selected strategy emphases and use these across classrooms. A literacy focus is apparent to all throughout a building.

Central to this focus is that teachers and administrators understand adolescents' existing literacies and the importance of these to adolescents' identity work (Gee, 2000). School staff learn to respect and understand adolescents' experiences and life choices, even those that do not match their own preferences for action. They are flexible and adjust their teaching in the face of teenagers' knowing insights about literacies required in the new millennium. They gently uncover adolescents' insights and competencies related to these experiences. They celebrate students' accomplishments in and out of school. They invite students to develop existing competencies.

Shared building-wide commitment to literacy goals is an essential feature of successful adolescent literacy programs (Davidson & Koppenhaver, 1993). For instance, if goals and objectives suggest that all students demonstrate understanding of important reading comprehension strategies (Fielding & Pearson, 1994), then staff orchestrate a plan whereby they emphasize particular aspects in each possible setting across the curriculum. Teachers read and study various recommendations for such instruction, searching professional journals and sharing relevant articles with one another. They talk to each other about difficulties in initial implementation of recommendations. Finally, they reconsider and redesign approaches in light of student outcomes.

A school system must make a commitment to ongoing literacy in-service education for staff members who work with adolescents. Anders and her colleagues (2000) describe characteristics of successful literacy-related in-service development. Sustained intensive commitment and support is essential. Volunteers seem to be the best at implementing any new approach.

Follow-up monitoring and coaching regarding key features of a particular instructional model can also be quite helpful.

Providing teachers time and incentive to reflect on the successes and areas for improvement in their literacy teaching has also been suggested throughout the literature on literacy staff development. Conversation and negotiation are also helpful features of successful change programs. Collaboration among different categories of staff and use of outside consultants, such as university professors or literacy coordinators from other schools, have been helpful in many literacy development projects.

Structures for Schoolwide Literacy Improvement

We hope the preceding section clarifies the idea that schoolwide comprehensive attention to all adolescents' literacy development is essential if a school is to develop an effective adolescent literacy program. Even students who appear to be successful need to develop a sense of participation in increasingly complex discipline-specific discourse communities. Others may need support with more basic aspects of reading and writing. All adolescents can benefit from extending nonacademic and academic literacies for postgraduation independence.

To provide such wide-ranging services, strong leadership involves classrooms across the curriculum and throughout the school. Literacy instruction occurs across the curriculum and in special academic literacy classes, staffed by literacy specialists, to help students develop and apply a generalized sense of important literacy practices. Intervention services, staffed by literacy specialists, address the needs of students who struggle as readers and writers. Resource support can be offered to students whose special needs are tied to an identified learning disability. Extension services can be developed for those adolescents whose literacy-related proclivity reflects out-of-school interests.

Literacy across the Curriculum

As Chapter 7 noted in the section on school structures, teachers across the curriculum should be encouraged to see their work as central to students' academic literacy development. After all, successful secondary school students actually join the discipline-specific language communities represented by the sciences, mathematics, and the social sciences, among others.

Kathy gained much insight into the nature of subject-specific discourse communities during a research collaboration with Patricia Zalewski, a tenth-grade global studies teacher (Hinchman & Zalewski, 2000). Pat's students told how they understood Pat during lectures, but that when she gives them a test or quiz, "she puts all these words in it" (p. 193). From this disclosure, we realized that we have to invite students to learn the language of her course, in the manner that Lemke describes literacy practices particular to *Talking Science* (see Lemke, 1990). Principles of language acquisition (e.g., immersion, modeling, experimentation, wide exposure, need) have come to seem more useful to us as a basis for planning instruction than principles of knowledge acquisition (e.g., reading texts and listening to lectures to learn facts for tests).

Once we figured this out, Pat worked with her colleagues to organize instruction with less lecture and reading as a safety net and more language immersion through inquiry. Her approach was consistent with suggestions by Moje (2000a) to invite students to participate in collaborative work as they read and reviewed multiple texts from multiple perspectives as well as in project-based teaching involving gathering, reporting, consolidating, and critiquing new information in pursuit of answers to critical questions. They implemented systematic use of daily learning logs. Assessment portfolios included more extensive discourse as well as reflection on discourse development, including bibliographies, selections from logs, writing samples, projects, and reflective pieces, shared via quarterly conferences, consistent with suggestions by Young, Mathews, Kietzmann, and Westerfield (2000).

Such approaches to instruction in discipline-specific study invite students with a wide range of reading and writing skills to participate in collecting, discussing, and analyzing information from a variety of perspectives. Even less-able readers contribute by looking things up in available and more easily read reference texts. All students can bring their out-of-school Internet research strengths to bear on such work. By helping each other in cooperative groups, students provide models to each other of their varying strengths in reading and writing. In such a setting, teachers can more easily modify expectations given students' varied skills. Teachers can also more easily observe needs for instruction and provide groups of students with mini-lessons so they develop the skills they need to proceed with their work.

Some secondary schools decide to emphasize reading for meaning and take a BDA (i.e., before, during, and after) reading approach to supporting students' work (Moore, Moore, Cunningham, & Cunningham, in press; Vacca & Vacca, 1998). They scaffold students' collaborative completion of activities such as anticipation guides, vocabulary development activities, graphic organizers, and study guides for finding and critique information in texts. They support students' writing with graphic organizers and other strategies described elsewhere in this text. Other schools demonstrate and reinforce a single, comprehensive strategic approach across classrooms, such as the predicting–questioning–summarizing–clarifying cycle of reciprocal teaching.

Academic Literacy Development Classes

Academic literacy classes are specific courses, separate from others, required of all students. Such classes typically are offered once in middle school and possibly again in the first year of high school. These classes come from a tradition of offering separate study skills classes to focus students' attention on reading-to-learn strategies. The classes are meant to set the stage for students' application of literacy strategies across the curriculum. To be sure, the skills presented in such classes are more likely applied in subject-area classes when the strategies are reinforced by subject-area teachers.

Separate academic literacy classes give students a chance for learning and developing competencies as well as provide a forum for discussing applications across classrooms and outside school. As with content-area literacy approaches, some classes emphasize strategies for time management, vocabulary development, BDA reading, writing, study, lecture note taking, and test taking. Others promote a single, overarching approach, such as reciprocal teaching.

Table 9.1 presents a list of topics covered in a traditional academic literacy class. For instance, students may be asked to organize a variety of materials received in a 6-week unit and implement a study schedule for a particular unit test or project. They may also learn to use context clues, structural analysis, and library resource materials to determine meanings for unknown words as well as engage in study of word parts needed for structural analysis. They may practice strategies such as prediction, previewing, scanning, and skimming as possible before-reading activities.

Students in these classes may also practice reading by segment, asking questions, and summarizing and clarifying the information contained in each segment. They might practice critiquing—recognizing how texts are positioned relative to other possible views of content being studied. Students might also learn split-page methods of taking lecture notes and practice with videotapes of teachers from their other classes.

Students might also be encouraged to develop the library research and note-taking strategies needed to write a research paper. They also need various organizational strategies, such as collecting notes, brainstorming, and webbing for writing other kinds of reports. Finally, students might learn study techniques, such as repetition and use of mnemonic devices, as well as test-taking techniques used for objective and subjective tests (e.g., reading over the test and setting a pace before beginning; always guessing T on true/false tests or B on multiple-choice tests).

A variation on the traditional academic literacy class is to embed reading and writing instruction in units that address uses of literacy (Schoenbach, Greenleaf, Cziko, & Hurwitz, 1999). For instance, students might participate in units that inquire into reading the self, reading society, reading the media, and reading history. Some secondary schools have discovered that drop-in learning centers support well the work begun in academic literacy and literacy-across-the-curriculum settings (Vacca, 1989). These classrooms are staffed by a literacy specialist, volunteer students, or community tutors (Rekrut, 2000). They serve as settings in which students can stop by for extra

TABLE 9.1   Sample Academic Literacy Class Topics

Class Orientation
Mission, connecting with academics, rules and procedures

Assessing One's Own Literacy
Survey of reading interests, habits, styles, strengths, and limitations

Reading Self-Selected Material
Locating and assessing books, setting aside times and places, reflecting on reading alone and with others

Learning How to Learn
Note taking, graphic organizing, reciprocal teaching (predict, summarize, clarify, question)

Analyzing Words
Context, morphemes (prefixes, roots, suffixes), external references (dictionary, glossary, annotations), syllabication

Recognizing Genres
Discerning the structure and style of different types of texts (narrative fiction, online home pages; assembly directions, poetry), adjusting to the situation

Interpreting Pictorial Aids
Understanding tables, graphs, charts, maps, and other text enhancements

Taking Tests
Preparing for tests, performing strategically and confidently

Conducting Research
Forming researchable questions, locating and synthesizing information, interviewing people, reporting findings

Analyzing the Media
Critically evaluating advertisements, entertainment, news reports, and legally binding documents.

support for completing the reading and study associated with particular subject-area study. Teachers who staff such classrooms become proficient in learning other teachers' expectations and mediate students' understanding accordingly. Finally, school success courses, such as the one described in Chapter 7, are another way to support literacy in a separate class outside the subject areas.

Intervention Services

During our many years of teaching literacy education classes in teacher preparation programs, we have heard many stories about young adolescents who seem interested in reading newspapers and song lyrics but whose teachers argue that these students will never learn to read, so teachers can't waste these students' time on literacy instruction. These teachers had given up on them! Similarly, we have heard of teenagers not willing to open even the cover of a textbook for selective scanning because they were waiting for the audiotape from the school district office. These students had given up on having even minimal access to the world of print! Either students' diagnosis of learning disabled or research suggesting that the most beneficial literacy interventions occur before grade 3 (Allington, 2001) had resulted in some students and teachers giving up on those who hadn't learned to read and write well by third grade!

We are unwilling to give up on those who struggle as readers and writers in adolescence. We have seen too many individual success stories among both teens and adults. Indeed, we feel that we owe even greater energy to helping older individuals develop literacy practices they will need as adults. Put another way, some struggling adolescent readers and writers continue to need basic reading and writing instruction. Secondary school is certainly not the place to give up on this effort!

Intervention services, as Chapter 6 describes, come into students' lives to alleviate difficulties. These services are difficult to fit into the busy, content-oriented schedule of secondary schools. Badly taught, they can create great cynicism in students (Nelson & Herber, 1982). Nonetheless, when adolescents do not read and write as well as they need to, such services can be essential to their survival in academic settings and in the world outside school. Intervention also may be the only way to invite some adolescents to the successes afforded by the new high-stakes assessments.

Students who need such services generally struggle in their academic course work. They often have difficulty with particular out-of-school literacy tasks. Intervention services can provide the extra boost of reading and writing insight that is more easily understood by adolescent readers and writers who are nearing adulthood.

The value of push in interventions—services that occur within the context of regular instruction across the curriculum (Barry, 2000)—is arguable for adolescents who struggle greatly with reading. It has been argued that such an approach is the best way to ensure that students get instruction they can then apply in their subject-area classes. This may be an appropriate way to orchestrate interventions if the instruction students need is provided using texts that serve them well in the regular class context. Push in instruction may provide students with the metacognitive insights needed to comprehend required class reading (Keene & Zimmerman, 1997).

However, some adolescents need more explanation than what can be gained from a classroom in which the focus is on learning subject-area material. They need an opportunity to build fluency by working with those out-of-school literacies with which they are most comfortable. According to Chapter

6, they need to spend time looking up information on the Internet and emailing other adolescents about what they find, with information that is of high interest, whether it includes song lyrics, car racing, basketball, or other out-of-school interests. They might also need instruction in strategies that help them figure out common words they do not know. Such approaches often do not fit easily into science, social studies, or even English classes. Ultimately students may feel more included in the larger school and world context if someone privately helps them develop some of the literacy practices they desire to develop.

In some schools, only a few adolescents need intervention services. However, in some schools marked with poverty, transience, and low expectations for literacy, many more teenagers need intervention support. They need reading and writing instruction that helps them more fluently approach their work in the multiple genres of discipline-specific study.

If only a few students need intervention, scheduling can sometimes be arranged during the school day. But when the number of students needing services is larger, an extended-day program might be a more appropriate setting. Such an approach should be carefully considered if it interferes with teens' abilities to work part time, as this can be a serious problem for some students.

Referring for literacy intervention everyone who struggles in a subject-area class—without having a clear sense that students' difficulties primarily lie with literacy-related needs—is counterproductive. It creates a negative intervention context that fails to allow literacy specialists to provide the differentiated responsive instruction described in Chapter 6. Instead, such programming yields classrooms that are wholly uncomfortable for struggling readers and writers.

A better practice is to consider the school's literacy goals and objectives for all students and how the intervention program fits these needs. The literacy team should ask itself which students can be best helped within the context of regular classroom subject-area instruction and an academic literacy class, and which students need literacy intervention. When students experience difficulty from lack of organizational skills or problems controlling behavior, then these needs can be addressed in other ways.

The literacy team should also determine which benchmarks qualify a struggling reader or writer for intervention services, and stick to those criteria. If misidentified students, or too many students, end up receiving services, then the literacy team should adjust the criteria for participation. Usually, interventions are provided to those readers and writers who are least likely to perform adequately on high-stakes assessment. These students are likely to struggle with basic skills such as decoding, fluency, basic comprehension, or the mechanical aspects of essay composition.

The smaller the intervention class size is, the more likely that a teacher will be able to provide appropriate responsive interventions. One teacher at a presentation looked Kathy directly in the eye and noted that she really could not do very much with the 15 adolescent nonreaders who had been assigned to one class because they all needed different kinds of literacy instruction. She had a point. No absolute number can be assigned here, but the difficulties faced by the students should be considered when decisions are made about whom and how many to enroll in a particular intervention class.

Resource Support

Resource teachers are scheduled to support classroom teachers and students in subject matter classrooms rather than proctor entire classes of students. Resource teachers should be integrally involved in the schoolwide comprehensive literacy program because a large percentage of students identified as having special needs have difficulties with reading and writing. Resource teachers should work closely with literacy specialists and English teachers to determine who has the expertise to extend these students' academic and nonacademic literacy practices.

Resource teachers can help subject-area teachers help students who may otherwise struggle with reading and writing to participate in and benefit from subject-area literacy activities. Subject-area teachers can invite discipline-specific inquiry of a central question, involving reading and writing in multi-leveled, multiperspectived texts. Resource teachers can offer an extra pair of hands during such project-based teaching (Moje, 2000a), helping all students with their research and reporting via responsive minilessons and tutorials planned in collaboration with watchful subject-area teachers.

It may also be helpful for resource teachers to work with subject-area specialists to determine ways to modify assignments suited to the needs of students who struggle with reading. For instance, some struggling readers may be better off scanning the headings, introduction, and conclusion of an assigned chapter, and then reading from another printed or electronic information source to enhance their insights related to an assigned topic. Some readers might benefit from reading along with a volunteer-made audiotape of a particular reading selection or a segment of a reading selection. Other readers may be helped to review assigned reading in pairs, so that students can work through segments of text together, vocalizing their implementation of recommended text-reading strategies as they work. Still other readers may need to have tests or assignments read to them.

Similarly, some writers may need to complete fewer, more closely teacher-mediated writing assignments. Having a teacher or other writing partner help with initial brainstorming and webbing of ideas for an essay can be invaluable to students who suffer from writing dysfluency. Other students may need to learn to dictate essays into a computer for revision and editing. Resource teachers can be excellent facilitators of such modifications, meant to include struggling readers and writers in regular classroom instruction.

Resource teachers who work with struggling readers and writers should remember that a fine line exists between offering scaffolding and doing the actual work for students; the latter is inappropriate. Kathy knew one misguided individual who photocopied completed study guides, inviting her charges to fill in their names before submitting the sheets to their teachers for credit. Resource teachers also should be careful to not give students unfair advantage as they read test items for them.

Resource teachers advocate for students who are identified as having special needs. They ensure that the students are getting the kind of instruction they need to improve their literacy practices sufficiently. Because of secondary school scheduling dilemmas, it may be tempting to suggest that struggling readers and writers receive only enough instruction in reading and writing to help them complete their subject-area homework. This might be possible when students struggle with reading comprehension or difficulties in writing answers to essay questions. However, this may not be the most effective or efficient way to help adolescents who need to learn strategies for decoding multisyllabic words, for comprehending multiple text types or for basic writing mechanics. Individual student needs must be considered and decisions made accordingly.

Out-of-School Extensions

As Chapter 7 showed, community volunteers can serve as reading buddies and role models for students who struggle with reading. Those who are trained as volunteers also can serve as tutors, with a teacher's supervision. The Literacy Volunteers of America (www.literacyvolunteers.org) training provides volunteers with reasonable ideas for approaching decoding, vocabulary, comprehension, and composition instruction for older students that can be quite effective with adolescents who are working at basic levels.

Some adolescents have developed their most effective literacy practices in out-of-school settings. These teenagers can be helped to continue to develop these skills within the contexts of internships and after-school programs. Special programs that encourage students to read, write, and reflect on out-of-school interests can be especially motivating.

It is important that out-of-school literacy practices not be appropriated by school to develop academic literacy. For instance, it is not appropriate to teach critical literacy skills with critiques of magazines and paperbacks that bring adolescents pleasure. Such actions can serve to drive reluctant academicians further underground in search of meaningful, independent identity work (Alvermann, Moon, & Hagood, 1999). At the same time, teachers who understand adolescents' out-of-school literacies can help to extend them in important ways, locating newspaper music or book reviews or organizing special interest clubs.

Conclusion

Comprehensive reading programs encourage the development of successful literacy practices by all adolescents, paying special attention to those who struggle with reading and writing. Developing such programs involves literacy teams, setting goals, involving all staff, and creating the right culture. The structure of such programs includes attention to literacy across the curriculum, academic literacy classes, intervention services, resource support, and out-of-school extensions. With attention to careful planning and respect across all involved staff, such a program results in more successful literacy practices by all involved adolescents, in and out of school.

CENTRAL QUESTION: THINK BACK

How can I involve my school administrators and colleagues with literacy?

To answer fully this chapter's central question, build on the following key concepts:

- Begin a schoolwide reading program that includes (1) assembling a literacy team, (2) setting goals, (3) involving staff, and (4) creating a culture.
- Provide structures for schoolwide literacy improvement that include (1) literacy across the curriculum, (2) academic literacy development classes, (3) intervention services, (4) resource support, and (5) out-of-school extensions.

REFERENCES

Allington, R. L. (2001). *What really matters for struggling readers: Designing research-based programs.* New York: Longman.

Alvermann, D. E., Moon, J., & Hagood, M. (1999). *Popular culture in the classroom: Teaching and researching critical media literacy.* Newark, DE: International Reading Association.

Anders, P. (1998). The literacy council: People are the key to an effective program. *NASSP Bulletin, 82*(600), 16–23.

Anders, P. L., Hoffman, J. V., & Duffy, G. G. (2000). Teaching teachers to teach reading: Paradigm shifts, persistent problems, and challenges. In M. L. Kamil, P. B. Mosenthal, P. D. Pearson, & R. Barr (Eds.), *Handbook of reading research* (vol. 3, pp. 719–742). Mahwah, NJ: Erlbaum.

Barry, A. (2000). High school reading programs revisited. In D. W. Moore, D. E. Alvermann, & K. A. Hinchman (Eds.), *Struggling adolescent readers: A collection of strategies* (pp. 317–325). Newark, DE: International Reading Association.

Buehl, D. (1998). Integrating the "R" word into the high school curriculum: Developing reading programs for adolescent learners. *NASSP Bulletin, 82*(600), 57–66.

Campbell, J. R., Hombo, C. M., & Mazzeo, J. (2000). *Trends in academic progress: Three decades of student performance* (NCES No. 2000–469). Washington, DC: US Department of Education, Office of Educational Research and Improvement, National Center for Education Statistics. Retrieved from www.ed.gov/NCES/NAEP.

Conley, M. W. (1989). Middle school and junior high reading programs. In S. B. Wepner, J. T. Feeley, & D. S. Strickland (Eds.), *The administration and supervision of reading programs* (pp. 76–92). Newark, DE: International Reading Association.

Davidson, J., & Koppenhaver, D. (1993). *Adolescent literacy: What works and why* (2nd ed.). New York: Garland.

Fabos, B. (2000). Zap me! Zaps you. *Journal of Adolescent and Adult Literacy, 43,* 720.

Fielding, L., & Pearson, P. D. (1994). Synthesis of reading comprehension research: What works. *Educational Leadership, 51,* 62.

Finders, M. (1996). *Just girls: Hidden literacies and life in junior high.* New York: Teachers College Press.

Gee, J. P. (2000). New people in new worlds: Networks, the new capitalism, and schools. In B. Cope & M. Kalantzis (Eds.), *Multiliteracies: Literacy learning and the design of social futures* (pp. 43–68). New York: Routledge.

Hinchman, K. A., & Zalewski, P. (2000). "She puts all these words in it": Language learning for two students in tenth-grade social studies. In E. B. Moje & D. G. O'Brien, (Eds.), *Constructions of literacy: Studies of teaching and learning in and out of secondary schools* (pp. 193–212). Mahwah, NJ: Lawrence Erlbaum.

Keene, E. O., & Zimmerman, S. (1997). *Mosaic of thought: Teaching comprehension in a reader's workshop.* Portsmouth, NH: Heinemann.

Langer, J. (2000). Excellence in English in middle and high school: How teachers' professional lives support student achievement. *American Educational Research Journal, 37*(2), 397–439.

Lemke, J. L. (1990). *Talking science: Language, learning and values.* New York: Ablex.

Luke, A., & Freebody, P. (1999). A map of possible practices: Further notes on the four resources model. *Practically Primary, 4.* Retrieved January 15, 2001, from http://www.alea.edu.au/freebody.htm.

Marzano, R., Pickering, D., Arredondo, D., Blackburn, G., Brandt, R., Moffett, C., et al., (1997). *Dimensions of learning teacher's manual* (2nd ed.). Alexandria, VA: Association for Supervision and Curriculum Development.

Moje, E. (2000a). *Adolescents' insights about literacy and learning in secondary schools.* Newark, DE: International Reading Association.

Moje, E. (2000b). "To be part of the story": The literacy practices or gangsta adolescents. *Teachers College Record, 102,* 651–690.

Moore, D. W. (in press). Secondary school reading programs. In B. Guzzetti (Ed.), *Literacy in America: An encyclopedia.* New York: ABC-CLIO.

Moore, D. W., Bean, T. W., Birdyshaw, D., & Rycik, J. A. (1999). *Adolescent literacy: A position statement.* Newark, DE: International Reading Association, Commission on Adolescent Literacy.

Moore, D. W., Moore, S. A., Cunningham, P., & Cunningham, J. (in press). *Developing readers and writers in the content areas, K–12* (4th ed.). New York: Longman.

Moore, D. W., Readence, J. E., & Rickelman, R. (1983). An historical exploration of content area reading instruction. *Reading Research Quarterly, 18,* 419–438.

Nelson, J., & Herber, H. L. (1982). Organization and management of programs. In A. Berger & H. L. Robinson (Eds.), *Secondary school reading: What research reveals for classroom practice* (pp. 143–158). Urbana, IL: ERIC Clearinghouse on Reading and Communication Skills and the National Council of Teachers of English.

New London Group. (1996). A pedagogy of multiliteracies: Designing social futures. *Harvard Educational Review 66,* 60–92.

O'Brien, D., Stewart, R., & Moje, E. (1995). Why content literacy is difficult to infuse into the secondary school: Complexities of curriculum, pedagogy, and school culture. *Reading Research Quarterly, 30,* 442.

Rekrut, M. D. (2000). Peer and cross-age tutoring: The lessons of research. In D. W. Moore, D. E. Alvermann, & K. A. Hinchman (Eds.), *Struggling adolescent readers: A collection of teaching strategies* (pp. 290–295). Newark, DE: International Reading Association.

Schoenbach, R., Greenleaf, C., Cziko, C., & Hurwitz, L. (1999). *Reading for understanding: A guide to improving reading in middle and high school classrooms.* San Francisco: Jossey-Bass.

Wepner, S. B., Strickland, D. S., & Feeley, J. T. (2002). *The administration and supervision of reading programs* (3rd ed.). Newark, DE: International Reading Association.

Wiggins, G., & McTighe, J. (2000). *Understanding by design.* Alexandria, VA: Association for Supervision and Curriculum Development.

Vacca, R. T. (1989). High school reading programs: Out of the past and into the future. In S. B. Wepner, J. T. Feeley, & D. S. Strickland (Eds.),

The administration and supervision of reading programs (pp. 93–105). Newark, DE: International Reading Association.

Vacca, R. T., & Vacca, J. (1998). *Content area reading: Literacy and learning across the curriculum.* Glenview, IL: Addison Wesley.

Young, J. P., Mathews, S. R., Kietsmann, A. M., & Westerfield, T. (2000). Getting disenchanted adolescents to participate in school literacy activities: Portfolio conferences. In D. W. Moore, D. E. Alvermann, & K. A. Hinchman (Eds.), *Struggling adolescent readers: A collection of teaching strategies* (pp. 302–316). Newark, DE: International Reading Association.

CHAPTER

10 Program Profiles

CENTRAL QUESTION: THINK AHEAD

*Where can I learn about specific reading programs and resources
that our school system might adopt?*

Not long ago a school district administrator telephoned Kathy with a
concern. His district's reading test scores were far less than satisfactory,
and upcoming subject matter tests, which relied on reading, promised
to yield similar results. The state was threatening to place at least one
of his secondary schools on probation because of low scores.

This administrator noted the limitations of evaluating his system on
the basis of a single assessment, but he reported that teacher dissatisfaction

as well as complaints from alumni, the community, employers, and post-secondary schools confirmed his system's need for literacy-based reforms. He wanted to help all readers and writers, but he was especially concerned about those who were struggling with academic reading and writing. He wanted to examine the adolescent literacy marketplace of ideas and products.

The more administrators inquire into programs for improving adolescent literacy, the more they tend to realize, as Allington and Walmsley assert in their 1995 text, "There is no quick fix!" Developing a comprehensive program, as presented in Chapter 9, is the best course of action. This chapter highlights resources that educators might find useful when producing comprehensive adolescent literacy programs. It profiles current selected resources.

We should note at the outset that our inclusion of any particular resource certainly does not mean that we endorse it. Our answer to the question, What works? always begins with the disclaimer, It depends. Teaching adolescents who struggle as readers in any setting, inside or outside school, is complex. We do not know of any magic potion to simplify these complexities. Indeed, we found no single set of instructional recommendations or packaged materials that constitute a comprehensive literacy program applicable to every school situation. Additionally, the profiles in this chapter illustrate what is available at the time this text was written; they do not exhaust all that is available. The items described here also might not be offered in the near future. The educational marketplace of ideas and products is volatile; resources come and go.

Furthermore, as we have emphasized throughout this text, relationships are central to any successful literacy program. The human elements of passion, purpose, partnership, and planning underlie effective instruction. The culture of a classroom and the countless decisions made each day influence learning more than a particular teaching method, instructional package, or school structure (Newmann, 1996). Programs must be enacted—and resources obtained—knowing that teacher–learner relationships matter tremendously in the tricky business of adolescent literacy and identity development.

At the same time, formalized program offerings bundle instructional ideas and materials together, often saving hours of planning and preparation. External resources can help educators reduce the complexity of their busy professional and personal lives. Such resources often protect educators from reinventing ideas and materials; in fact, they can provide opportunities to improve what is offered by adapting it to particular local situations. Formalized programs and resources often present opportunities to collaborate with other educators and find solutions to common problems. These benefits are not to be underestimated and should inform decisions about whether to acquire particular offerings.

Two sections follow. The first section, entitled Schoolwide Offerings, concentrates on literacy initiatives that encompass all teachers and students—in all departments or teams—in a secondary school. The second section, Intervention Offerings, extends Chapter 6 by profiling specific resources available for literacy improvement classes.

Schoolwide Offerings

This text has presented elements of schoolwide literacy programs that serve the needs of adolescents. Some of the more important ones include the following:

- A schoolwide literacy *focus,* orchestrated by a well-respected school-based literacy team, that directs access to many, varied genre and experiences
- Teacher preparation of instruction that integrates literacy *apprenticeships* with subject-area study, building desire and competence to read increasingly complex materials
- School, home, and community *partnerships* to help adolescents develop a complex repertoire of academic and out-of-school literacy practices
- *Assessment* that helps adolescents understand the strengths and needs in their literacy practices, and that helps teachers to plan differentiated instruction
- Teacher–student negotiation of print-rich, meaningful classroom *culture* with expectations for success

Schoolwide offerings that encompass these elements can be divided between those produced and disseminated by service agencies and those presented in the professional literature that need to be designed locally.

Service Agencies

Table 10.1 lists the names and website addresses of service agencies that have full-time staff members who initiate schoolwide literacy programs. Staff developers interact with school personnel to guide initial literacy improvement efforts along a certain path. These resources have a research base and sound, if sometimes competing, theoretical assumptions. It is important to realize that none of the resources presented next qualify as comprehensive programs; they all address only certain program elements. Through negotiation, they have the potential to be part of effective, context-specific, comprehensive adolescent literacy programs.

TABLE 10.1   Schoolwide Programs through Service Agencies

America's Choice	www.ncee.org
Creating Independence through Student-Owned Strategies (Project CRISS)	www.projectcriss.org
Great Books program	www.greatbooks.org
Literacy Volunteers of America (LVA)	www.literacyvolunteers.org
Mulitcultural Reading and Thinking (McRat)	www.ecs.org/ecsmain.asp?page=/html/issues.asp?am=1
Strategic Literacy Initiative (SLI)	www.wested.org.stratlit
Strategic Teaching and Reading Project (STRP)	www/ncrel.org/sdrs/areas/issues/educatrs/profdevl/pd21k199.htm
Success for All (SFA)	www.successforall.net

The agency-initiated resources presented next also vary somewhat in orientation. All provide for aspects of literacy development for all adolescents, noting strategies for including adolescents who struggle as readers and writers. Some are resources designed for literacy strategies across the curriculum; some concentrate on separate reading classes.

America's Choice.   According to its website (www.ncee.org), America's Choice, produced by the National Center on Education and the Economy, "offers comprehensive standards-based school design that focuses relentlessly on results, using assessments, curriculum, an instructional program, and a planning, management and organizational system all aligned with standards." At the secondary level, this resource calls for restructuring into a small system focused on an academic core. Specific literacy practices then are offered. A staff member offers continuous technical assistance, and participants have access to an annual conference and networking with other America's Choice schools from around the country.

Creating Independence through Student-Owned Strategies   Carol Santa and colleagues in the Kalispell School District, Kalispell, Montana, developed one well-researched schoolwide literacy resource called Project CRISS, which stands for Creating Independence through Student-Owned Strategies. The resource received both state and national recognition in the 1980s and early 1990s, suggesting strong positive evaluation results. Lest anyone think that it only suits the needs of students in the Rocky Mountains, the resource has been replicated in many elementary, middle, and high schools across the United States.

In up to 24 hours of staff development, subject-area teachers learn strategies for text analysis and teaching the author's craft, discussion strategies, active strategies for encouraging learning and organizing, writing, vocabulary development, and assessment. They learn to explain and model, provide support systems, and help students extend independent learning strategies. They develop skills for planning a gradual release of responsibility as students learn to apply CRISS strategies on their own. The challenge to teachers and curriculum leaders who decide to implement Project CRISS is to invite other teachers to learn how generalized teaching strategies can be applied to their particular students and subject areas.

Great Books. The Junior Great Books and the Great Books programs offer middle and high school students the chance to read what are described as outstanding literature selections. Reading books on the Great Books lists and engaging in text-based discussion called the shared inquiry model is said to strengthen critical thinking and civil discourse, promote reading and the appreciation of literature, and provide tools for social engagement and life-long learning.

Initial training to be a Great Books discussion leader takes 2 days. It involves step-by-step instruction in how to use shared inquiry discussion and interpretive activities, including questioning strategies that keep discussions lively and focused, questions to help children develop their own ideas, techniques to involve children of all ability levels, and before- and after-discussion activities that reinforce good reading and discussion and build children's thinking and writing skills. Implementing either of these two resources might prove difficult because some students would struggle with some of the texts.

Literacy Volunteers of America. Literacy Volunteers of America (LVA) provides training and matching for thousands of volunteers who work with adult beginning readers and speakers of English as a second language. As a resource that is designed to respect those who do not learn to read in school or who are new to the United States, LVA tutoring has been used successfully with adolescents who struggle as readers and writers. Tutors learn how to select or compose passages to be used for instruction as well as how to teach decoding, vocabulary, comprehension, and writing. Even adolescents have been trained as LVA tutors, and they can work with other adolescents, children, or adults using the LVA tutoring model.

Multicultural Reading and Thinking. Multicultural Reading and Thinking (McRat) was developed by the Arkansas Department of Education in collaboration with reading specialists and classroom teachers throughout the state. Meant for all students in grades 3 through 8, it is described as a supplementary program that uses available literature on culturally diverse themes to teach students to read reflectively, develop and supply evidence for their opinions, and communicate ideas effectively in writing. There is an authentic assessment system that includes both student portfolios and McRat written assessments. The resource is implemented by teachers who participate in extensive staff development.

Strategic Literacy Initiative.   The Strategic Literacy Initiative (SLI) is a consulting model developed by Ruth Schoenbach, Cynthia Greenleaf, and colleagues at the Oakland, California, office of WestEd, a nonprofit educational research, development, and service agency. Focused on improving student literacy at the secondary school level, this work is described in the 1999 text *Reading for Understanding: A Guide to Improving Reading in Middle and High School Classrooms* (Schoenbach, Greenleaf, Cziko, & Hurwitz, 1999). This text describes a reading apprenticeship framework that was developed with teams of teachers in the San Francisco Bay area and nationally. To learn this framework, interdisciplinary teams of teachers participate in 3-day summer institutes and 4 days of school-year professional development. This framework is implemented in both an academic literacy class and in classrooms across the curriculum.

The SLI reports positive evaluation results for the more than 90,000 middle and high school students it has affected so far, with reading comprehension gains that are sustained as students progress to higher-level courses and encounter more complex texts in various disciplines. Arguing that most adolescents do not need isolated instruction in phonics or word attack, the reading apprenticeship model emphasizes teaching via metacognitive conversations. These are orchestrated from teachers' knowledge of the social, personal, cognitive, and knowledge-building dimensions necessary for the development of flexible comprehension strategies (Greenleaf, Schoenbach, Cziko, & Mueller, 2001). As with project CRISS, the challenge to teachers and curriculum leaders implementing the Strategic Literacy Initiative is to help teachers apply generalized teaching strategies in particular classrooms and to manage the scheduling of an academic literacy class.

Strategic Teaching and Reading Project.   Implemented as part of *Pathways to School Improvement,* the Strategic Teaching and Reading Project (STRP) was developed at the North Central Regional Educational Laboratory (NCREL) as a long-term, professional development resource implementing current research with reading as the focus. Students are said to learn the what, where, why, and how of the reading process. More specifically, the curriculum attends to metacognition, prior knowledge, inferencing, word meaning, and text structure, all of which can be studied in the *Strategic Teaching and Reading Guidebook,* available through the NCREL web page.

STRP's emphasis on professional development means that schools who implement the resource must be committed to making change, organizing study groups to explore effective practice and to develop a school improvement plan that is implemented with extensive support. It is said to work because of team collaboration and peer support; administrative support and active participation; ongoing professional development; integration of STRP into the school's existing initiatives; willingness of the staff to implement research-proven practices; time to plan, meet, and evaluate the project; and providing STRP materials for each team member. The difficulty with STRP, as with Project CRISS and SLI, would be fitting the instructional strategies to a specific school context. Helpfully, the NCREL website also includes a Literacy Program Evaluation Tool (http://www.ncrel.org/literacy/eval/).

Success for All.   Initiated as a resource meant to improve school achievement in urban elementary schools, Success for All (SFA) (Slavin, Madden, Dolan, & Wasik, 1996) is now being piloted at the middle school level. The resource involves thematic integrated science, social studies, and language arts units so that students learn effective strategies for extending knowledge and thinking critically. Its goals are to increase the number of students reading at or above grade level by 20 percent a year; to produce integrated, academically rigorous curricula that increase student achievement on performance-based measures in reading, mathematics, science, and social studies; and to improve school climate by increasing attendance, academic self-concept and self-esteem, and parent and community involvement and by decreasing discipline problems. The language arts instructional component of Success for All, Cooperative Integrated Reading and Composition (CIRC), is also available for implementation apart from Success for All.

     To become a Success for All middle school, schools must commit to a 90-minute humanities period that incorporates social studies and language arts, with at least 40 minutes to be spent on reading. They must orchestrate heterogeneous groups of students, except for flexible homogeneous reading groups. They must develop interdisciplinary houses consisting of four classes that keep students together for the day, with the exception of reading. In addition to incorporating required SFA curricula, schools must provide reading tutoring to at least 20 percent of all sixth graders. Although the jury is still out on middle school SFA programs, elementary SFA programs have been critiqued for promoting heavily teacher-directed instruction that does not respond quickly to students' needs (see, for example, www.alt-sfa.com).

Local Designs

Table 10.2 shows program plans (and their references to the professional literature) that need to be designed locally. The offerings consist of plans from the professional literature that school district personnel need to implement

TABLE 10.2   Schoolwide Programs Designed Locally

Collaborative staff development	Fisher, 2001; Taylor, 2001
Home–school partnerships	Epstein, 2001
Peer and cross-age tutoring	Rekrut, 1994
Providing Opportunities with Everyday Reading (POWER)	Weller & Weller, 1999
Sustained silent reading	Pilgreen, 2000

on their own. Many emphasize the importance of ongoing staff development (e.g., Fisher, 2001; Taylor, 2001). Although these references provide appropriate general guidelines, numerous specifics relative to local situations need to be addressed.

Home–School Partnerships.   As Chapter 7 described, a variety of home–school partnership programs can be implemented to include secondary school students, either as parents (Johnson, Pflaum, Sherman, Taylor, & Poole, 1995/1996) or as reading partners (Handel, 1995). Such programs might teach young parents to serve as their children's first teachers by helping them engage in interactive play and by teaching them to engage in effective storybook reading (Taylor, 1999; www.familylit.org). Indeed, learning such skills can end up aiding the fluency and metacognition of adolescent parents who struggle with more sophisticated reading and writing themselves. Teenagers can also be trained as intergenerational tutors of siblings or other family members using any one of a variety of peer and cross-age models.

Peer and Cross-Age Tutoring Programs.   Many schools institute peer and cross-age tutoring programs to aid all students in a secondary school (Rekrut, 1994). Touting effects that can be greater than those of computer-assisted instruction, such pairings can be concerned with work in any subject area, including reading and writing, and can occur within or across grades. The most frequent pairings involve fifth graders working with younger students, or high school students working with intermediate or middle grade students. Most programs include some training to help tutors develop interpersonal skills, management skills, and lesson planning.

Literacy tutoring can include paired reading and writing or development of word recognition, fluency, or comprehension skills, depending on the pairings involved. Any population can benefit from tutoring or being tutored, depending on program design and students' need. For instance, less fluent middle school student readers can benefit from rehearsing and reading aloud to younger children. Similarly, the same students might be helped by more fluent high school student readers who engage in paired oral reading and discussion with them.

Providing Opportunities with Everyday Reading (POWER).   Weller and Weller (1999) describe a schoolwide program developed in and replicated throughout Georgia that targeted independent reading and reading in the content areas. Begun with strong administrative support, teachers took an initial and, during a second year, an advanced summer content-area reading course designed to offer reading strategies for preparation, assistance, and reflection. The program also included a twice-per-week, 25-minute sustained silent reading component. The program resulted in increases in students' reading comprehension test scores, changes in teachers' use of and appreciation for reading strategies in their subject-area classes, and positive student attitudes toward reading.

Sustained Silent Reading (SSR).   In an effort to encourage adolescents to read widely and often, many secondary schools, middle schools especially, initiate sustained silent reading or Drop Everything and Read (DEAR) (Pilgreen, 2000). Such initiatives usually invite everyone in a school or, sometimes, in a classroom to read for a certain period of time each day or each week. Reading is supposed to be completed for pleasure, and book reports are not required.

Most models of SSR suggest initiating such programs with a public relations campaign that touts the benefits of wide, frequent reading. They also suggest that teachers and other school staff join in to serve as role models of proficient readers. If a school decides to implement SSR, it is recommended that classrooms be well stocked with all kinds of reading materials, and that teachers regularly use book talks to entice students to become interested in these texts.

School Restructuring

We should note that the preceding schoolwide initiatives all report evaluation results that suggest their value to secondary schools as they are presently structured. However, from the point of view of some school reform movements, this perspective could represent a limitation to these programs. The last decade has seen many critiques of secondary school structures as too compartmentalized. One might query programs that are designed to invite teenagers to become adept at the narrow, inflexible practices associated with academic literacy as now perpetuated in many schools (Luke, 2000). To illustrate, *Literate Futures* (Luke & Freebody, 2000) presents an alternative curriculum framework that was constructed for use in Queensland, Australia, in response to such concerns.

Numerous initiatives across the United States now address general issues of restructuring secondary schools. These initiatives might be helpful for literacy study groups to consider as they begin constructing a vision for alternative, more literate schooling. For instance, Daniels, Bizar, and Zemelman (2001) describe best practices for restructured high schools, and Marzano, Pickering, and Pollock (2001) present research-based teaching practices for increasing new school achievement.

As Chapter 7 indicated, restructuring efforts have addressed personalized schools and full-service schools that indirectly mark literacy. Other efforts represent quite varied political views and include approaches to developing school choice, service learning, and social justice initiatives. Any of these programs can become a context for purposeful literacy instruction. Some organizations exploring secondary school restructuring are included in Table 10.3.

TABLE 10.3   Secondary School Restructuring

National Center for Restructuring Education, Schools and Teaching, Teachers College at Columbia University (www.tc.columbia.edu/~ncrest)	Works to develop learner-centered, knowledge-based, responsible, and responsive schools with changed accountability and assessment
Center on Organization and Restructuring of Schools (now closed), University of Wisconsin–Madison (www.wcer.wisc.edu/archives/completed/cors)	Studied efforts to change students' school experiences, teachers' professional life, school leadership, and community resource use
Coalition of Essential Schools (www.essentialschools.org)	A national network promoting higher student achievement and humane school communities through changes in practice
Annenberg Institute for School Reform (www.whannenberg.org)	Funds K–12 public school restructuring and reform
Center for Leadership in School Reform (www.clsr.org)	Supports the transformation of the existing system of rules, roles, and relationships that govern the way time, people, space, knowledge, and technology are used in schools
Comprehensive School Reform Program (www.ecs.org)	Federal grants to help low-performing schools implement research-based, schoolwide reform

Intervention Offerings

Interventions to help adolescents who struggle as readers and writers are especially controversial partly because they have been shown to have limited impact beyond the third-grade level (Allington, 2000). Yet we feel as though we would be needlessly giving up if we did not recommend such work for older students who struggle significantly with reading and writing. Doing nothing to help them would be immoral—especially because we have seen many older students improve their reading substantially and because the cause of reading difficulties so often is inappropriate instruction.

The answer to the question of whether to provide push-in or pull-out interventions depends on the adolescents involved. In the push-in, or inclusion, model, students who struggle with particular aspects of reading or writing participate in subject-area study along with a reading specialist or resource teacher who helps them with literacy activities. Push-in resource teachers generally plan with subject-area teachers, help teach content, and work with students other than the struggling readers they are required to target. The premise for this model is that the less struggling readers feel the stigma associated with special classes, the more likely they will be able to reconstruct themselves as successful readers and writers. Most students can be helped with such push-in help within the context of literacy instruction that should be available for all students, such as those programs described in the schoolwide section.

At the same time, others argue that the needs of all adolescents cannot be met in regular educational settings. For instance, when a teenager needs extra support to develop basic word-level decoding and fluency, teaching needs to be quite individualized. Such help could be quite distracting during subject-focused study in a classroom where most students do not have such needs. With differentiated instruction, such students can and should be helped to participate in subject-area classes. But an additional, separate pull-out literacy class for some students may also make sense. The numbers represented by the students who could benefit from such intensive instruction are quite small yet, we think, well worth attention.

Status of Interventions

Barry's (1997) survey of U.S. high school principals clue us about the state of programs and practices available in high schools for students with reading difficulties. Sixty-seven percent of respondents note that they maintain such a program as part of their regular education department, 17 percent say they do so through their special education departments, and 11 percent note that no special programs exist and that regular classroom teachers try to accommodate struggling readers. Existing programs try to address needs equally in grades 9 through 12, usually, but not always, during the school day.

Barry (1997) reports that intervention classes are called by names such as Reading Improvement, Developmental Reading, and Remedial Reading and range from isolated skills approaches, to immersion-in-reading approaches, and, in a compromise, to something the author calls interactive approaches, a combination of word skills, vocabulary development, and free reading. These programs report using skill development materials marketed by publishers such as Jamestown, Scholastic, SRA, Readers' Digest, EDL, and Globe. Trends reported by principals include reductions in the number of secondary school reading specialists, use of more performance-based assessment, and a move toward collaborative, consultative, push-in models.

Cases for Pull-Out Support

Several authors have presented cases for pull-out support of adolescents who struggle as readers. The authors of "A Case Study of Middle School Reading Disability" (Morris, Ervin, & Conrad, 1996) argue that push-in models do not work as the only literacy instruction for all adolescents. Instead, presenting a case study of one seventh grader, Brett, they suggest the kind of pull-out teaching and teacher expertise needed for effective intervention for a student who continues to struggle with pronouncing multisyllabic words, spelling, fluency, and basic reading comprehension. At various points, Brett's quite effective intervention consists of guided reading with texts at his instructional level, word study, writing, and easy reading.

Some schools provide interventions by putting secondary students into a special class. For instance, in "A Second Chance to Learn to Read," Showers and Joyce (1998) describe a California high school course for students who were 2 or more years below grade level in reading. It involves inductive models of teaching, direct instruction in vocabulary and comprehension, cooperative learning, reading at home and at school, dictation activities, writing exercises, and regular assessment.

Similarly, Tatum (2000) describes a very successful yearlong reading class for below-level urban eighth graders, using culturally relevant literature along with explicit word study, fluency, writing, and comprehension study to make significant gains in reading performance. Heath and Mangiola (1991) describe teachers' efforts to create literacy lessons that are more engaging for culturally and linguistically diverse students, including a middle-to-elementary cross-age tutoring program. Allen (1995), Krogness (1995), and Mueller (2001) present detailed and inspiring descriptions of classroom successes with adolescents who struggle as readers and writers.

Avoiding Stigma

Some alternative interventions suggest models that explicitly work to avoid stigmatizing adolescents with pull-out programs. Mehan, Hubbard, and Villanueva (1996) report an effort that removes students from a remedial track and provides appropriate academic and social supports so that they meet expectations. Rex (2001) similarly describes the remaking of a high school reader, showing the features of the student's move from low track to gifted and talented and illustrating the central relationship between individual readers and their membership in a reading culture.

Harwayne (2000) wrote about the Manhattan New School's reading and writing workshop to encourage students to read and write enthusiastically and to perform well on high-stakes assessments. David (1999) developed a middle school program within which she switches roles from that of a tutoring reading specialist to that of an educational resource teacher.

After-School Programs

After-school programs have begun to provide alternatives to the usual public school literacy instruction. After-school literacy or book clubs offer great potential for helping all adolescents extend their literacy practices (Alvermann, Young, & Wisenbaker, 1999; Knowles & Smith, 1999). These out-of-school efforts may be especially potent when they are organized around adolescents' interests and current literacy practices (Fabos, 2000; Finders, 1996; Moje, 2000b).

For instance, Alvermann and her colleagues have begun to speak at conferences and to write about a 15-week media club that involved 30 adolescents ranging from 12 to 15 years of age and mostly of African American heritage. The study took place after school in a public library that was adjacent to a middle school in Athens, Georgia. Alvermann (2001) tells the story of a student in this program who she names Grady. When the Internet-based curriculum turned to Grady's interests, he could demonstrate profoundly improved reading and writing skills as well as interest in his own progress.

Commercial Resources

Many commercial resources exist that purport to solve all, most, or some of the difficulties faced by adolescents who struggle as readers and writers. Educators often are tempted to purchase such resources and think that mass application offers a solution to most problems. However, teenagers who struggle with academics have already faced a multitude of in- and out-of-school pressures to learn to read, including varieties of instruction. Each adolescent has understandings and needs that are as individual as every literacy-related situation she or he has encountered.

Commercial resources may contain literature or explicit instruction that may seem useful, but these needs vary considerably by student. We know of no quicker way to frustrate an adolescent than to push him or her through an inappropriate or meaningless resource, especially if the resource involves the

TABLE 10.4   Commercial Programs

Academy of Reading, Academy of Reading 2000 (Autoskill International)	www.ecs.org/clearinghouse/18/78/1878.htm
Accelerated Reader (Permabound)	www.perma-bound.com/accelreader.htm
Corrective Reading (Science Research Associates)	www.sra-4kids.com/teacher/directin/index.html
Failure Free Reading (Failure Free Reading)	www.failurefree.com
Language! (Sopris West)	www.language-usa.net
Reading 180 (Scholastic)	www.teacher.scholastic.com/read180/index.htm
Soar to Success (Houghton Mifflin)	www.eduplace.com/rdg/soar/
Wilson Reading System (Wilson Language)	www.wilsonlanguage.com/catalog.html

isolation and meaningless repetition common to computer or workbook-based skill-and-drill exercises. Thus, we present materials in Table 10.4 with the pronounced caveat that they are to be used carefully, with negotiation about how one aspect or another might suit particular students.

Academy of Reading; Academy of Reading 2000.   The Education Commission of the States presents Academy of Reading and Academy of Reading 2000, published by Autoskill International, as examples of resources being used to initiate schoolwide reform. They are described as comprehensive, computer-based remediation programs to complement language arts instruction in grades K–12. They are said to accommodate readers' needs with modules for phonemic awareness (which may not be needed for any adolescents we've meet), reading subskills, and oral and silent reading comprehension paragraphs. Two days of teacher training and an assessment tool are provided. In addition to difficulties associated with individualizing the resource, the passages may be too short to align in an authentic way with those that older students need to read in class, for assessment, and outside school.

Accelerated Reader.   Accelerated Reader is a rather popular, heavily marketed computer-based resource that is said to invite students to practice reading. The resource's main components include computer-based quizzes used to match students with trade books and assess performance with the books. Avoiding the tedium of regular computerized testing and matching is a challenge of this resource.

Corrective Reading.   Science Research Associates (SRA) publishes Corrective Reading for literacy interventions in grades 4 through 12. The resource is said to allow students to work in a decoding resource, a comprehension resource, or both. A management system guides student participation in the sequenced, scripted lessons and application activities said to be most suited to their needs. Teacher training is provided. Students may have difficulty finding connections between everyday literacy practices and the activities in this resource.

Failure Free Reading.   Grandly titled, Failure Free Reading is described as a supplemental program for struggling and English as a second language readers in the lowest 10 percent of the reading population. It consists of three instructional elements: repetition of reading exercises to increase fluency and vocabulary; use of materials containing simplified sentence structure; and age-appropriate, meaningful content that forms a connected story across selections. Also accompanying the program are a computer management system and instructional software, to be implemented by teachers or paraprofessionals following training.

Language!   Sopris West publishes Language! as a comprehensive language intervention resource for grades 1 through 12. Its 15 strands are said to address phonemic awareness, decoding/encoding connected text, decoding/encoding isolated words, syllabication in word structures, comprehension, pragmatic language, syntactic embedding variations and sentence patterns, grammatic structures of English and their interrelated functions, abstract language, mechanics, principles of composition, morphology, and vocabulary expansion via morphology. It is structured so that students enter at their initial proficiency levels. Progress depends on mastering the concepts in a unit of study. The resource provides a trainer-of-trainers model that assists districts in certifying in-service providers within their own districts. A potential weakness is that students may have difficulty finding connections between their day-to-day literacy practices and the skills that are practiced in this resource.

Reading 180.   Scholastic's Reading 180 resource describes itself as a balanced technology and print program that builds essential reading skills and develops fluency. In the instructional reading portion of the resource, students read leveled passages and complete activities to build fluency, word recognition, comprehension, vocabulary, and spelling skills. In the modeled/ independent reading portion of the resource, students either listen to a book on tape or read a text at their independent level. In the teacher instruction portion of the resource, students and a teacher work together on comprehension, word study, vocabulary, and writing. Many varied materials and 2 days of teacher training are provided. Related Scholastic intervention resources suitable for middle school include Reading XL, with subject-specific reading materials, and Project Achievement Reading, meant to address skills needed for test performance.

Soar to Success. Soar to Success is a reading intervention offered for students in grades 3–8 who are reading below grade level. It is published by Houghton Mifflin. It uses literature, reciprocal teaching, and graphic organizers in small-group lessons. Teachers who use the resource participate in 2 days of staff development to teach them to orchestrate the fast-paced interactions required by the approach. Ensuring that reading materials are at an appropriate instructional level for a particular student within this group context could be problematic with this resource.

Wilson Reading System. Wilson Reading System is said to be a comprehensive intervention system for students who have difficulty with learning to decode. It is a mastery approach with a 10-step lesson plan that also attends to sight-word instruction, vocabulary, oral expressive language development, and comprehension. The resource ends with fluency and comprehension work. The code-emphasis approach represented by this resource will appeal most to adolescents who recognize their needs in this area.

Conclusion

This final chapter of *Starting Out* closes with resources available for adoption, replication, or purchase that are meant to serve the needs of adolescents who struggle as readers or writers. Due to the complex nature of adolescents' prior literacy experiences, of course, no single set of instructional packages could be expected to resolve the problems faced by all the students in a given school.

Successful programs include those with a schoolwide literacy focus, in- and out-of-school partnerships, and supportive cultures, apprenticeships, interventions, and assessments. The chapter delineates schoolwide offerings, including efforts to bolster literacy across the curriculum, middle school reading classes meant to extend literacy development beginning in elementary school, and a host of tutoring and wide-reading program complements. Interventions for adolescents who struggle in significant ways with reading or writing are best designed to suit the needs of particular adolescents. Interventions may be designed as either push in or pull out.

We encourage those of you who have read our text to work with others inside and outside your school to design your own comprehensive literacy programs. As we said throughout this text, consider the needs and interests of all the adolescents with whom you work as you determine goals and objectives for your program. Don't overgeneralize from the criticisms typically levied toward particular kinds of resources as they may cause you to overlook an approach that might provide a solution for a teenager for whom nothing else has worked. Good luck as you join us in this exciting and critical work!

CENTRAL QUESTION: THINK BACK

Where can I learn about specific reading programs and resources that our school system might adopt?

To answer fully this chapter's central question, build on the following key concepts:

- Begin searching with the mindset that teacher–student relationships—not commercial promises of quick fixes—are central to reading programs.
- Search for schoolwide offerings provided by service agencies
- Search for models of schoolwide offerings such as (1) home–school partnerships, (2) peer and cross-age tutoring, (3) Providing Opportunities with Everyday Reading, (4) sustained silent reading, and (5) school restructuring.
- Search for models of interventions such as (1) pull-out support classes and (2) after-school programs.
- Search for commercial resources.

REFERENCES

Allington, R. L. (2001). *What really matters for struggling readers: Designing research-based programs.* New York: Longman.

Allington, R. T., & Walmsley, S. (1995). *No quick fix: Rethinking literacy programs in America's schools.* New York: Teacher's College Press.

Allen, J. (1995). *It's never too late: Leading adolescents to lifelong literacy.* Portsmouth, NH: Heinemann.

Alvermann, D. E. (2001). Reading adolescents' reading identities: Looking back to see ahead. *Journal of Adolescent and Adult Literacy, 44,* 676–690.

Alvermann, D. E., Young, J. P., & Wisenbaker, J. M. (1999). Adolescents' perceptions and negotiations of literacy practices in after-school read and talk clubs. *American Educational Research Journal, 36,* 221.

Barry, A. (1997). High school reading programs revisited. *Journal of Adolescent and Adult Literacy, 40,* 525–531.

Daniels, H., Bizar, M., & Zemelman, S. (2001). *Rethinking high school: Best practice in teaching, learning, and leadership.* Portsmouth, NH: Heinemann.

David., M. (1999). Reading at the middle level: Change may be good, but not always easy. *NASSP Bulletin, 83,* 95–100.

Epstein, J. L. (2001). *School, family and community partnerships: Preparing educators and improving schools.* Boulder, CO: Westview Press.

Fabos, B. (2000). Zap me! Zaps you. *Journal of Adolescent and Adult Literacy, 43,* 720–725.

Finders, M. (1996). *Just girls: Hidden literacies and life in junior high.* New York: Teachers College Press.

Fisher, D. (2001). "We're moving on up": Creating a schoolwide literacy effort in an urban high school. *Journal of Adolescent and Adult Literacy, 45*(2), 92–101.

Greenleaf, C., Schoenbach, R., Cziko, C., & Mueller, F. (2001). Apprenticing adolescent readers to academic literacy. *Harvard Educational Review, 71,* 79–129.

Handel, R. (1995). Family reading at the middle school. *Journal of Reading, 38,* 528–540.

Harwayne, S. (2000). *Lifetime guarantees: Toward ambitious literacy teaching.* Portsmouth, NH: Heinemann.

Heath, S. B., & Mangiola, L. (1991). *Children of promise: Literate activity in linguistically and culturally diverse classrooms.* Washington, DC: National Education Association.

Johnson, H. L., Pflaum, S., Sherman, E., Taylor, P., & Poole, P. (1995/1996). Focus on teenage parents: Using children's literature to strengthen teenage literacy. *Journal of Adolescent and Adult Literacy, 39,* 290–296.

Knowles, E., & Smith, M. (1999). *More reading connections: Bringing parents, teachers, and librarians together.* Englewood, CO: Libraries Unlimited.

Krogness, M. M. (1995). *Just teach me, Mrs. K: Talking, reading, and writing with resistant adolescent learners.* Portsmouth, NH: Heinemann.

Luke, A. (2000). Foreword. In E. B. Moje & D. G. O'Brien (Eds.), *Constructions of literacy: Studies of teaching and learning in and out of secondary schools* (pp. ix–xiii). Mahwah, NJ: Lawrence Erlbaum.

Luke, A., & Freebody, P. (2000). *Literate futures: Report of the literacy review for the Queensland State Schools.* Queensland: State of Queensland Department of Education. Retrieved January 15, 2001, from www.education.gld.gov.ua.

Marzano, R. J., Pickering, D. J., & Pollock, J. E. (2001). *Classroom instruction that works: Research-based strategies for increasing student achievement.* Alexandria, VA: Association for Supervision and Curriculum Development.

Mehan, H., Hubbard, L., & Villanueva, I. (1996). *Constructing school success: The consequences of untracking low achieving students.* London: Cambridge University Press.

Moje, E. (2000b). "To be part of the story": The literacy practices of gangsta adolescents. *Teachers College Record, 102,* 651–690.

Morris, D., Ervin, C., & Conrad, K. (1996). A case study of middle school reading disability. *The Reading Teacher, 49,* 368–377.

Mueller, P. M. (2001). *Lifers: Learning from at-risk adolescent readers.* Portsmouth, NH: Heinemann.

Newmann, F. M. (1996). *Authentic achievement: Restructuring schools for intellectual quality.* San Francisco: Jossey-Bass.

Pilgreen, J. L. (2000). *How to organize and manage a sustained silent reading program.* Portsmouth, NH: Boynton/Cook.

Rekrut, M. D. (1994). Peer and cross-age tutoring: The lessons of research. *Journal of Reading, 37,* 356–362.

Rex, L. (2001). The remaking of a high school reader. *Reading Research Quarterly, 36,* 288–314.

Schoenbach, R., Greenleaf, C., Cziko, C., & Hurwitz, L. (1999). *Reading for understanding: A guide to improving reading in middle and high school classrooms.* San Francisco: Jossey-Bass.

Showers, B., & Joyce, B. (1998). A second chance to learn to read. *Educational Leadership, 55,* 27–30.

Slavin, R. E., Madden, N. A., Dolan, L. J., & Wasik, B. A. (1996). *Every child, every school: Success for all.* Newbury Park, CA: Corwin.

Tatum, A. (2000). Breaking down barriers that disenfranchise African American adolescent readers in low-level tracks. *Journal of Adolescent and Adult Literacy, 44,* 52–64.

Taylor, D. (1999). *Family literacy: Young children learning to read and write.* Portsmouth, NH: Heinemann.

Taylor, R. (2001). Teacher's challenge. *Journal of Staff Development, 22*(4), 56–59.

Weller, L. D., & Weller, S. J. (1999). Secondary school reading: Using the quality principle of continuous improvement to build an exemplary program. *NASSP Bulletin, 83,* 59–68.

INDEX

Academy of Reading, 204
Accelerated Reader, 204
accommodations, test, 167–168
acrostics, 78
administrators, 178
Adolescent Literacy Commission, 172–173
agencies, service, 193–197
agenda, shared, 109
aliteracy, 15
aloud
    reading, 31, 53
    think, 31
America's Choice, 194
analogy, decoding by, 117–118
analyzer
    reader as, 12, 61–63, 82–83
    text, 114–115, 123–124
applying, 8
apprentice, reader as, 12–13, 193
approach, language experience, 116
arrangement, room, 5, 27–29, 89
assessment, 151–169
    classroom-support, 155–162, 193
    high-stakes, 153–155
    spelling, 161
    uses of, 152–156
assignments
    modification of, 122–123, 186
    communicating, 32–33, 95
associations, professional, 142–143
author, questioning the, 82–83
autobiographies, literacy, 71, 95–96

behaviors, observable, 38
brainstorming, 54–56
breaker, code, 114–118
builder, reader as, 6–12, 61–63, 64–67

cards, getting to know you, 90–91, 95
categorizing, 119
centers, family resource, 135
centers, library-media, 144–145

chart
    data, 68
    information, 75–76
choices, instructional, 101–103, 109
cinquain, 79
class, academic literacy development, 181–182
coaches, 178
collaboration, 5
commitment, building-wide, 179
compacts, 134–135
components, grading, 163–164
conferences
    teacher-student, 160–161
    writing, 161
consequences, 39
context clues, 8, 120
Corrective Reading, 204–205
courses, school success, 145–146
Creating Independence through Student-Owned
        Strategies, 178, 194
credit, extra, 168
culmination, unit, 50–51
culture
    classroom, 22–27, 193
    popular, 116–119
    school, 179–180
curriculum, literacy across the, 144, 180–181

designs, local, 197–199
development
    professional, 141–143
    staff, 197–198
diagram, Venn, 68–69
disabilities, remediating, 16–18
disruptions, chronic, 40–41
diversity, 87
doer, reader as, 11–12, 61–63, 74–81

education, culturally responsive, 87
evaluating, 8
expectations
    assignment, 33

expectations *continued*
    classroom interaction, 25–26, 37
    school success, 24–25
    signaling, 26–27
experiencer, reader as, 9–10, 61–63, 71–74
experiences, prior, 7
extensions, out-of-school, 187

fading, 88, 101
Failure Free Reading, 204, 205
fairness, 166–168
features, of standards-based outcomes, 47–48
flowchart, 69
fluency, 116, 123
focus, schoolwide literacy, 193
frames, story, 69–70
framing, unit, 44–52

goals
    for literacy program, 175
    for students' literacy, 6
grading, 162
Great Books, 194, 195
groups
    cooperative, 119, 121
    literature discussion, 72–75
    study, 141–142, 178

haiku, 80

identity, adolescent, 16–18, 108, 110, 124, 130, 179
images, 121
importance, determining, 8, 121, 121
improvement, grades based on, 166
information, literal, 8, 121
in-service, literacy, 179
instruction, differentiated, 86–104
intervention
    behavior, 39–41
    literacy development,106–126, 183–184,
        201–206
    pull out, 184, 201–203
    push in, 184, 201
interviews, 133–134
introduction, course, 91–92
inventories, diagnostic, 161–163

journal, 111, 113

KWL, 54

Language!, 204, 205
launching, unit, 52–57, 108–109, 119
learner, reader as, 8–9, 61–63, 68–71
list-group-label, 54–56, 119
literacies, multiple, 15–16, 107–108, 110–111, 114,
    172
Literacy Volunteers of America, 194, 195
literacy
    assessment, 124, 176
    basic, 14–15
    four resources model of, 113–115
Literate Futures, 199–200

makers, meaning, 114–115, 118–123
make-ups, facilitating, 33
materials, multi-level, 101–102, 111, 112
minilessons, 120–121
miscues, oral reading, 161
Multicultural Reading and Thinking,
    194, 195–196

National Assessment of Educational Progress,
    14, 172
norms
    curriculum-referenced, 166
    performance, 166
    social behavior, 36
note taking, 31, 70–71

observing/participating, real-world, 52–53
opening, school, 89–101
organization, text, 8, 121
organizers, graphic, 86–70
outcomes
    standards-based, 45–48
    unit, 45–48

pantomime, 77
paperload, 33–34, 91
paraphrasing, 8
partnerships, 4–5, 94–95, 97, 100, 103, 130–148,
    192–193
    community-school, 130–135, 137–139, 198
passages, graded, 161
passion, of teachers, 3, 99, 192
performance, monitoring student, 34

planning, 5–6, 100–101, 192
    classroom culture, 22–27
    discipline, 36–41
poems
    comparisons, 81
    found, 78
    list, 79
    permissions, 81
    question-answer, 80
    repetitions, 79
    to a topic, 81
    understandings, 80–81
    Wh, 80
poetry, patterned, 78–81
portfolios, 159–160
positives, general, 26–27
predicting, 8, 119, 121
previewing, 53–54
procedures, classroom, 29–36
programs
    after-school, 139, 203
    bilingual, 87
    literacy, 172–188, 193–201
    special education, 87
Providing Opportunities with Everyday
    Reading, 198, 199
purpose
    classroom literacy, 23–4, 3–24, 92, 99, 192
    for literacy development, 4

questions, essential, 48–50, 119, 124

rank, class, 166
Reading 180, 204, 205
reading
    buddy, 136–137
    repeated, 116
    self-selected, 92–93, 96–97
    shared, 116–117
    supporting, 120–121
    sustained silent, 198–199
relationships
    letter-sound, 116
    positive, 108–109, 161, 192
ReQuest, 121
resources
    commercial, 203–206
    program, 192–207

responsibility, gradual release of, 88, 111
restructuring, schoolwide, 199–200
resubmissions, 168
role-play, 77–78
routines
    closure, 32
    during class, 31–32
    entering, 34–35
    exiting, 36
    extra help, 32
    leaving during class, 35–36
rubrics, 121, 156–159
rules, classroom, 37

samples, of achievement, 167
sayings, common, 37–38
scale, reading strategies rating, 98–99
scheduling, block, 146
schools
    beating the odds, 63
    full-service, 147
    personalized, 146
self-assessment, 155–156
setting, effective classroom, 3–6, 89
share, quick book, 72
signals, 35
Soar to Success, 204, 206
space, third, 109
staff, literacy program, 177–178
statements, main idea, 64–64
strands, literacy, 60–83
Strategic Literacy Initiative, 178, 194, 196
Strategic Teaching and Reading Project, 194, 196
strategies, reading, 7, 8, 98–99, 121
structures
    classroom, 27–41
    school, 144–147, 180–187
students, bilingual, 103
Success for All, 194, 197
summarizing, 8, 63–64, 121
synthesizing, 8

tactics, low profile, 38–39
talks
    family book, 132–133
    guest book, 71–72
T-chart, 69
teachers, resources, 186–187

teaching, reciprocal, 24, 31, 60, 65–67, 118, 121, 154
teams
  curriculum planning, 44–45, 61
  interdisciplinary, 146
  literacy, 174
test taking, 75–77
texts
  interrogating, 83
  selecting, 101–102, 111, 112–113
  taped, 122–123
ties, cultural, 140–141
timeline, 68
topics, unit, 45
toss, bean bag, 95
transitions, 34–36
tutoring, 135–137, 198
types, syllable, 118

unit, coherent framing of, 51–52

updates, continual, 168
user, text, 114–115, 122–123

vision, classroom literacy, 4, 92
vocabulary, 31, 93–94, 96–97, 119–120, 144
volunteers, community, 138–139, 178

weights, in grades, 164–165
Wilson Reading System, 204, 206
words
  graded lists of, 161
  key, 117
work, bell, 30–31, 94, 97
workshops, 115, 154
write
  extended personal, 56–57
  quick, 56
writing
  during interventions, 121
  in units, 56–57